C. BEN ROSS AND THE NEW DEAL IN IDAHO

C. BEN ROSS

AND THE NEW DEAL

IN IDAHO

By MICHAEL P. MALONE

UNIVERSITY OF WASHINGTON PRESS · *Seattle and London*

The photographs facing pages 40 and 41 are used through the courtesy of the Idaho Historical Society

Copyright © 1970 by the University of Washington Press
Library of Congress Catalog Card Number 69-14207
SBN 295-95068-9
Printed in the United States of America

To Gail, my wife, and to Elmo Richardson, my mentor

FOREWORD

This scholarly examination of the career of C. Ben Ross will need no introduction to those who are interested in Idaho. Ross was not only a colorful character fully entitled to the nickname "Cowboy Ben" but a political independent in a state noted for the propensity of its voters to honor "the man, not the party." The state which has sent to the United States Senate such varied types as William E. Borah, Fred T. Dubois, Glen Taylor, and Frank Church—people who have "put Idaho on the map" for national audiences—has also had more than its share of spectacular governors. But none, I think, can compare with Ross for drama and sheer excitement. And none, at least until Robert Smylie (who served three four-year terms as governor, 1955–67), was as important as C. Ben Ross.

During his three two-year terms (1931–37), Ross led Idaho through the Great Depression as head of one faction of the badly divided Democratic party. His work set the tone for state government in Idaho until the coming of Governor Smylie and his liberal brand of Republicanism. This careful and judicious study by Michael Malone will make Ross known to new generations of Idahoans.

While C. Ben Ross was an important man in Idaho history—and worthy of scholarly attention for that fact alone—his era almost completely coincides with the first term of Franklin D.

Roosevelt. Thus Malone is here making an important contribution to our understanding of the impact of the New Deal on a single state and, consequently, of the workings of our federal system. James T. Patterson has put the matter succinctly in his book, *The New Deal and the States* (Princeton, N.J.: Princeton University Press, 1969): "Pennsylvania Avenue offered a fascinating view of American federalism in the 1930's. But is was hazy and unreliable compared to the perspective from the states." Malone gives us the perspective from Boise, and an enlightening one it is.

Few books and articles have been published on state politics in the 1930s, a fact frequently deplored by New Deal scholars. Manuscript collections have often been dispersed or (even more frequently) lost altogether, since heirs have been slow to see the importance of papers belonging to "mere" state politicians, even when those people have served as governors. Rich manuscript collections of state legislators, incidentally, are exceedingly rare and should be pursued by archivists with real fervor. In a few states serious efforts to collect recent history have long been under way. Fortunately for Mike Malone—and for all of us interested in twentieth-century American history—Idaho is one of those states. Under the imaginative leadership of Dr. Merle W. Wells, director —and for many years before that, historian-archivist—the Idaho Historical Society has gathered in a comprehensive manuscript collection and has made it readily accessible to scholars. In addition, Wells is a master at putting students on the trail of subjects for interview. Malone not only benefited from Wells's generosity, as he acknowledges, but he has duplicated it in assisting others, including the present writer, as they pursue their own researches.

I am delighted to see this important study become a book, the only form in which it can reach the wide audience it deserves. I hope that publishers will find similar works and have the courage to accept them. State history in the twentieth century is a scholarly

Foreword

frontier which needs the fullest exploration if we are to understand our nation's recent past.

ROBERT E. BURKE

Seattle, Washington
November, 1969

PREFACE

Who was C. Ben Ross? And what conceivable relevance might there be in the Idaho New Deal that could merit a monographic study? Both questions will occur, no doubt, to many who come across this volume. Neither Ross nor, for that matter, the state of Idaho are familiar to most Americans. But hopefully, those who read this book will conclude that the subject amply merits the attention which I have devoted to it.

I have sought neither to inflate the reputation of Ross nor to write a rigidly patterned New Deal "case study." My purpose has been rather to describe the impact of the depression and the New Deal upon this unusual state and to narrate Idaho's hectic political, social, and governmental experience during the turbulent decade of 1929–38. Ross himself is too little known. Overshadowed like most of his Idaho generation by the towering figure of William E. Borah, Ross nonetheless played a much greater role in his home state than Borah did. In fact, as this study attempts to demonstrate, he was the central figure of Idaho's political life during the depression era. Students of both the New Deal and the Northwest will find much that is familiar and much that is a bit bizarre in both C. Ben Ross and in the Idaho New Deal.

Many people have contributed to the making of this book. It began as a Ph.D. dissertation at Washington State University under the guidance of Professors Elmo R. Richardson, David H.

Stratton, and Thor Swanson, all of whom contributed generously of their expertise and advice to its creation. To my mentor, Elmo Richardson, I owe a special debt of gratitude—for his sound scholarly guidance, the example of his own achievement as an historian, and his warm personal friendship. Professor Robert E. Burke of the University of Washington and Dr. Merle Wells of the Idaho Historical Society have contributed a great deal to the revision of the manuscript and to its progress toward publication, and I also extend a heartfelt thanks to them.

Several good citizens of Idaho have been especially generous with their assistance. These include Dr. Wells's associates at the Idaho Historical Society, Idaho's leading political analyst, John Corlett, Robert Coulter, James H. Hawley, Jr., Truman Joiner, C. Ben Reavis, Mrs. Ethel Steel, Calvin Wright, and many others. Professors William E. Leuchtenburg of Columbia University, James T. Patterson of Indiana University, Leonard W. Arrington of Utah State University, Marian C. McKenna of Manhattanville College of the Sacred Heart, Ross Peterson of the University of Texas at Arlington, and Dean Orde S. Pinckney of Central Oregon College all supplied me with helpful advice and information. And, far from least, my wife Gail has stood by, aided, and tolerated me during the many trying stages of this endeavor.

As is customary in extending these thanks and acknowledgments, I wish to add the obvious, that any errors are entirely my own.

MICHAEL P. MALONE

Bozeman, Montana
August, 1969

CONTENTS

FOREWORD BY ROBERT E. BURKE		vii
PREFACE		xi
INTRODUCTION		xvii
I	C. BEN ROSS: AGRARIAN DEMOCRAT	3
II	THE DARK AGE OF THE IDAHO DEMOCRATS: 1918–30	14
III	DEPRESSION IDAHO: 1931–32	31
IV	WORKING WITH THE NEW DEAL: 1933–34	51
V	THE HIGH TIDE OF REFORM: 1934–36	77
VI	1936: "THE BATTLE OF THE IDAHO TITANS"	101
VII	DEMOCRATS IN DECLINE: 1937–38	117
NOTES		137
BIBLIOGRAPHY		171
INDEX		183

ILLUSTRATIONS

	facing
C. BEN ROSS	40
JAMES P. POPE	41
WILLIAM E. BORAH	41
BARZILLA W. CLARK	41
D. WORTH CLARK	41

INTRODUCTION

The Great Depression of the 1930s was a decisive turning point in the history of the United States. Only the Revolution and the Civil War had comparable impact upon long-term national development. The panic of 1929 shook the entire structure of American civilization to its foundations and seemed for a time to threaten the collapse of the nation's economic and social order. Most Americans at first viewed the depression as a temporary aberration in a basically sound economic system and believed that in time the situation would naturally stabilize again. In the meantime, as they had in the past, most citizens trusted in local government and private initiative to deal with the dislocations which the financial debacle had caused in society.

As the depression ground into its third year, however, it became increasingly apparent that neither time nor local action would bring genuine recovery. Only large-scale planning and financing could meet the challenge of the depression, and neither the cities nor the states commanded the resources necessary for such endeavors. The federal government alone had the potential to take decisive action. Through a mammoth expansion of federal relief, reform, and recovery efforts, President Franklin D. Roosevelt's New Deal program set out in 1933 to meet the threat posed by the depression. The New Deal, then, marked a revolution in federal-state relations and began that tremendous expansion of federal authority into every aspect of American life which so differentiates the new from the old America.

The rapid acceleration of federal activity under the New Deal also began a coinciding decline in the prerogative of the state governments. As William E. Leuchtenburg has said: "For the first time for many Americans, the federal government became an institution that was directly experienced. More than state and local governments, it came to be *the* government, an agency directly concerned with their welfare." [1] Obviously, therefore, the decade of the depression was a time of trauma and confusion for the states and for the state governments. This aspect of the New Deal period has generally been neglected by the historians, who have tended to view their subject almost exclusively from the national perspective. Despite the new magnitude and importance of federal activity during this era, such a viewpoint can be misleading and incomplete. For, like all broad, national movements, the New Deal developed differently in different geographical regions of the country. Relatively few state and regional New Deal studies now exist. But James T. Patterson's excellent ground-breaking work, *The New Deal and the States: Federalism in Transition,* points the way for future state New Deal studies and raises many of the questions which must be answered for each separate locality.[2] Before the historical mosaic of the "Roosevelt Revolution" can be completed, each state and region must be examined in depth, for in a true sense each is peculiar unto itself.

Basically urban and liberal in orientation, the New Deal confronted an inhospitable environment in a spacious but sparsely populated state like Idaho. The response to the New Deal in Idaho naturally differed from that of the more populous and industrialized states of the East and somewhat resembled the reactions of similar farming states of the South and West. The Idaho depression was a rural, agricultural problem, and as such it presented especially complex difficulties to national administrators who were often unfamiliar with conditions in the more remote regions of the country.

Introduction xix

Much of the chaos of the New Deal years in Idaho stemmed from the inability of federal authorities in Washington, D.C., and state officials to understand or sympathize with each other's problems.

In one sense, the New Deal in Idaho typified the situation only in the rural states. But in a broader sense, Idaho's problems were those of all the states. President Roosevelt's federal programs relieved many of the desperate problems confronting the states, such as large-scale unemployment, bank failures, industrial stagnation, and disastrously low farm prices. New difficulties, however, arose with the New Deal effort. The state governments were to a large extent bypassed by the federal government as the New Deal intervened directly on the grass-roots level with its basic reforms. Yet some federal programs demanded the cooperation of the state governments and placed heavy burdens upon them. The result in both cases was tension and confusion. Idaho's New Deal experience was typical in some instances and unique in others. To trace the impact of the New Deal years upon this one state is the purpose of this study.

No other state in the Union is quite like Idaho, and a basic understanding of the state's geographical peculiarities is essential to the study of its politics. It is a large, oddly shaped state, a patchwork of many divergent parts. Of its fifty-four million acres, less than eight million were under cultivation in 1930, while 39 per cent of its surface was covered with forests and 36 per cent was devoted primarily to grazing.[3] As one scholar has observed, Idaho is a "geographical anomaly," for it is one of the strange tricks of history that such an area ever became encompassed within the borders of one body politic.[4]

In general, the population of Idaho follows the "fishhook" of the state's principal resource, the Snake River. From Lewiston in the north, upstream to Boise in the southwest and Pocatello and Idaho Falls in the southeast, the state's small urban areas are geographically linked only by the river. The northern part of Idaho is separated from the southern by vast and primitive ranges of mountains, and the southeast is drawn by geographical and other affinities to neighboring Utah rather than to Boise in the southwest. It is geography, therefore, which fundamentally underlies the longstanding social, economic, and political sectionalism so characteristic of Idaho. Neither the state nor its people can be understood until these sections and their traits are comprehended.

Northern Idaho, generally called the "Panhandle," consists of the ten northernmost counties and is divided from the south by the wild Salmon River and the mountains through which it pours. This is an upland region, much of it being mountainous and almost all of it more humid than the south. Its major resources are its valuable stands of white pine, its extensive mineral deposits, and the rich farmlands of the Camas and Palouse areas. In 1930, these counties contained 26 per cent of the population, 30 per cent of the wealth, and 25 per cent of the total area of the state. The three small cities of Lewiston, Moscow, and Coeur d'Alene were the population centers of the area, as they are today.[5]

South of the Salmon River, the terrain is drastically different from that of the north, breaking into broad, arid prairies. The sixteen counties southwest of the Salmon contained 36 per cent of Idaho's population, 36 per cent of its wealth, and 37 per cent of its area in 1930. Dominated by the state capital of Boise, which is flanked by the smaller cities of Nampa, Caldwell, and Twin Falls, this was and is the least provincial of the three sections and the least inclined to sectional jealousies. The major economic interest of this area is its irrigated farmland, supplemented by considerable mining and lumbering.[6]

Comprised of the remaining eighteen counties, southeastern Idaho in 1930 contained 39 per cent of the population, 34 per cent of the wealth, and 38 per cent of the total area of the state. Southeastern Idaho in the 1930s was in a dynamic state of growth, as much of the state's 2,405,000 acres of irrigated farmland was

Introduction xxi

located there. Most of Idaho's 110,000 Mormons lived in and about the two principal cities of this region, Pocatello and Idaho Falls, and cultural, religious, and economic ties drew them south toward Salt Lake City rather than toward Boise.[7]

The antagonism and estrangement among the three geographical sections of Idaho is still a problem today. But during the 1920s and 1930s it presented a much greater difficulty, largely because of the rudimentary nature of the state's transportation system. Although four transcontinental railroads crossed the state from east to west, three were in the far north, en route to the northwest coast, and only one traversed the main population belt in the south. There was and is no north-south railroad in Idaho. Similarly, while the national movement for paved highways was then in full swing, most of Idaho's roads remained unpaved and at times impassable. The long-contested north-south highway, running from Boise to Lewiston, was practically completed by 1933, but for years it included stretches of rough gravel surfacing and was often closed during the winter months.[8]

Another factor contributing to sectional disunity in Idaho was its lack of any major metropolitan center. The state's largest city, Boise, numbered a mere 21,544 inhabitants in 1930 and dominated only its own subregion in the southwest. The other two sections were actually economic hinterlands of what Benjamin E. Thomas has called "external capitals." The north, whose largest city in 1930 was Lewiston (population 9,403), looked to Spokane, Washington, as its economic and cultural urban hub, while the southeast looked toward Utah.[9]

Geographical sectionalism naturally expressed itself in politics as well as in economics. The south was generally conservative and usually Republican, while the north has tended since Populist days to be Democratic. Typical of intersectional rivalries was that which flared between the north and the southeast over the state college issue. At that time, the small two-year college in Pocatello, which is now Idaho State University, was a branch of the University of

Idaho at Moscow; and the southeasterners met constant frustration from the north in their efforts to make it an independent, four-year institution. The Boise area tended most often to play the other sections against each other and usually held the balance of power. For that reason, this area produced more than its share of state political leaders, while the other regions, particularly the north, traditionally felt neglected in political affairs. This constant bickering and jealousy among the three sections of the state has been a potent factor in the political contests of Idaho from territorial days to the present.[10]

Regardless of the dissimilarity of its component regions, it is still possible to generalize about Idaho as a whole. It has always been most noteworthy for its abundance of natural resources and its sparsity of population. The 1930 census strikingly revealed the rural-agricultural nature of the state's social order. In 1930, Idaho contained 445,032 people, only 38,015 of whom lived in cities of over 10,000 population. The state numbered, in fact, only two cities of over 10,000 (Boise and Pocatello) and only five other cities of over 5,000 (Idaho Falls, Lewiston, Twin Falls, Coeur d'Alene, and Nampa). The most significant fact of all was that 315,000 of the state's 445,032 people lived in actual rural areas, that is, on farms or in towns of under 2,500 population.[11]

Idaho was and still is a rural and agricultural state whose major social, economic, and political interest group consisted of its 41,-674 farmers and ranchers.[12] One observer calculated in 1933 that the total agricultural wealth of Idaho was $628,507,746, whereas the two leading industries of the state, lumbering and mining, totaled only $265,501,658 and $86,945,589, respectively.[13] Thus, while industry and labor organizations were far from being nonexistent, agriculture was the dominant economic and political force in Idaho. The silver, lumber, and public- or private-utility interests could muster powerful lobbies and blocs of votes, but only the Grange, the Farm Bureau, and their allies could produce the constant majority vote.

Introduction

Idaho in the early 1930s, therefore, presented a unique and perplexing environment in which to apply the liberal-nationalistic reforms of the New Deal. The rural-agrarian philosophy of the Idahoans, even of the reform Democrats among them, would perforce differ basically from the philosophy of the typical eastern, urban New Deal administrator and politician. This difference in outlook no doubt lay at the root of the many misunderstandings and bitter feuds that so often characterized the new federal-state relationship inaugurated by the New Deal in Idaho. But personalities also loomed large in these episodes, and the man who, more than any other, left the imprint of his personality upon Idaho during the decade of the depression was C. Ben Ross.

C. BEN ROSS AND THE NEW DEAL IN IDAHO

I

C. BEN ROSS: AGRARIAN DEMOCRAT

Charles Benjamin Ross (1876–1946), governor of Idaho from 1931 to 1937, was one of those unusual individuals who, through the force of his personality and the intensity of his ambition, is still remembered when his peers are forgotten. The first native-born governor of his state and the first man to serve three terms in that position, Ross was an innovator and a proud individualist who seemed to thrive on the controversy which he always inspired. Few Idahoans have exercised such political power as did he, and fewer still led a more colorful public life. Like all other figures of recent Idaho history, his stature has been dwarfed by the reputation of Senator William E. Borah. Yet, while Borah was undoubtedly Idaho's most prominent citizen of the 1930s, Ross exercised far greater real power within the state itself. He was, in fact, the central figure of Idaho political life from 1928 through 1938.

Governor Ross took pride in tracing his ancestry back to the early pioneers and was fond of comparing himself with them. The comparison was appropriate. A strain of religious piety and individualism ran throughout this clan of Rosses, beginning with the original emigrant from Scotland in the 1740s, and including Ben's great-grandfather, who fought in the Revolution, and his father, who was a schoolmate of Jay Gould.[1] This family trait no doubt climaxed in C. Ben Ross.

His father was John M. Ross of Vermont, about whose origins very little is known. Apparently John Ross was drawn to the sea as a young man and worked as a sailor for several years. He rounded Cape Horn en route to San Francisco in 1850 and prospected in California with little success for most of the next decade, until the lure of another mining boom drew him north to Portland, Oregon, in 1860–61. From there he followed the gold rush to the Boise Basin of Idaho with a string of pack mules in 1862, and he continued his search for fortune until 1864, when he met his future wife at the now extinct mining town of Rocky Bar.[2]

Jeannette Hadley was only sixteen years old in 1864. She had arrived in Idaho earlier that year with the Piercy family of Illinois, which had adopted her. Evidently she had little difficulty in taming the wanderlust of John Ross, for they were married the next year. The Rosses homesteaded near the present town of Eagle but soon abandoned that site for the rich river-bottom soil near the confluence of the Boise and Snake rivers in what is now Canyon County. The 160-acre plot which John Ross purchased in 1875 had been homesteaded by Herman Hass in 1866 and was one of the first farms to hold adjudicated water rights on the Boise River.[3]

The farming country nestled in the bend of the Snake River began to prosper when the railroad traversed it in the early 1880s, and John Ross's farm grew with the country. Located only a few miles from "Old Fort Boise," where Francois Payette used to welcome travelers on the Oregon Trail, the property still known as the Ross farm is situated between the two villages of Parma and Roswell. The town of Parma, which became C. Ben Ross's home for most of his life, sprang up when the Fouch brothers moved their store to its location from the short-lived railroad boom town of St. Paul. By the early 1930s, Parma numbered six hundred inhabitants and differed little from dozens of other such small Idaho farming communities. John Ross expanded his farm holdings in time to include three hundred acres of diversified grain and vegetable crops and one thousand acres of pasturage for cattle, hogs, and

C. Ben Ross: Agrarian Democrat 5

sheep.[4] It was on this ranch that Charles Benjamin Ross was born, on December 27, 1876.

The boyhood of "Ben" Ross probably differed little from that of most of his friends on neighboring ranches. At the age of eight, he was already an experienced cowhand and was helping to herd fifteen thousand head of cattle over the sagebrush prairies of southwestern Idaho and southeastern Oregon. Ross worked and lived as a cowboy until he was eighteen.[5] These were his favorite years, and he never really outgrew them. As a mature man, he remained a cowboy in actions and appearance and seldom neglected a chance to exhibit his excellent horsemanship in rodeos and parades. His lifelong nickname of "Cowboy Ben" was authentic and was always a political asset.

Even as a lad, Ross was apparently a unique and unusual individual. Reminiscences of his friends, no doubt liberally colored by folklore, attest to his youthful ambition and somewhat eccentric self-discipline. There are many reports of his boasts to fellow cowhands that they should be proud to be riding with the future governor of the state. One story even has it that, when his father once took him to visit the governor, the boy remarked that he too would one day occupy the statehouse of Idaho. From his earliest years, a rigidly moralistic attitude made him a man apart. He would never join his companions in those heralded pastimes of the cowboy—drinking, smoking, and gambling.[6] As the future would prove, Ross was inclined by temperament toward political activism, self-righteous progressivism, and especially that supreme chimera of his age—prohibition. He was constantly goaded by a sense of inner compulsion for self-improvement and a desire to attain worldly fame.

One of Ross's early and lasting regrets was his lack of education. He ended his career at the country school near Parma after the sixth grade, not, apparently, because of a lack of ability but, as he later claimed, only because of an inborn dislike of the restraint of school. In order to remedy this shortcoming, Ross left the ranch in 1894, at the age of eighteen, and spent the next three years attending business college classes in Portland and Boise. He returned to the ranch in 1897, a mature man; and for the next seventeen years he and his brother, W. H. Ross, managed the holdings which their father had developed. The Ross brothers became widely known as prominent farmers and stockmen. Their range lands extended north to the Weiser area and west and south into the Owyhee country.[7] Ben Ross was obviously a capable and farsighted farmer and a shrewd businessman as well. He was one of the pioneers of large-scale irrigation in Canyon County.

On February 14, 1900, three years after his return to ranching, Ross married Edna Reavis, the daughter of John and Ellen Reavis of Midvale, Idaho. She was a physically large and exuberant woman with a warm and attractive personality. To her many friends she later became known as "Governor Edna"; in fact she was as natural a politician as was her husband and was always an asset to his political career. Her roots too were deep in the frontier, for she had been born in a covered wagon somewhere on the Wyoming prairie, June 6, 1878. Her parents settled in Midvale, and there she grew to womanhood. After attending the old Weiser Institute, she returned to teach school and was doing so when she met Ben Ross.[8]

C. Ben Ross was a natural politician and, as noted, had harbored political ambitions from his early years. His reputation as a stockman gained him considerable local renown, and he became an active civic leader in Parma at an early age. His outgoing personality and enthusiasm made him an instinctive "joiner"; he was a member of the Congregational Church, an Odd Fellow, an Elk, and a member of the Woodmen of the World.[9] Local politics was the obvious next step.

The Ross family was by long tradition Republican in political affiliation. But Ben Ross turned his back on the Grand Old Party just before his twenty-first birthday in 1896. He later maintained that he had abandoned the party because it had strayed from the principles of Abraham Lincoln, but it seems more plausible to assume that, like many other Idahoans, he was lured from his traditional political moorings by the appeal of Populism and of William Jennings Bryan.[10] At any rate he soon became a Democrat, and a Democrat he remained for the rest of his life.

Like the other counties of Idaho, Canyon County was then governed by three elected commissioners. This agricultural county had a reputation of political radicalism, especially the agrarian radicalism of populism and later of the Nonpartisan League, which has endured until recent times. Because of its pivotal location in the southwest and its comparative density of population, Canyon County has always produced more than its share of Idaho's political leadership. State commentators still refer to this county as the "Mother of Governors," and its roster of prominent citizens includes many of Idaho's most powerful political leaders—Frank Steunenberg, John T. Morrison, H. C. Baldridge, and Charles Gossett, as well as Ross. In 1915, after campaigning as the "farmers' friend," C. Ben Ross was elected a commissioner of Canyon County, and he served in this position until 1921. Although the county was large and heavily Republican—it then included present-day Gem and Payette counties as well—Ross twice won reelection as a Democrat.[11]

Ross's philosophy of government seemed to change little over the years. His message was directed to the farmers, and his slogan was "The Cow, The Pig, and The Hen." [12] He captured and held the loyalty of Canyon County voters by his two major programs—farm-to-market roads, and economy and honesty in government. His lamp burning long after midnight in the courthouse became a familiar sight in Caldwell. As Ross later recalled, it was during these years that he developed that "crusader spirit" of which he loved to boast as governor. He told Lamont Johnson in 1932:

When I first wanted to be governor I knew I had to prepare myself. There is no mere happenstance about doing worthwhile things. You've got to plan for it. That's why I went to business school, and that's why I stayed up at nights in the courthouse at Caldwell. I studied tax records at night and travelled the roads by day to see how things were being handled. As a young man I cut out cards and dances and poolhalls. I couldn't waste time on those things when I had something else in mind.[13]

The long hours eventually paid off when Ross uncovered fairly extensive tax fund irregularities in the county administration; his exposure of them brought him acclaim and seemed to fulfill his promises of economy and honesty in government. He also endeared himself to local farmers by leading the road improvement movement in Canyon County. During his six-year term he saw the county's mileage of crushed rock roads increase from seven to three hundred miles.[14]

But local fame was one thing and statewide renown quite another. The latter came to Ross through two efforts: his Farm Bureau activities and his political career in Pocatello. Long an advocate of farmers' organizations, Ross was one of the founders of the Idaho State Farm Bureau during and after World War I. As such he lectured for the Farm Bureau in every county in the state. Ross served as secretary and later as president of the state organization and made a mild sensation in an appeal before the Interstate Commerce Commission on behalf of the wheatgrowers which resulted in a considerable scaling down of railroad freight rates in Idaho.[15] The acquaintances which he made in every remote corner of the state through these organizational activities were to be of great political benefit to him later.

Ben Ross left Canyon County in 1921 and moved with his family to Bannock County, where he had purchased some farm land in the Michaud Flats irrigation district. He sold the old farm, planning to invest the money in his new holdings. But the agricultural depression of the 1920s had by then fallen heavily upon Canyon

C. Ben Ross: Agrarian Democrat 9

County, and he was forced to repossess the Parma ranch. During his gubernatorial term, he would again make it his family home.[16]

In his new location, Ross achieved immediate success and became a leader in developing the Michaud Flats area. A resident of Pocatello, he also made sizable investments in urban real estate, the best known of which was the old Ross-Davis building there. Ross's political reputation followed him to Pocatello, and within two years he had made himself the leader of the progressive wing of the local Democratic party. It is a fair indication of the man's dynamism that in 1922, less than two years after his arrival in Pocatello, he was running for the office of mayor. Despite the fact that the city was normally Republican by at least a one thousand-vote plurality, Ross threw all of his native enthusiasm into the effort and campaigned on a platform of clean and thrifty government. The result was that he was the only Democrat to be elected.[17]

The years as mayor of Pocatello (1923–30) were in some respects the most successful and happy of Ross's political career. He quickly gained the reputation of being a strong, energetic executive, and the results he achieved sufficed to win him re-election three times, each time by a larger majority. When Ross took office, Pocatello had only a few blocks of paved streets and a few more which were graveled. The city's streets were 94 per cent oiled by the end of his mayoral term. Mayor Ross promoted the digging of the first wells in what is now known as Ross Park in Pocatello and thereby vastly improved the city's water supply. As a reform mayor in the old progressive tradition, he also cleaned up Pocatello's police force and modernized its fire department. At the same time, by practicing strict economy, he managed to reduce the bonded indebtedness of the city by over one million dollars.[18]

It was an impressive record in all, and by 1928 it had made Ross one of the most famous men in Idaho. The editor of the *Pocatello Tribune,* a critical observer of most Democrats, voiced a common sentiment as Ross's term as mayor drew to a close in

1930: "It is rather remarkable, but Ben Ross is nearing the end of a period of six years' continuous service as mayor of Pocatello, just as popular, if not more popular, than he was when he was first a candidate, an accomplishment which rightly belongs in Ripley's 'Believe It or Not' column." Despite the fact that Ross had not been involved in Democratic politics on the state level and was not even well-known by the Democratic state leaders, he was able to move immediately to the forefront of state politics on the basis of his reputation as the mayor of Idaho's second largest city.[19] He did so as an independent, and an independent he always remained.

C. Ben Ross was an impressive man, both in physical appearance and personality. He was a large, strong, and erect man, with a full head of graying black hair, a firm jaw, and a determined gaze. His demeanor radiated self-confidence and force, which moved many if not most people to accept him at once as a leader. And his driving energy made him a tireless worker; in fact, his long hours on the job eventually ruined his health. Yet these same qualities also made him a great egoist, "a supreme political egoist," as political analyst John Corlett remembered him.[20] In his dealings with others, Ross always remained a man unto himself and seldom seems to have enjoyed the intimacy of close personal friendships. He was a man apart, with little social life, no hobbies excepting an occasional rodeo, and no visible means of relaxation. Even in reading, he found no escape. "I never read books," he once said. "They spoil original thinking." [21] He drove himself to success but also to ultimate frustration and collapse.

There is perhaps a thin line dividing such earnest individualism from eccentricity, and in his religious beliefs Ben Ross crossed that line. Although a member of the Congregational Church, Ross always viewed religion as a highly personal affair. He became more and more inclined, as he grew older, toward spiritualism and an obsession with his own special mission in life. In 1936 he ex-

C. Ben Ross: Agrarian Democrat 11

plained his philosophy as follows: "I have my own philosophy—you might call it an Indian philosophy. What I desire to achieve I concentrate on. If one concentrates his thoughts upon a goal or purpose long enough and hard enough—Indian philosophy—to the exclusion of all else, one is bound to arrive." [22]

The most bizarre aspect of Ross's spiritualism was his relationship to one Minnie Green, a woman who lived near Pocatello and practiced the art of fortunetelling. Ross was evidently impressed by her ability to foretell certain events, and even at the height of his political career he came to her for advice.[23] Just how much and what kind of advice she gave him is uncertain. Rumors at the time, some of which found their way into print, had it that Minnie Green had predicted Ross's three gubernatorial victories and had proceeded to foretell that he would defeat Senator Borah in 1936 and then be elected President of the United States.[24] Such stories cannot be substantiated. Only this much is certain, that she reinforced his sense of mission and his belief in his own infallibility. "Johnny," he told reporter Corlett just before his death, "because of my religion and the facts it has revealed to me, I know I am right and everyone else is wrong." [25]

Ross was certainly no orthodox New Dealer. His basic political beliefs were heavily tinctured with Populist dogma, and he might best be grouped with such Neo-Bryanite, prairie Democrats of the 1930s as Elmer Thomas and "Alfalfa Bill" Murray of Oklahoma. Though widely publicized, this group played only a minor role in the New Deal period and was most powerful in Congress and on the state level. Ross resembled the Populists of the 1890s in his thoroughgoing monetary inflationism and his vociferous fear of Wall Street. Like them also, he placed the farmer at the peak of the American social order and was an isolationist in his view of foreign policy. But Ross was neither an intellectual nor even an amateur political theorist. As Richard L. Neuberger phrased it: "Great problems of governmental philosophy and international relations are not his concern. He is more interested in whether the water in irrigation ditch 12-A has sufficient gravity pressure to reach Seth Withers' south potato field." [26]

The fundamental source of C. Ben Ross's political strength was his uncanny ability to capture the emotions and the votes of farm people. Like Theodore Roosevelt, he understood the "psychology of the mutt." Before a group he was at his best, gesturing wildly, spicing his monologue with well-chosen profanity and Biblical allusions, walking down the aisles and addressing members of the audience by their first names, offering to return to his rusty old plow tomorrow if the people no longer desired him. To a critical and detached obserer, like famous Idaho author Vardis Fisher, such performances were revolting: "C. Ben Ross was a wholly uneducated man who thought he was the center of the universe." But to a typical agrarian, like Will Rogers, who met Ross at Lake Tahoe in 1933, the appeal was irresistible: "We didn't think there was anybody in Idaho but my old friend Bill Borah. But they sho know they got this Ben Ross. He is a fine chap, plain and no frills, but genuine." After watching Ross perform at Driggs, Idaho, in 1936, a young entertainer named Glen Taylor was greatly impressed and decided to apply his own considerable theatrical talents to politics, a decision which would later result in his election to the United States Senate from Idaho.[27]

Beyond dispute, there was much of the demagogue in C. Ben Ross. This excerpt from a 1934 speech is a good example.

> I want to say to you folks. I want to talk to you about agriculture because that is a thing that is dear to my heart. I expect it always will be. Now, I told my legislature, last winter I wanted them to give me the right to issue moratoriums, and they did. There is talk of running a lawyer against me. And there are several Republicans, who are lawyers, who want to be Governor.
>
> Now, you farmers, who have mortgages on your farms, know what I have done for you with that moratorium. Two or three courts have declared my moratoriums were unconstitutional but that hasn't made any difference to me. I've kept right on issuing moratoriums. Every sixty days I've issued a new one. And I'm still doing it. Do you think

C. Ben Ross: Agrarian Democrat 13

a lawyer, if he had been your Governor would have done that, and kept them from foreclosing the mortgage—kept them from taking your farms?

No, sir-ee! All the lawyers say I'm wrong.[28]

Many observers over the years have characterized Ross as an outright demagogue, sometimes comparing him to the most radical charlatans of the depression era. Frank Burroughs, the caustic editor of the Republican *Idaho Pioneer,* likened him to Huey Long as a political adventurer who had "Barnumized" the masses. Richard Neuberger, the Pacific Northwest's foremost political commentator of the 1930s, agreed: "Ross is the first public figure of considerable political skill to apply even a modified Long-Bilbo-Talmadge technique to the Pacific seaboard." And Charles M. Gates, noted Pacific Northwest historian, concurred: "There was a hint of Huey Long and Theodore G. Bilbo in him, something of the same art of demagoguery and the same consuming political ambition."[29]

But such characterizations can be misleading. While Ross often played upon the sentiments and even the frustrations of the people for votes, he was actually more of a radical in speech than in action. Governor Ross was a sincere and pragmatic reformer, despite some of the dubious schemes which he professed at various times. There were many radicals in Idaho during the 1930s who veered much farther to the left—or to the right—than did C. Ben Ross. He was an idealist and a reformer, but his philosophy was anchored in a deep respect for tradition and for the law. While he did bear a certain resemblance to such depression radicals as Governor Floyd Olson of Minnesota or even Senator Long of Lousiana, Ben Ross was first of all a local product, and he can only be understood when viewed in the historical and political context of his own state. He was an individualist and an independent in the same Idaho tradition which has produced Fred T. Dubois, William E. Borah, Glen Taylor, and Frank Church. Idaho politics have always been amazingly unique, confusing, and colorful, no less so during that twenty-year period between the world wars than today.

II

THE DARK AGE OF THE IDAHO DEMOCRATS: 1918-30

Since the earliest days of statehood, two persistent hallmarks of Idaho politics have been rampant factionalism and unrestrained personal ambitions. This was especially true during the formative 1890s, when the Populist movement mushroomed in the state and divided each party in half, into orthodox Republicans and "Silver" Republicans, Democrats and Populists.[1] It was also true during the post-1900 period, an era of Idaho politics which might well be called the Age of Personalities.

The Progressive Era opened in Idaho when colorful and powerful Senator Fred T. Dubois and his Silver Republicans moved into and took control of the Democratic party in 1900. Dubois's favorite issue of anti-Mormonism proved to be too weak a reed to lean upon and resulted only in the internal division and impotence of the party. The anti-Dubois Democrats, led by the stately progressive John F. Nugent, eventually managed to regain control of their party in 1908, but they were unable really to heal the divisive wounds which Dubois had left upon their organization. The Democrats could control the statehouse from 1910 to 1912 and from 1914 to 1918 only because of a divided opposition.[2]

Meanwhile, the Republicans had problems of their own. Their most capable and popular leader, young Senator William E. Borah, followed a course of independent progressivism and refused to ally himself directly with his own party's organization. The rise

Dark Age of Idaho Democrats: 1918-30

of the national Bull Moose Progressive party under Theodore Roosevelt in 1912 further weakened the Republican party in Idaho, just as it undermined the strength of the national party. With the coming of World War I, the Progressive Era ended in Idaho just as it had begun, with both parties divided.

The election of 1918 marked the end of the reform era in Idaho and the disruption of the Democratic party. Since its initial triumph in 1916 in North Dakota, the Nonpartisan League—a radical, neo-Populist farmers' organization—had been rapidly expanding into Minnesota, Montana, Canada, and finally even as far as Idaho. League organizer Ray McKaig came to Idaho in 1917, advocating a program of state-owned or -controlled banks, railroads, stockyards, and packing houses. After he secured the support of the Idaho Federation of Agriculture for his program, the political power of the league grew tremendously.[3]

A favorite Nonpartisan League tactic was to use the direct primary nominating system to capture an established party. The Democratic party was particularly vulnerable to such a plan because it was once again divided, this time as a result of Senator Nugent's unsuccessful efforts to expel several leading conservatives from the party.[4] The league entered a complete slate of its own candidates in the Democratic primary election in September of 1918. When its entire ticket won in the primary, the league gained momentary domination of the Democratic party and thereby shattered its organization. In the general election, the well-organized Republicans crushed the Nonpartisan-Democratic opposition. Only Senator Nugent managed to survive the landslide. The triumph of the Nonpartisan League, however, was short-lived. In the conservative reaction which immediately followed this episode, the state legislature in 1919 repealed the 1909 Idaho Direct Primary Law and thus sealed off the opening through which the league had come to power.[5]

The repeal of the Direct Primary Law effectively drove the agrarian radicals out of the Democratic party and forced them to campaign as independents in 1920. But the party had been damaged almost beyond repair. In the meantime, shrewd and calculating Frank Gooding had been buttressing the Republican organization which was to rule the state for the next decade. The Democrats lost their last bastion of power in the 1920 election, when Gooding deprived Nugent of his seat in the Senate. Senator Gooding's conservative organization gained a firm and lasting grip upon the GOP and for the next ten years scored one victory after another. During the 1920s, every elected congressional and state official in Idaho was a member of the Republican party. The one exception was a Democratic Supreme Court justice who had been elected in 1916 and whose term did not expire until 1922.[6]

Idaho exemplified the national trend toward Republican conservatism after 1919, voting for Harding, Coolidge, and Hoover by large majorities. But the state did not share in the growth and prosperity which the nation as a whole experienced during the 1920s. The agricultural depression which began shortly after World War I deadened the state's economic growth throughout the "prosperity decade." From 1920 to 1930, Idaho's population increased by only 3 per cent, and almost all of this growth took place in the small urban centers. Of its forty-four counties, twenty-five actually lost in population as hard times drove the farmers from the land.[7] Continuing hardships kept the coals of agrarian radicalism, which had flared in the Populist and Nonpartisan League movements, smoldering throughout the decade.

Following their defeats of 1918 and 1920, Ray McKaig and his followers in the Nonpartisan League chose to maintain their independent status rather than seek a reconciliation with the Democrats. In 1922 the league joined forces with the state organization of the Old Bull Moose Progressive party of the prewar era. Although most of the members of this new Progressive party were former Nonpartisan League members, they adopted the Progressive label both to avoid the radical connotations of the league's reputation and to identify themselves with national Progressive leaders.[8] The new party's program was almost identical to that set forth by the Nonpartisan League, calling for the public ownership of utilities, government control of money and credit, and state guarantee of bank deposits. The Progressives entered independent slates in the elections of 1922, 1924, and 1926, and in 1922 and 1924 they outpolled the Democrats to become the second strongest party in Idaho.

Typically, the Progressives were the most active and enthusiastic campaigners in the state. They focused their attention upon the reinstitution of the direct primary. Quite correctly, they asserted that the "machine" which sustained the power of Senator Gooding and his colorless allies in the statehouse relied upon the closed, convention nominating system for its effectiveness and that the return to the direct primary system would weaken the grip of conservative leaders upon the Republican party. They were supported in this aim by Senator Borah, who, as an old independent progressive himself, looked with disdain upon the return to the convention nominating system of 1919.[9] Much of Borah's political support, in fact, came from the Progressives. The Senator was angered by the consistent opposition of Gooding and his friends to all efforts at restoring the direct primary system, and he remained at loggerheads with his party throughout the 1920s.[10]

The Republican party was able to hold sway in Idaho from 1920 to 1930 only because its opposition was divided. The Democrats and the Progressives held the majority of votes between them and might have triumphed through fusion. The major factor prohibiting this action was the turbulent state of the Democratic party. Senator John F. Nugent had estranged the conservative Democrats by his successful acceptance of Nonpartisan League support in the 1918 election, but his subsequent defeat in 1920 had sapped his power. Following 1920, therefore, the Democrats remained hopelessly split between pro- and anti-Nugent factions.

The hardest fought struggle of the Democratic factions occurred in the 1922 nominating convention when the conservative, anti-Nugent forces tried to thwart the gubernatorial nomination of Nugents' ally Moses Alexander by changing the rules so as to require a two-thirds majority in order to be nominated. This maneuver left the Democrats bitterly divided and impotent. Thus, despite his veto of a new direct primary bill in 1923, Republican Governor C. C. Moore was re-elected in 1924. Moore polled over 50,000 votes, while the Progressive candidate received over 40,000 and the Democrat only 36,810.[11] Idaho Democrats seemed doomed either to extinction or to a permanent third-party status.

During these dark years, a small group of loyal Democrats financed the operations of their party and ran for office with little hope of immediate gain. They sometimes cooperated but more often squabbled among themselves. The conservative, anti-Nugent faction drew upon the financial resources of the Day brothers of Wallace, who had amassed a fortune in mining. Among the most prominent figures in this group were the Days, William Morgan of Boise, Ramsay Walker of Coeur d'Alene, and Asher B. Wilson and W. Orr Chapman, two prominent lawyers from Twin Falls.[12] The progressive, Nugent faction was led by Nugent himself and former Governor Moses Alexander. Its key younger members were lawyers James P. Pope of Boise and Theodore A. Walters of Caldwell, and also State Representative Robert Coulter of Cascade.[13] There were no clear-cut lines dividing these groups; and many prominent Democrats, such as former Governor James Hawley and even Ross himself, were not specifically aligned with either group. Yet the basic antagonism between them endured into the 1930s and was further aggravated by the prohibition issue. In general the Day-Morgan group was "wet" and the Nugent group "dry."

Things had become so bad for the Democrats by 1926 that they even found it difficult to put forward a complete ticket. Five of the

Dark Age of Idaho Democrats: 1918–30

candidates chosen at the poorly attended nominating convention at McCall soon withdrew their candidacies. One of those to withdraw was gubernatorial nominee William Morgan; another was Second District Congressional candidate C. Ben Ross, who had been nominated *in abstentia* and who offered no explanation for his withdrawal.[14] The Democrats were swamped again in the general election of 1926. This time the Progressives failed to support Nugent in his attempt to regain his Senate seat, and he was beaten by Frank Gooding for the second time. Republican H. C. Baldridge, also of Parma, succeeded C. C. Moore as governor.

It seemed that Democratic fortunes might quickly improve following the disaster of 1926. The Republicans' heavy reliance upon the ad valorem property tax for revenue was causing increasing unrest among farmers who thought that they were being forced to carry too large a share of the tax burden. Such dissatisfaction might have driven them into the Democratic party in 1928 had not national factors intervened. The candidacy of Al Smith and the issue of prohibition repeal alienated rural voters from the Democratic party in Idaho and undercut Democratic chances to capitalize upon the widespread public dissatisfaction with conservative Republican rule.

The Democratic factions took opposite views of Al Smith. The conservative, anti-Nugent wing of the party welcomed his candidacy because, like many other wealthy Bourbons across the country, they shared Smith's contempt for prohibition and admired the economic conservatism of his campaign manager, John J. Raskob. Oddly, the Nugent forces, though more liberal, were dry; and many of them, like James Pope, had supported William G. McAdoo against Smith at the Democratic national convention in 1924. The Republicans followed Herbert Hoover in his view of prohibition as a "great social and economic experiment." Idaho's experience certainly lends credence to William E. Leuchtenburg's claim that the biggest issue of the 1928 election was the revulsion of rural voters against Al Smith. Like its neighboring state of Washington, Idaho evidently was almost as dry in 1928 as it had been in 1920.[15]

The impact of the repeal issue in Idaho may be easily seen in the action of the Progressives. They were dry almost to a man; in fact, many of them had been associated with the Anti-Saloon League. Senator Borah used the wet, corrupt stereotype of Smith as a prod to drive them back into the Grand Old Party. According to Borah's biographer C. O. Johnson, the Senator's personal influence upon Ray McKaig, H. F. Samuels, and other old Progressive leaders was decisive. So the agrarian reformers gave up their independent status and supported conservative Republicans Hoover for President, Baldridge for governor, and John Thomas for senator,[16] all because of Al Smith.

As the campaign season approached in 1928, the Democrats were unable to generate much enthusiasm. The wet conservatives among them were from the beginning better organized and more highly motivated than the dries. In early February of 1928, the wet forces, led by W. Orr Chapman and Asher B. Wilson of Twin Falls, scored a victory in the factional struggle over appointing a state national committeeman. They succeeded in installing Wilson in the position, defeating Beecher Hitchcock of Sandpoint, who was being pushed by Coulter and Pope.[17]

The wets were able to gain control of the party organization probably because most Democrats were tired of the prohibition issue and willing to let them have their way. As the party's elder statesman James H. Hawley wrote: "I have no patience with prohibition or its supporters, and while I am no drinking man, I really believe that prohibition is the source of more intemperance and is doing more to immoralize the American people than any other evil that is afflicting them at the present time." The Idaho delegation to the Democratic national convention in Houston in late June was thus solidly wet and instructed to vote for Smith.[18]

Whatever their enthusiasm for or against prohibition, however,

Dark Age of Idaho Democrats: 1918–30

few realistic Democratic politicians had any illusions about the possibilities of victory in Idaho in 1928, knowing full well that they had little chance of unseating any of the Republican incumbents. As in 1926, candidates were hard to find. One of the few contestants to emerge was Mayor C. Ben Ross of Pocatello, who sought the gubernatorial nomination. Ross took this step at the behest of the Nugent and Hawley Democrats, and especially because of the backing of popular and respected former Governor Hawley himself. But Ross held little hope for the struggle ahead, and he wrote to Pope: "This letter may seem to you that I am a little independent, but I do know this, that the man that makes the race for Governor on the Democratic ticket in this state is going up against a hard fight and it is my opinion that he should not be asked to make too much of a sacrifice." [19] He probably had little confidence in success but hoped to build for the future.

The Democrats held their nominating convention in Grangeville on August 27, 1928. Led by Chapman and Wilson, the conservative-wet faction maintained its party hegemony and installed E. M. Holden of Idaho Falls, a dripping wet, as state chairman. Robert Coulter, the pro-Nugent candidate and a pronounced foe of the wet leadership, was defeated for the position. The pro-Smith leaders chose not to enter a man in the gubernatorial race, and Ross received the unanimous nomination. An indication of the lack of enthusiasm at the convention was the fact that neither Ross nor the Senate nominee, Chase A. Clark of Idaho Falls, was even in attendance.[20]

The Democratic platform of 1928 accurately reflected the grievances of Idaho farmers and incorporated many of the planks of past Progressive campaign platforms. It spoke emphatically for a new, state-wide direct primary law and a nonpartisan judiciary, called for a more equitable distribution of taxation, and endorsed the national platform. But the Progressive leaders would not rise to the bait; the prohibition issue made conciliation with the Democrats impossible for them. Two of their key leaders, Ray McKaig and W. Scott Hall, announced that the party would put forth no ticket and endorsed Hoover. The Republicans met in convention at Kellogg on August 27 and with litttle discussion renominated Governor Baldridge and Senator Thomas, who had assumed leadership of the Gooding organization. They completely endorsed the national platform and made no concessions to Progressive sentiment.[21] They did not need to.

Ross put on an exciting campaign during September and October, making fifty-five speeches throughout the forty-four counties, and easily stole public attention from the other candidates. His position, however, was made difficult by the fact that he was a pronounced dry, surrounded by an enthusiastically wet party organization. Naturally, a friction developed between Ross and State Chairman Holden and National Committeeman Asher Wilson. Ignoring his own party platform, Ross struck out on an independent campaign, dwelling upon the issues which would later bring him success. He criticized the Gooding-Thomas organization as an "invisible government" and promised to destroy it by bringing back the direct primary; he attacked governmental extravagance and promised to save the state one million dollars annually by rigid economizing; he took full advantage of his farming connections to promise better marketing roads for agriculture. But, as an instinctive politician, he never once mentioned the bothersome issue of prohibition.[22]

Aside from Ross's strenuous efforts, it was a dull campaign in Idaho. Baldridge and Thomas did little except defend the status quo in both state and nation and, with customary rationalizations, extol the virtues of the protective tariff for agriculture. The Republican organization had never been more efficient or better financed. Under the nominal direction of Senator Thomas and State Chairman John McMurray of Oakley (and the actual, brilliant planning of W. Lloyd Adams of Rexburg), the old Gooding machine operated smoothly and effectively. The Democrats, on the other hand, were both poorly organized and broke. They received practically

Dark Age of Idaho Democrats: 1918–30

no money from the national party headquarters, with the result that the candidates for major offices in large part financed their own campaigns, and those for minor positions scarcely campaigned at all.[23]

The proportions of the Republican triumph in Idaho in the November 6, 1928, election exceeded all expectations. Hoover swamped Smith by an astounding 44,396-vote plurality, 97,322 to 52,926. Otherwise, the Republican margin of victory ran from 25,000 to 40,000 votes. Ross lost to Baldridge by a 24,635-vote plurality, 87,681 to 63,046. Most striking of all was the degree to which the old strongholds of third-party, Progressive strength—Minidoka, Canyon, Jerome, Gooding, Payette, and Gem counties—all went for the GOP. In only two of Idaho's forty-four counties did the Republican vote decline from 1924.[24] The north went overwhelmingly for Hoover, some counties by two-to-one margins, and the southwest was almost as solid. Only in the southeast was the Republican front even slightly broken.

Ross, the strongest major Democratic candidate, was fortunate to carry the ten counties he did. Not only Idaho but the entire Pacific Northwest recorded a blanket repudiation of Smith and the ticket he headed. Fremont County, Idaho, was the only county in the states of Oregon, Washington, and Idaho to vote for Al Smith. Democratic fortunes had seemingly reached their lowest ebb.[25]

Political winds, however, shifted radically during the second Baldridge administration of 1929–30. Long-standing discontent with the heavy property tax came to a head in the legislative session of 1929, when progressive legislators tried to establish a new system of income, inheritance, and tobacco levies to relieve the burden upon the property tax. Governor Baldridge was a moderate conservative, not a reactionary, and he was not closely affiliated with the arch-conservative Gooding-Thomas organization. But he was not a dynamic executive, and he refused till too late to espouse the tax reform program. As a result, the session broke into warring factions and failed to deal with the tax problem at all.[26]

This impasse had the effect of weakening the newly forged loyalties of the ex-Progressives to the Republican party and thereby undermining the victorious coalition of 1928. Clearly, a progressive Democrat, not stigmatized as a wet, might wean these disenchanted reformers away from the GOP. Mayor Ross read the situation correctly and took every opportunity to make speaking tours around the state during these two years. He shrewdly publicized his contempt both for Al Smith and for the repeal cause.[27] But both the Nugent and the Day factions of the party also recognized the new prospects for victory in 1930, and they began to develop their own ambitions. Lacking any solid organizational support from either faction, Ross seemed to have little chance of recapturing the gubernatorial nomination, now that it was really worth something.

Political rumblings became audible in 1929. Following the close of the legislative session, the formerly independent, progressive Republicans began conspiring to wrest control of the party from Senator Thomas and his cronies. The leader in this effort was Lewiston lawyer and amateur historian Byron Defenbach, a Borah-style western progressive who started campaigning for the governorship in late 1929 on the promise of returning the GOP to popular control and destroying "machine rule" by reincarnating the direct primary. The Thomas organization retaliated in February of 1930 with the announcement by State Chairman John McMurray, a staunch ally of Thomas, that he too would seek the office. Backers of Attorney General W. D. Gillis promoted his candidacy as a possible compromise choice.[28]

As the prospects of a divided opposition brightened, Democratic hopefuls began scenting the wind. Ross announced for the governorship on May 2, 1930, upon fundamentally the same program he had espoused in 1928: reinstitution of the direct primary, a nonpartisan judiciary, tax reform, more support of agricultural interests, better roads, and economy in government. Again he evaded the prohibition issue. The wet-conservative Democrats reciprocated Ross's dislike and tried to check his ambitions by running wealthy—and wet—Twin Falls attorney Asher B. Wilson against him. In his announcement of candidacy on June 26, Wilson concurred with most of Ross's indictments and maintained silence on prohibition too. But his ally, State Chairman Holden, had been clamoring for repeal since May 3.[29]

The dry-progressive Democrats now found themselves in a predicament. They had men of their own whom they wished to run, especially Mayor James P. Pope of Boise, but in doing so they faced the likelihood of dividing the dry vote and handing the nomination to Wilson. Robert Coulter, a key organizer of the progressive Democrats, reasoned that "though Ross is a splendid fellow and would make a good governor, . . . we have other men who could get more votes. Standing at the head of the list is J. P. Pope of Boise." Coulter toyed with the idea of putting up a decoy as a third candidate and then bringing out his real choice as an apparent compromise. Ross had told Coulter that he would back down for anyone but his old foe Wilson, but the passage of time made it apparent that he was in the race to stay. Rather than risk a wet candidate, the old Nugent forces fell in line behind Ross by August.[30]

By convention time, most Democrats believed that Ross would be a better vote-getter than Wilson, and he entered the convention as the almost certain victor. Both parties convened on August 26, 1930, the Democrats at St. Anthony and the Republicans at Idaho Falls; and each promised an explosive intra-party fight. But at St. Anthony it quickly became apparent that the Ross-Nugent combine held the upper hand. Ross overpowered Wilson on the first ballot for the gubernatorial nomination, and Wilson moved to make the vote unanimous. The Ross forces clinched their victory when Ross's henchman G. P. "Gub" Mix of Moscow was easily nominated for lieutenant governor and when T. A. Walters of

Caldwell was chosen to replace E. M. Holden as state chairman. After considerable debate, they decided to run Joe Tyler of Emmett as the sacrificial lamb to oppose Borah for the Senate.[31]

The Democratic platform of 1930 closely followed the Ross line. It denounced the GOP for "the extravagance and inefficiency of its machine domination and subservience to special interests," and criticized the national administration for its failure to provide agricultural relief and its dedication to the ruinously high tariff. Again, it called for the direct primary, nonpartisan judiciary, and an old-age pension plan. It placed responsibility for the depression, which was just beginning to be felt in Idaho, on the Hoover administration, but again failed to mention prohibition.[32]

The Republican progressives were less successful. As their convention opened at Idaho Falls, it appeared that Defenbach and his supporters might be able to carry the day. But candidate Gillis refused to withdraw in Defenbach's favor, and the convention fell into a thirty-six-hour deadlock, during which the progressives came to within two and one-half votes of victory. Then, although Defenbach was the obvious popular favorite, the Gooding-Thomas machine turned the scales in McMurray's favor by backing Ralph Scatterday of Caldwell for state chairman and thereby capturing the large Canyon County vote for their man. The nomination of McMurray and all incumbents followed. The Republican platform was a blanket endorsement of Hoover's and Baldridge's policies. The conservative organization had held the line, but at the price of jeopardizing its winning coalition of 1928.[33] In two short years the Republican conservatives' unyielding obstinacy had undermined the unity of their party.

The Democratic strategy in 1930 was almost entirely geared toward the governorship. Walters and Ross realized that they had no hope of defeating Senator Borah, Representatives Burton French and Addison Smith, or many of the state elective officials. Therefore, they directed their attack upon McMurray as a tool of the "invisible government" of the Gooding-Thomas organization. The "machine," they claimed, could sustain itself only through the manipulation of the undemocratic convention nominating system; a return to the direct primary system of nomination would weed out the political charlatans by returning party government directly to the people. Ross constantly kept the issue of the "machine" before the people, characterizing it as a soulless monster which could exist only on patronage and undemocratic chicanery. But he was careful to separate the "machine" from the honest rank and file of Republicans.

> I have no quarrel with the rank and file of the Republican Party of Idaho. I was raised a Republican, and though I have left that party I feel that it still contains some of Idaho's finest citizenry. They themselves, however, agree with me that their only relief from the intolerable system now oppressing the state is to destroy them utterly.[34]

Obviously, Ross was aiming his remarks at the independent progressives among the Republican fold. He had taken over Defenbach's issues.

Republican ineptitude helped the Democrats make the "machine" issue the key factor in the campaign. John McMurray, a wealthy farmer and banker from Oakley, suffered a double disadvantage in being a somewhat worldly Mormon. The gentiles distrusted him because of his faith, and the orthodox Mormons disowned him because he was rumored to have enjoyed an occasional drink or cigarette.[35] In addition, McMurray was an ineffective campaigner. Although a successful political broker as party chairman since 1928, he lacked the flair of enthusing the voting populace.

The tragicomic crowning blow against McMurray and his friends came when the Democrats uncovered and publicized positive evidence that, although he was not a state employee, McMurray had been using a state car and state-purchased gasoline to tour the state on his campaign.[36] As Ross and Walters carried this well-documented news to all corners of the state, Senator Borah and like-minded progressives eventually concluded that they could not support the Republican candidate. There is even some evidence, not entirely convincing, that the Democrats induced Borah to keep quiet during the campaign by promising not to push his Democratic opponent.[37] At any rate, the campaign closed with public attention focused on the gubernatorial race and with the Gooding-Thomas organization discredited. It is perhaps a sad but accurate reflection on the low caliber of local political debate that, in the throes of the most serious depression in American history, the decisive issue in the Idaho campaign of 1930 was the use of a state car for partisan purposes.

The Idaho election returns of November 4, 1930, indicated a clear repudiation of the organizational leadership of the Republican party, but only a limited Democratic "comeback." Senator Borah easily crushed his opponent by a whopping 58,776 plurality, and both Republican representatives and almost all the elective state officials were re-elected. But in the gubernatorial race, Ross exactly reversed this trend, defeating McMurray by a plurality of 15,894 votes, 73,896 to 58,002. His strength, however, did not extend to other Democrats on the ticket. Only G. P. Mix, the candidate for lieutenant governor, rode into office on Ross's coattails, and by an extremely slender margin at that. The legislature remained solidly Republican.[38]

Any sweeping generalization to the effect that the 1930 elections in the United States went heavily Democratic as a result of a protest vote against the depression would not conform to the facts in Idaho. The depression was not yet of crucial magnitude in Idaho by 1930. Representatives French and Smith and Senator Borah all supported Hoover and all won easily. Of the ten northernmost counties, where many of the mines and lumber mills were being shut down, Ross won only six. But of the remaining thirty-four counties to the south, he carried all but four. The southwest, where progressive and radical sentiment had always been strongest, went almost solidly Democratic, and so did the agricultural and Mormon southeast.[39]

Clearly, then, the depression issue did not elect Ross. Nor, apparently, did the religious issue. With a few isolated exceptions, the Democrats in 1930 refused to use Dubois's favorite old cudgel of anti-Mormonism against McMurray. Ross and Walters also succeeded in muffling the repeal controversy which had dominated the spring and summer Democratic primary feuds. The winning issue in 1930 was obviously Ross's promise to abolish "machine rule" in state politics through the direct primary. Ross's constant pursuit of this theme, which was indeed a page out of the old Progressive Bible, caused that decisively large group of ex-Progressives who had entered the GOP in 1928 to turn to the Democrats in 1930.[40]

The mistake of the Gooding-Thomas Republican organization in thwarting reform demands in 1930 proved fatal. Within a year's time, almost all of the leaders of the so-called "machine" had abandoned the game of politics. Gooding himself was dead, and most of his old allies now willingly retired from the scene. Only W. Lloyd Adams and Senator John Thomas, who had two years left in his term, remained active.[41] The Republican party of Idaho faced a new and uncertain future, divorced from the organizational leadership which had secured for it twelve years of undisturbed control of the state. Yet the great majority of Republicans seemed to welcome its passing. The rigidly conservative *Idaho Daily Statesman* summarized the sentiment of the Republican press:

> The voters of Idaho defeated John McMurray because they knew his defeat meant smashing the machine. And the Republican leaders have only themselves to blame. When a party organization develops into a machine whose members are more interested in advancing personal ambition than in the welfare of the party and in good government, that machine deserves to be smashed.[42]

Finally, after more than a decade of frustration, the Democrats had breached the Republican wall. But theirs was a limited victory, and they commanded only a minority of the state's votes. Whether they could sustain their gains and build for future success depended in large part upon the executive ability and political acumen of C. Ben Ross.

III

DEPRESSION IDAHO: 1931–32

Their first taste of victory in a dozen years had an invigorating effect upon the Idaho Democrats. Every party faction and county organization sought more than its share of those appointive positions which promised patronage. The Bonneville County headquarters, for example, recommended men for the positions of state purchasing agent, state insurance commissioner, state land commissioner, deputy commissioner of public welfare, state game warden, matron of the state mental institution at Blackfoot, and an opening on the public utilities commission. Party leaders set up a "sifting committee," dubbed by some as the "pie counter" or the "Committee of St. Peter," to make recommendations for the various positions. Meeting at the Owyhee Hotel in Boise, the committee consisted of State Chairman T. A. Walters, Ben Davis of Pocatello, Ramsay Walker of Coeur d'Alene, W. Orr Chapman of Twin Falls, and Sam Tannahill of Lewiston, and thus represented all party factions.[1] Naturally, its recommendations favored Democrats.

It was the Governor-elect, however, who held the actual appointive power, and Ross raised many hackles among the organization men by selecting in the end just about whomever he pleased for the various positions. Ross did make some concessions to the desires of party stalwarts, most notably by awarding the fairest plum of all, commissioner of public works, to Chapman's protégé, Alvin Harbour of Twin Falls. But, whereas he cleaned out most of the

Republican incumbents in office, Ross replaced them almost entirely with his own personal devotees.[2] The "Old Guard" Democrats recognized this fact and resented it.

From the beginning of his first administration, Governor Ross's relations with the so-called "professional" politicians were strained. He was not a party man and privately expressed himself as being above and independent of the organization.[3] Such an attitude grated harshly on the party leaders of the previous decade, whose appetite for the spoils of office had been whetted by twelve years of exclusion from power. This lack of rapport between Ross and the "Old Guard," although existing only in embryonic form in early 1931, would in time grow and eventually destroy the Democratic coalition which had achieved unity and victory in 1930.

Idaho's new Governor greeted the new year of 1931 with an outpouring of optimism.

> I feel just the way Jeremiah did—"vineyards and fields and lands will once again be sold"—and any statement I would make would be bound to be optimistic. The present depression is due just to the same causes in the business cycle as all the others, and recovery is bound to come shortly. And you will see ultimately a higher level of living than before. That has been the way in all panics since the day of Jeremiah. . . . The recovery will be slower than the slump, but it is in the air for this year of 1931.

It was in such an atmosphere that Democratic Governor C. Ben Ross, his Republican official family, and the state's twenty-first legislature were sworn into office in Boise on a sunny January 5, 1931. The inauguration marked the first mixed party administration in twelve years. Immediately following the inaugural ceremony, the heavily Republican legislature met to organize. The Republicans succeeded in installing C. A. Bottolfsen of Butte County as house speaker and George W. Grebe of Ada County as president pro tempore of the senate. The Democrats in turn selected Robert Coulter as their floor leader in the house and E. G. Van

Hoesen as the senate minority leader.[4] The legislature then met in joint session to hear the Governor's message.

The program which Governor Ross outlined to the 1931 legislature flowed logically from his campaign platform. He proposed, first of all, a reduction in the ad valorem property tax commensurate with the decline in property value resulting from the economic slump. This reduction would be compensated by a graduated income tax and other tax levies which would tap new sources of revenue. Ross tried throughout his career to end the property tax or at least to scale it down drastically in order to relieve the tax burden upon his fellow farmers. Next in priority came the reinstitution of the direct primary nominating system, which had been a Democratic campaign promise throughout the previous decade. Ross also recommended judicial reform which would reduce the number of state judges and would make their appointment nonpartisan, an old-age pension plan, a nonpartisan procedure of selecting educational officials, and the submission of an amendment to the state constitution which would require only a simple majority of votes cast to pass referendum and recall measures in general elections.[5]

Neither Ross nor the Republican majority leaders seized the initiative through effective leadership, and the legislative session quickly mired down into a partisan struggle over its number one problem, tax reform. Against Ross's income tax plan, the Republicans eventually espoused a dubious tax proposal conceived by Roy Dodge, a Seattle tax consultant. When the majority leadership hired Dodge as a special advisor to the legislature against heated Democratic protest, a partisan split over the tax issue was assured. The "Dodge Plan" provided for a license tax on all persons and corporations financially involved in the state. The tax would have been based on net earnings, inversely graduated according to the amount invested within Idaho, and levied upon all tangibles, but with deductions allowed for the property tax.[6] It was an overly complicated scheme, amounting in effect to a softened and camouflaged income tax measure.

Until early February, the session remained deadlocked over the tax issue, and in the meantime discontent mounted among farmers distressed at the legislature's failure to relieve property taxes. A bipartisan "farm bloc" emerged to push a sales tax plan as an alternative but neither Ross nor the Republican majority would consider it. The impasse was finally broken when the progressive Republicans became convinced that their party's leaders were insincere in espousing tax reform and when the Republican leadership, by default, allowed Ross to take the initiative in pressing for a direct primary bill.[7]

The log jam began to break in the senate on January 30, when all the Democrats and six progressive Republicans, led by Senator J. Wesley Holden of Bonneville County, pushed through the Direct Primary Bill. On the same day, a similar coalition in the house passed Ross's Old-Age Pension Bill. Both measures were then pushed through the other houses and signed into law by the Governor by February 15. The Direct Primary Law provided for primary elections to be held on the fourth Tuesday of May, 1932, and biennially thereafter, and for party platform conventions to be held at least sixteen days after the primary elections. The Old-Age Pension Law established in each county an old-age pension committee, composed of the probate judge and the county commissioners, which would rule on claims by persons over sixty-five for pensions up to twenty-five dollars monthly.[8]

The victorious coalition then disposed of all pressing issues except tax reform. A bill providing for the distinct lettering of all state cars, an outgrowth of the 1930 campaign, passed both houses by February 18; and a bill liberalizing the state Workmen's Compensation Law immediately followed. In a lighter moment, the syringia was declared Idaho's state flower. Another bipartisan coalition pushed through both houses a ninety-day divorce law, which reduced the time of state residence necessary for a divorce in order to compete with the Nevada divorce trade. Ross vetoed the bill because he feared that it would "put the State of Idaho and its citizens in an unfavorable light with the sister states of the Union." But the legislature disagreed and overrode his veto.[9]

Despite his general success so far, Governor Ross continued to vacillate on his tax program throughout the regular session. He always believed that the most painless method of relieving the heavy property tax was through the introduction of a wide variety of "hidden taxes," each of which would pinch only a small segment of the populace. So, in addition to his income tax proposal, Ross also introduced a "kilowatt tax" plan which would levy a tax of one-half mill per kilowatt hour of electricity generated within the state. These "hidden taxes" generally pleased the public but ran afoul of the economic conservatism of most legislators. The regular session thus ended on March 6 without having come to terms with the demand for tax reform.[10]

Realizing that public sentiment was behind him, Governor Ross immediately convened the legislature in special session and demanded passage of the Income Tax and Kilowatt Tax Bills. The Republican conservatives, under the leadership of Senator Donald Callahan of Shoshone County, still tried to hold back the tide. But with Senator Holden and the progressive Republicans eventually backing his measures, Ross finally attained the necessary majority and succeeded in putting over his entire tax program. The special session adjourned March 13 in a major Democratic victory and a serious defeat of the badly divided Republican majority.[11]

The passage of Ross's tax program did not bring immediate relief to distressed property owners. The kilowatt tax was too limited to produce much revenue. The income tax, which was graduated from 1 per cent on the first two thousand dollars of net income to 4 per cent on net income over six thousand dollars, was calculated to produce approximately one million dollars annually. But the Income Tax Law would not take effect until March 15, 1932, and there was thus little hope of scaling down the ad valorem property levy until 1932. Ross's tax measures did succeed, however, in arousing the conservatives and pressure groups. Led by the Utah

Power and Light Company, the power companies operating in Idaho contested the kilowatt tax in court, but the federal district court in Boise upheld the law in August of 1931. And in a test case brought by the Ross administration, the Income Tax Law of 1931 was upheld by the state supreme court on March 11, 1932.[12]

Even if Ross's tax reform was more apparent than real, he still made the most of it by announcing that by the end of his term he would have relieved the taxpayers to the extent of four million dollars—two million dollars in new revenue and two million dollars saved through rigid economizing. He went on to claim that the 1931 legislature had enacted "more constructive legislation than any legislature in the last ten years."[13] This boast was largely true, for Ross had succeeded in enacting much of the reform program called for in his 1930 campaign. He did so by dividing the opposition and capturing progressive votes from the Republican column, just as he had done in the 1930 election. The cornerstone of his victory was, of course, the new Direct Primary Law, which the more optimistic progressives thought would revolutionize state politics. Whereas the tax relief measures of 1931 would soon prove inadequate as the depression dried up the wellsprings of state revenue, they were at least a step in the right direction. Of his key programs, only the nonpartisan judiciary proposal completely failed.

Governor Ross's legislative victory won him considerable acclaim as a pragmatic reformer and as the first strong governor Idaho had seen in over a decade. The Direct Primary Bill, sometimes called the "Bill Borah Bill," was actually drawn up by ex-Progressive leaders and was only passed with liberal Republican aid. But Ross claimed and received credit for it because the conservative GOP leaders erred in allowing him to feature it as solely an administration measure. A new executive with virtually no legislative experience, Ross had faltered at first and lost the initiative; but in the end, with luck on his side, he gained control of a legislature dominated by the opposition party and thereby succeeded in enacting most of his program into law. In the meantime, he had firmly established his authority over all executive departments under his jurisdiction. His reputation as a strong governor was made.[14]

The year 1931 was by far the most tranquil of the six years of the Ross administration. But during its final months, the national depression began to set in; and in 1932 the Idaho depression reached the depths of its severity. The depression posed probably the greatest challenge which had ever confronted state government in Idaho, and the state's response was at once both typical and unique.

About one-half of Idaho's population depended directly upon agriculture for its livelihood at this time, while only one-tenth of it relied directly upon manufacturing. Of this latter one-tenth, 90 per cent were involved in the lumber industry, and most of the others were in mining.[15] Thus the primary shock waves of the national depression were transmitted to Idaho through these basic industries and were diffused throughout the state economy.

Both lumber and mining in Idaho were hard hit by the depression before 1931. The nationwide decrease in construction undercut the demand for Idaho lumber, and the sluggishness of eastern industrial tempo caused a drastic cutback in Idaho mining activity. Northern Idaho, where most of these industries were located, experienced the shutdown of local plants and large-scale unemployment long before the south. But the major cause of the depression in Idaho was naturally the decline in value of farm products, which began during the 1920s, worsened in 1931, and fell to disastrous levels in 1932.[16]

Following a visit to Idaho in September of 1932, popular columnist Mark Sullivan concluded that "Idaho was literally the last community in the United States to feel the depression." Sullivan apparently did not realize that the agricultural depression was then in its twelfth year in Idaho and was thus no new phenomenon. But he was quite correct in describing the abrupt drop in crop totals and values during the 1932 farm season. Wheat, the major farm crop in Idaho, held up fairly well both in production and prices, and so did sugar beets. But sheep prices were in decline, as were the prices of dairy products and dry beans. Cattle prices in 1932 hit their lowest level since 1911. The production of potatoes in 1932 fell 20 per cent below the already low level of the two preceding years. The important hay crop brought prices equal to only 50 per cent of the previous year's level.[17]

The farm crisis of 1931–32, then, combined with the prevailing industrial depression in the north to drag down the entire state economy. One of the most accurate indexes of agrarian depression was the rate of mortgage foreclosures. These reached their peak in the eighteen months following December, 1931, totaling in that period 1,145. Delinquent taxes were another revealing barometer of economic dislocation. At the opening of the 1931–32 biennium, these totaled $11,501.67 and at the end of it $438,319.28. The total resources in Idaho banks decreased by over $39,000,000 from 1930 to 1933, and the number of unemployed rose from 6,194 in 1930 to 20,000 in late 1932.[18]

Social disorder and protest accompanying the Idaho depression resembled that which arose throughout the country: demands for lower prices and taxes, protests against mortgage foreclosures, bank runs, and pleas for work relief or the dole. The suicide rate in late 1931 was up 600 per cent from January of 1930. Settlers living below the Big Lost River reclamation district, a privately owned Carey Act project near Arco, had for some time been angry at being excluded from the irrigation facilities nearby. Twice in late June of 1931 mobs dynamited the reservoir controls and diversion works at Mackay Dam, and even worse was threatened. The Utah Construction Company, which owned the dam, could not rely on local police for protection and had to import special deputies. The company apparently knew who the offenders were but also knew that no local jury would convict them. Ross and Reclamation Commissioner R. W. Faris intervened and prevented further violence, but the matter remained unsettled until 1935, when a Reconstruction Finance Corporation loan was secured to buy out the rights of the Utah Construction Company to the dam.[19]

During the summer of 1931, the state of Idaho, and especially the Boise Basin, experienced one of its worst epidemics of forest fires. In Gem, Boise, Idaho, Valley, Adams, and Lemhi counties, arsonists systematically ignited fires in the tinder-dry forests in order to obtain employment as fire fighters. The situation finally became so serious that Ross declared those counties to be in a state of insurrection, placed them under martial law, and ordered the National Guard to close off the forests to public access.[20] Such open manifestations of discontent never became widespread, but they pointed to the growing insecurity and fear which prevailed throughout the state.

The Ross administration attempted to adjust to the hard times by the traditional method of reducing expenditures and waiting for the economy to right itself again. Governor Ross ordered all department heads under his direct authority to cut expenditures by at least 10 per cent in August, 1931. And in March, 1932, he ordered all state employees' salaries over three thousand dollars per year to be cut 10 per cent, voluntarily reducing his own wage by that amount. Wherever possible, Ross and his administrators consolidated offices and eliminated extra functions and employees. The result of this economizing was that the state spent $546,775.41 less than the legislature had appropriated for the biennium.[21] But, while these efforts did keep the state on a sound financial basis and did hold down taxes, they obviously could contribute nothing toward alleviating the general economic crisis.

These economy drives, however ineffective, proved to be popular with the public, and Ross dramatized them whenever possible.

The most spectacular episode of this sort occurred in the fall of 1931. A special investigation of the Lewiston Highway Office disclosed widespread purchasing irregularities and indicated that Henry Gusman, a Russian-born Boise and Lewiston machinery dealer, had for years been defrauding the state through collusion with highway bureau personnel and through the sale of faulty or nonexistent parts to the Lewiston office. Gusman was subsequently tried and convicted of fraud following a Lewiston grand jury investigation.[22]

The grand jury probe revealed a general condition of laxity in the Department of Public Works and raised a cloud of suspicion over the head of Public Works Commissioner Alvin Harbour of Twin Falls. Governor Ross allegedly became suspicious of Harbour after looking into a contract which he had negotiated with Gusman's firm paying fifty-six thousand dollars for some snow removal equipment. After securing a bid of thirty-seven thousand dollars for similar machinery, Ross fired Harbour on November 23, 1931. The Governor seemed on solid ground in dismissing Harbour, but he exploited the episode to the utmost by heralding it as an example of his pursuit of honesty and economy in government. This action added to Ross's popularity with the public, but it also aggravated Harbour's Democratic cohorts. Harbour was a prominent member of the old Day wing of the party and a confidant of W. Orr Chapman. Arguing that Ross had destroyed his friend unfairly, Chapman became Ross's most bitter Democratic enemy.[23] Significant is the fact that, while Ross heralded his exposure of wrongdoing, he made no serious effort to reform the Public Works Department or to straighten out its clumsy method of accounting. This failure would return to haunt him later.

A growing number of Idahoans came to regard Ross as their protector and bulwark against venal politicians and dishonest businessmen. He endeared himself to the common people by attacking those whom they viewed as their oppressors. Another instance of this tactic occurred in the summer of 1932, when popular resent-

C. BEN ROSS

JAMES P. POPE

WILLIAM E. BORAH

BARZILLA W. CLARK

D. WORTH CLARK

ment was running high against oil companies who were charging higher gasoline prices in Idaho than elsewhere in the Northwest. Ross wired the five major oil companies operating in the state and threatened to establish state-owned and -operated filling stations for public use unless the prices were reduced. When gasoline prices were scaled down in some areas, Ross won a rich reward of popular acclaim.[24] But, regardless of their political effects, such efforts had little bearing upon the economic plight of the state, and Ross probably knew it.

As the depression deepened in 1932, it became more and more apparent to state leaders that local efforts to combat it were inadequate. Because of the small size of most Idaho towns, local work relief projects on the community level were almost impossible to sponsor. Absence of tax revenue also ruled out any possibility of large-scale public works on the state level. Only the extensive highway construction and maintenance program, initiated in 1929 with federal aid, could hire many of the unemployed; and even this project was far too limited to be of much over-all benefit to the economy of the state. Basically a realist, Governor Ross never followed the states' rights argument regarding unemployment relief. He always contended that only the federal government could effectively deal with the problem.

> The responsibility of taking care of the unemployed must rest upon the Federal government because of the fact that the policy of the government over the last several years brought on the depression which threw millions of men out of employment; therefore, the Federal government should pay the bill. The states can properly be called upon to take care of the indigent poor, as they have in the past.[25]

President Hoover's attitude toward relief was directly contrary to that expressed by Ross; Hoover felt that local government and private charity could and should provide for the needy. It was with reluctance, therefore, that the President finally turned to a limited program of federal assistance. In January of 1932 Congress authorized the Reconstruction Finance Corporation (RFC). The act created a new federal agency, capitalized with a stock of five hundred million dollars and authorized to make loans to needy banks and other financial institutions.[26]

The hub of Idaho banking was Boise, whose three major banking organizations were the First Security Corporation, controlled by the Eccles family of Utah, the Idaho First National, and the Boise City National. The presidents of the three banks organized the Reconstruction Corporation of Idaho in February of 1932, in order to secure RFC loans. Eventually, the RFC helped to alleviate the sad condition of Idaho banking and by 1938 had loaned $2,902,146.39 to banks in the state. But it came too late to stave off near disaster in 1932, one of the most calamitous years in the history of Idaho banking. In that one year alone, sixteen banks failed, and the total banking resources in the state dropped twenty-three million dollars. According to Marriner Eccles, only the First Security banks kept their doors open without interruption throughout the critical year.[27]

Hoover was even more reluctant about loaning money directly to distraught states for relief and emergency public works, but by the summer of 1932 the pressure for such aid had become almost irresistible. In July, Congress passed the Emergency Relief and Construction Act, which set aside a fund of three hundred million dollars which the RFC would loan to the states at 3 per cent and which the states would repay over a five-year period.[28]

The states could employ this RFC money according to their own discretion. Like many of the later New Deal administrators, especially Harry Hopkins, Governor Ross firmly opposed the "dole," which merely involved parceling out money to the counties on the basis of population for direct relief. Instead, he favored keeping the money under his own control and spending it on useful public works projects. Like other small, rural states, Idaho had no state relief commission; the county commissioners still held responsibility for care of the indigent. Over heated protests, Ross set out to bypass the county relief system and to use federal relief loans as he saw fit. He made his personal secretary, Parker Carver, director of state relief. Regional RFC Director Pierce Williams favored formation of a nonpartisan state relief commission and criticized Ross's choice of Carver as relief director since, he felt, Carver lacked the strength of personality and the free time to do an adequate job. But, as usual, Ross had his way.[29]

Idaho received from the RFC loans of $150,000 each in September and November, 1932, and three more grants from January to April 1933, for a grand total of $950,616. Governor Ross, who held full responsibility for its use, generally spent the money wisely, most of it for highway construction. But such a policy demanded careful selection of only a few projects and was bound to anger county and municipal officials whose areas were not so favored. Ross added credence to the arguments of his critics by spending half of the first $150,000 stipend on one project, the Sandpoint Bridge.[30]

The leading critic of Ross's relief policy was popular Democratic Mayor Barzilla Clark of Idaho Falls. Clark insisted that such work projects did not benefit enough people and that the only fair way of using the funds was to distribute them among the counties on the basis of population. And the Twin Falls Board of County Commissioners, represented by the law firm of W. Orr Chapman, unsuccessfully attempted to secure a court order compelling Ross to follow this method.[31] None of these criticisms deterred the Governor. Ross was essentially correct in avoiding the outright dole, for by selecting certain worthwhile public works projects he could both concentrate spending in hardest pressed areas and use the money for projects of enduring value. But he could have tempered much local criticism by sponsoring more and smaller projects rather than a few large ones.

The efforts of the federal government to provide relief in Idaho through the RFC in late 1932 and early 1933 were only marginally successful. Supplying less than one million dollars through loans, the RFC simply did not pour enough money into Idaho either to employ more than a small fraction of the state's twenty thousand idle men or to stimulate its languishing economy. But on the local level at least, the RFC revealed how controversial the allocation problem would be and acquainted local officials with most of the difficulties which would accompany the more concentrated relief efforts of the New Deal.

In state politics, the deepening of depression further widened the breach which the Democrats had opened in the Republican front in 1930. Reform and repeal sentiment grew rapidly, and so did the ambitions of many Democrats, who became more liberal with the times. While the Democratic party enjoyed a rejuvenation, the GOP fell deeper into inertia, suffering from both lack of leadership and the onus of the Hoover image. The Republican hold upon most state offices was obviously weakening, and the Democrats sensed that it was their year to turn the scales.[32]

The most important political development in Idaho during 1931 and 1932 was undoubtedly the rise of a new force to dominance, the Ross organization—or "machine," as the Governor's many enemies preferred to call it. The Ross organization was less a machine—in the true sense of a tightly knit political group maintaining power by material give and take—than it was a bipartisan, loosely organized group of voters who were held together only by their fervid dedication to the Governor. As an administrator, Ross completely dominated his appointees, and he personally supervised the hiring of all personnel, making sure that they were loyal to him. As a politician, he largely ignored the Democratic organization and the established leaders of his party and dispensed patronage as he saw fit.[33] He thereby developed his own bloc, which some hostile observers called the "Statehouse Gang," within the Democratic party. The repercussions of his strategy were to become apparent only late in the campaign of 1932.

The degree to which Ross had overturned the old party leadership was revealed early in 1932. At a Pocatello "victory dinner" on January 13, Ross and his devotees held undisputed sway and vaunted their own choice candidates and issues. In the main address, Ross heatedly blamed the tight-money policies of Treasury Secretary Andrew Mellon for causing the under-consumption which had brought on the depression, and he called for a coalition of the South and West to overthrow the rule of Hoover and Mellon. But, most conspicuously, Ramsay Walker and W. Orr Chapman, two chief spokesmen for the old Day wing of the party, did not even attend. At the meeting of the Democratic State Central Committee in Caldwell on February 18, the reason for their absence became clear. Leaders of both the Nugent-progressive and Day-conservative factions protested Ross's habit of ignoring them and catering to those progressive Republicans who had carried him into office in 1930.[34] The conservatives were particularly disgruntled over the firing of Public Works Commissioner Harbour.

The ripest plum sought by the Democrats was the Senate seat held by Republican John Thomas. Because of his bland conservatism and lack of many noteworthy accomplishments, Thomas was vulnerable. J. Wesley Holden, a liberal Republican from Idaho Falls, had been campaigning against him for the nomination since 1931. By the spring of 1932, five Democrats had joined the race. The contest originally centered upon the wet-conservative W. Orr Chapman of Twin Falls and the dry-progressive mayor of Boise, James P. Pope. Lieutenant Governor G. P. Mix, the brother-in-law of Chapman's main ally J. J. Day, dealt Chapman's cause a serious blow by also entering the race and thereby neutralizing the Day influence. Very probably, Ross put his good friend Mix up to this strategy in an effort to keep his sworn enemy Chapman out of power.

Finally, two extremist candidates also filed—State Senator Owen T. Stratton of Lemhi County, a radical wet, and Harry Kessler of Boise, an outspoken prohibitionist of long standing. Pope was the leading candidate of the five. Chapman and Mix were ineffective campaigners, and Kessler and Stratton seemed more concerned with the prohibition issue than with their own political fortunes.[35]

As in the Senate contest, a large number of Democratic candidates emerged in contention for all major offices. Neither faction, however, put up a man against Ross. Mayor Clark of Idaho Falls announced his candidacy for the governorship, apparently without the backing of either wing of the party, but he quickly withdrew when he saw the impossibility of success.[36] Russ refused to endorse any of the senatorial aspirants, although he probably avoided supporting his friend Mix only in order to hold the support of Pope and the old Nugent group.

Such political ferment among the Democrats contrasted sharply with the inertia which had fallen upon the GOP. The Republican party had not yet recovered from the collapse of the Gooding-Thomas machine following the 1930 election. Many of the progressive Republicans, furthermore, now supported Governor Ross. Byron Defenbach, the old liberal who had almost won the nomination in 1930, was the single Republican contestant for governor. Of the congressional delegation, only Senator Thomas faced primary opposition.

Idaho's first primary election since 1918 was held May 24, 1932. Its results disproved the warnings of those who had feared that the return of the direct primary would again disrupt party organization. All those established in office won renomination: Ross, Senator Thomas, and the two veteran Republican Congressmen Addison T. Smith and Burton L. French. Pope easily won the Democratic Senate nomination, and Defenbach captured the Republican gubernatorial position unopposed. Two new Democratic personalities emerged as congressional nominees: Compton I. White of Clark's Fork for the First District, and Mayor Thomas C. Coffin of Pocatello, a liberal wet, for the Second District. The Liberty party, a leftist splinter group advocating the retention of prohibition and the abolition of "usury," nominated Barzilla Clark for governor and threatened to capture a significant percentage of the old Nonpartisan League–Progressive element.[37]

With the nominating conventions struck down by the Direct Primary Law, the party platform conventions became the scenes of intra-party power struggles. The Democratic convention, held at Weiser on June 10, at once evidenced a coalition between the Ross forces and the old Nugent faction—now led by Pope and State Chairman T. A. Walters—which was bent on driving the wets and conservatives out of power. With impressive ease, the coalition elected its own man, Sam O. Tannahill of Lewiston, as national committeeman, defeating the anti-Ross incumbent Asher Wilson. The platform, most of which was written by Pope, applauded Ross's achievements, scored Hoover for the depression and the Smoot-Hawley Tariff, and called for an international conference on the remonetization of silver. Over the violent protest of congressional nominee Coffin, Pope quietly ignored the repeal issue. Idaho's eight votes at the national convention were committed to Governor Franklin D. Roosevelt of New York for President and to Governor George H. Dern of Utah for Vice-President.[38] Ross's and Pope's ally T. A. Walters continued as state chairman.

The Republican platform convention, held at Boise on June 10, was relatively uneventful and devoted most of its time to lauding Borah and Hoover. R. B. Parry of Twin Falls, who had earlier been elected as a compromise choice, stayed on as state chairman. Like its Democratic counterpart, the Republican platform demanded the remonetization of silver and kept silent on the issue of prohibition repeal. It naturally voiced approval of Hoover's policies and spoke out for a thorough investigation of various state agencies.[39]

The gubernatorial race of 1932 was interesting in that it pitted two progressives, who agreed on all fundamentals, against each other. Both Ross and Defenbach followed the successful Ross formula of the 1930 campaign. Defenbach charged the Ross administration with being "the most extravagant administration in the history of the state." He further argued that property taxes were too high in the face of property devaluation, promised to cut the budget "at least 25%," and repeatedly voiced his heartfelt sympathy for the common man. Ross said about the same thing, except that he rather understandably disagreed about the merits of his own record. Whereas Defenbach had accused him of grandstanding in his highway investigation, Ross capitalized on his image as a fearless foe of corruption in government, as is seen in this advertisement:

> HE STANDS UNAFRAID. Here is the man—the one who tore the lid off certain things which had not been revealed for 3 administrations—all of them Republican—before him. He had the searchlights of justice turned on in full glare into dark corners of state government and drove graft out. This man has no keep-it-dark policies.[40]

Otherwise, the campaign centered around national issues, with all Democratic candidates following the Roosevelt line against Hoover. Almost every prominent Democrat in the state greeted Roosevelt when he stopped at Pocatello on September 19 on his western railroad tour. A large and somber crowd voiced thorough agreement with F.D.R.'s criticism of the status quo and his promise "to restore the purchasing power of the farm dollar." Candidate Roosevelt promised Idahoans what they wanted and expected of him: a new farm policy, recovery, and economy in government. Whereas Al Smith had been a liability to Idaho Democrats in 1928, Roosevelt was an asset in 1932. Since the Democratic leaders in Idaho remained dry in 1932, they frowned upon the repeal plank in the national platform; but, sensing national victory, they quietly accepted it.[41]

While the 1932 election might well be termed a "landslide" on the national level, the word "earthquake" would better describe it in Idaho. In a state which had normally been safe for most Republican candidates, the Democratic New Deal ticket ran well over 15,000 votes above its opposition. Roosevelt trounced Hoover, 109,479 to 71,312; and Pope beat Thomas for the Senate, 103,-

020 to 78,325. But the most surprising result of the election was the decisive defeat of both well-entrenched Republican congressmen. First District Representative Burton L. French of Moscow had been in Congress for twenty-six years; and Addison T. Smith, the Second District Representative, had been in office for twenty years. Both were toppled by margins exceeding ten thousand votes. In the state legislature, the margin of victory was astounding— only three Republicans held their house seats, and a mere nine remained in the senate. Seldom has any state seen such a drastic overturn in its political status quo. The only Republican elective official remaining in high office was Senator Borah, who had carefully remained aloof this time from the national administration. Since 1896, Idaho had not seen such a Democratic victory. The arch conservative *Wallace Miner* headlined its lament: "Rampant and Unreasoning Democracy Rides Ruthlessly over Republican Opposition in Shoshone County." [42]

The entire far West experienced a political revolution. The only western Republican to win a Senate contest was Frederick Steiwer of Oregon. In Utah, university professor Elbert Thomas unseated prominent Republican Senator Reed Smoot, a Mormon leader. In Washington, liberal Democrat Homer T. Bone defeated incumbent Wesley L. Jones. Four western states elected governors, and each of them chose a Democrat. The dimensions of the political revolution in the Pacific Northwest were overwhelming. Hoover had carried all but one of the counties in Washington, Oregon, and Idaho in 1928. In 1932 he carried only two. Idaho not only shared in this western Democratic trend, it undoubtedly exceeded it.[43] The Republican leadership of the previous decade had been completely overthrown.

The Idaho election of 1932 was, above all, a personal triumph for Governor Ross. By defeating Defenbach 116,663 to 68,863, he won more votes than any other candidate, surpassing even Roosevelt himself.[44] The voters not only repudiated the Republicans, they approved of Ross and his programs. Thus, while the other

Democrats obviously owed their victories at least in part to the long coattails of F.D.R., Ross could and did boast that he was stronger than his party. But the Governor actually had less cause for jubilation than it might have seemed. On the surface, it appeared that the New Deal avalanche had strengthened Ross's position by surrounding him with fellow Democrats. It actually had just the opposite effect of raising to the fore other Democratic leaders in the state whose first loyalties were not to C. Ben Ross.

Ross had pretty well alienated the conservative wing of the party in 1931 by his firing of Public Works Commissioner Harbour, but he had held the more powerful progressive wing of the party with him throughout the 1932 campaign. During that campaign, however, Ross offended candidate Pope and State Chairman Walters by virtually ignoring party headquarters and the Pope entourage and running his own campaign his own way with the help of his men in the statehouse. Ross and his followers were kept well supplied with information and publicity by this so-called "Kitchen Kabinet," but Pope and the other candidates were left to their own devices. As James H. Hawley, Jr., recalls, Ross and Pope were not even on speaking terms following the election, and Ross was the aggressor.[45]

At the very pinnacle of his power, therefore, Ross had already sown the seeds of party division which were to bring about his own downfall in the future. Increasingly, the old lines of division between Nugent and anti-Nugent Democrats became blurred, and the new division of the Idaho Democratic party into Ross Democrats and anti-Ross Democrats began to coalesce. The two new factions were formed, not on the basis of conservative or liberal ideology, but on the basis of personal loyalties, rivalries, and ambitions. Caught in the tensions of this local dispute, the Democratic party of Idaho was never able to form a united and lasting New Deal coalition to compare with the apparent Roosevelt coalition on the national scene.

IV

WORKING WITH THE NEW DEAL: 1933–34

As the year 1933 dawned in Idaho, a confused and desperate population, caught in the grip of the worst depression the state had ever seen, looked to the Governor and the legislators to give it some sort of relief. The farmers were unable to pay their taxes or to stave off creditors, and they feared and resented the prospect of losing their farms. It was a bleak prospect which confronted the Democratic party as it assumed full control of state government for the first time in a generation. As conditions worsened and the sense of crisis mounted, the time for action seemed to be running out.

The 1933 legislature was so heavily Democratic that the Republican opposition was scarcely a factor at all. So many legislators were new in their positions that few of them had any experience to guide them. Many were farmers whose single goal was the improvement of the agricultural situation and who looked to the farmer in the statehouse for leadership. Ross's leadership of this legislature would perhaps be his greatest achievement as governor. Assisted by House Speaker Coulter and President pro tempore of the senate E. G. Van Hoesen, Governor Ross exercised a firm and responsible control over the turbulent session and expertly guided its course between the extremes of radicalism and reaction.[1]

In his opening address to the joint session, Governor Ross maximized the obligations of the federal government and minimized those of the states. The first duty of the federal government, he said, should be a controlled program of currency inflation; the first duty of state government should be to economize and to aid the harried taxpayer. "The states can do but little through their legislative bodies to increase the income of our people. But what they can do is to ECONOMIZE. . . . It is not a matter of what we think we need or what we are entitled to, but the whole question before us is what we can pay for." [2]

With the Income Tax Law of 1931 now in effect, Ross proposed to cut back the ad valorem levy and to place a temporary moratorium on the collection of overdue property taxes. In the interest of economy, he suggested putting certain governmental departments which served only limited economic groups on a self-supporting, fee basis. Again, as in 1931, he asked for a nonpartisan judiciary and educational system and for reform of the initiative, referendum, and recall laws.[3]

Ross's crash economy program failed to satisfy many agrarian spokesmen who were in a mood for radical action. The farm bloc of 1931 re-emerged with its sales tax proposal and also sought to enact a law halting all mortgage foreclosures. Most radical of all was the proposal by Senator Owen T. Stratton of Lemhi County, who introduced a bill to nullify the debts of all political subdivisions of the state and to allow the courts to declare ninety-nine-year debt moratoriums. A growing number of Democrats and Republicans alike pushed for legislation to legalize the sale of 3.2 per cent beer, but Ross held fast to his dry stand.[4]

Spearheaded by State Senator Chase Clark of Idaho Falls and House Speaker Coulter, the Ross-sponsored bills flowed through both houses with remarkable ease. The two tax moratorium measures—one allowing a two-year moratorium on the payment of delinquent property taxes, the other prohibiting the collection of interest on the outstanding taxes due—passed both houses unopposed on January 4. Likewise, the Governor's ad valorem levy, which was slashed from four and one-half million dollars to two and one-half million dollars, and his budget, cut by almost two million dollars, passed with only light opposition. The legislators quickly approved and submitted to the voters at the forthcoming 1934 general election amendments to the state constitution calling for the nonpartisan selection of supreme court and district judges and for reducing the number of votes required to pass referendum and recall legislation to a simple majority of the votes cast in an election. The legislature also approved submission of an amendment to repeal the state Prohibition Law of 1915.[5]

By early February, Governor Ross had already pressed his fundamental program to enactment, but in the meantime agrarian unrest and pressure for further debt and foreclosure relief mounted rapidly. Ross naturally sympathized with these complaints, especially those against the dreaded mortgage foreclosures, but he was wary of endorsing the farmers' pet relief schemes because of their doubtful legality. Pressure from rural areas, however, was fast becoming irresistible. The threat of violence was omnipresent. On February 21, a mass meeting of several hundred southwestern Idaho farmers served "demands" on the Governor and the legislators for a two-year holiday on mortgage foreclosures and a law requiring jury trials in foreclosure cases.[6]

Ross finally took action on February 10, intervening to halt the sheriff's sale of the Henry Maw property near Roswell. Maw, an old friend and neighbor of the Governor, had homesteaded and cleared the land himself. Ross explained this drastic action to a Nampa newspaper:

> In these times when mortgages threaten to deprive farmers of their homes because of conditions for which they are in no way responsible, I feel that the mortgagee must take his share of the loss along with the farmer. The loans were made when farm values were high, but now that four bushels of wheat are required to pay for what one bushel did a few years ago, I don't think we should take a man's farm

away from him. It will be my policy, until the prices of farm products return to the point where the farmer can meet his obligations, to discourage the disposal of land by sheriff sale upon which the state holds mortgages.[7]

Ross's response to agrarian demands for tax reform and foreclosure relief was a limited compromise. Instead of backing the sales tax which many farm groups wanted, he introduced and pushed through two new "hidden taxes." The first was a Gasoline Tax Law, which required an annual five-dollar license for all gasoline distributors and levied an excise tax on gasoline of five cents per gallon. The other new levy was a Chain Store Licensing Tax Law, which required an annual licensing fee of all such stores operating in the state, steeply graduated according to how many branch stores any firm had within the state.[8]

While he opposed two radical measures for a general debt moratorium and a rent moratorium, the Governor finally satisfied discontented farmers by sponsoring a General Moratorium Law, which authorized him to declare sixty-day holidays on mortgage foreclosures and to renew such sixty-day holidays consecutively. Based on similar laws of Minnesota and other states, Ross's bill became law on March 1. The Governor tried to be selective in halting foreclosures at first, but when this proved impossible he issued the first blanket sixty-day moratorium in late March. Despite a constant running battle with the courts, he continued to reissue them at two-months intervals thereafter until the law expired in 1935. Compared to the actions of some other depression governors, Ross's policy on mortgage foreclosure relief does not seem quite so radical. Governor Floyd B. Olson of Minnesota, for instance, proclaimed a general moratorium on his own authority until the legislature could act. Governor William Langer of North Dakota even called out the state militia to halt foreclosures.[9] While of dubious legality, Ross's action was undoubtedly humane and may well have averted widespread violence and a serious breakdown of law and order.

Working with the New Deal: 1933-34

The General Moratorium Law was the final reform enactment of the 1933 regular session. After authorizing a special election to be held at some time before the 1934 general election on the subject of repealing the Eighteenth Amendment, the legislature adjourned on March 1, 1933.[10] It had been a tense and nerve-racking session, and the agrarian reformers who constituted its majority would gladly have taken much more radical steps than Ross encouraged them to do. The Governor and his lieutenants held the radicals in line and systematically put through every one of the administration measures.

As one awe-struck editor saw it, the legislature had given the Governor "powers that would make Benito Mussolini blush with envy."[11] Yet, in the pathos of the moment, many frightened conservatives no doubt forgot that in general the laws passed were the more moderate of the original measures proposed. Unlike a genuine radical or demagogue, Ross toned down and compromised the extreme demands of the true radicals, rather than nurturing their growth. Like many another reformer, he found the radicalism of his ideas mellowed by the responsibility of office. As an administrator, he often behaved more like a conservative than a radical.

The inauguration of President Roosevelt on March 4, 1933, and the hectic period of reform known as the "100 Days" which followed, began a tumultuous era in federal-state relations. The mammoth intrusion of the federal government into what had before been the domain solely of the state governments was a response to an urgent demand and need. But in its early stages, the coming of the New Deal initiated a period of great confusion, misunderstanding, resentment, and readjustment. People often failed to realize the considerable accomplishments of the New Deal in the clamor of local political activity.

Governor Ross went to Washington, D.C., early in March of 1933, to attend the inauguration of President Roosevelt, and he remained to attend the special governors' conference which the new President called on March 6. At the conference, Ross made a considerable stir by presenting his so-called "Ross Plan for National Rehabilitation." The Ross Plan was a soft-money scheme, not unlike those submitted by other Democrats of the time, which harked back to the Greenback-Populist era of economic radicalism on the prairies.

Ross looked upon the depression as the beginning of a financial revolution, overthrowing the gold standard and the power of Wall Street. He asked that the new administration "issue up to $20 billion in non-interest bearing notes, payable within 38 years at 3 per cent on the principle." These federal "Liberty Notes" would be issued as legal tender to pay approximately six million men working on agricultural and industrial public works projects recommended by the various states. As a result of this infusion of buying power, all the other unemployed would be hired.[12]

The Ross Plan was a panacea. The employment of six million men and their payment in government scrip would have disrupted not only the stability of the nation's currency but the entire capitalistic system of the United States, and it would have helped little in the vital area of production. But Ross's scheme did strike a sentimental vein among the old Bryanites of the Democratic party, and it was endorsed by Governors O. K. Allen of Louisiana, Eugene Talmadge of Georgia, W. A. Comstock of Michigan, and Leslie Miller of Wyoming.[13]

While Governor Ross was in Washington, D.C., banking conditions in Idaho had deteriorated to the point that complete failure in some areas became imminent. Total resources in Idaho banks had fallen to their 1914 level, and in neighboring states banking holidays were already in effect. The result was a series of disastrous "runs" on banks located in the northern "panhandle" area. It was to protect these banks that Lieutenant Governor George Hill declared a general state banking "holiday" on March 2; his action was supplanted by the President's declaration of a nationwide "banking holiday" on March 6.¹⁴

Banking conditions were quickly stabilized in Idaho. In line with the President's decree, Ross and Finance Commissioner Ben Diefendorf began to allow reopenings on a limited basis within a few days. By March 14, Ross was convinced that the worst was over, and he lifted the state moratorium. The Federal Reserve banks opened their doors as soon as they had guaranteed the Treasury Department of their soundness, and the state finance commissioner likewise supervised the reopening of state banks. Most Idaho banks were doing business as usual by March 19 except in the Lewiston area, which had been hardest hit by out-of-state runs; normal banking activities did not resume there until June.¹⁵

In Idaho, as in the nation at large, the closing of the banks seemed to mark the low point of the depression; and their reopening seemed to spark the beginning of recovery. Statewide and nationwide attention focused on the White House and the Congress in anxious anticipation of the President's relief, recovery, and reform programs.

The greatest interest in Idaho centered upon the administration's farm program, which was presented to Congress on March 16, and after considerable debate and modification, enacted as the Agricultural Adjustment Act on May 12, 1933. This complex legislation was designed to restore the economic position of the nation's farmers to a parity with that of 1914 through a fourfold program: (1) restraints on production to raise prices, (2) direct federal payments to farmers who voluntarily participated in production control programs, (3) levying excise taxes on farm-produce processors to defray costs of administration, and (4) the regulation of marketing through voluntary agreements among processors and distributors or through compulsory licensing to eliminate unfair practices or charges.¹⁶

The Roosevelt farm program was administered by the United

States Department of Agriculture and the Agricultural Adjustment Administration (AAA). Unlike most of the new federal agencies, the AAA did not rely upon the state governments for administrative cooperation or assistance. Complying with the suggestion of Agriculture Secretary Henry Wallace, Ross established a State Advisory Committee to the AAA, consisting of the Governor, the director of the agricultural extension service at the state university, and the state commissioner of agriculture, the chief justice of the state supreme court, and one farmer to be chosen by the Governor.[17] But this committee had no administrative functions. Each farmer who enrolled in the production control program signed a contract with the federal government and dealt directly with AAA authorities. More than any other New Deal agency, the AAA bypassed the state governments altogether and established federal authority on the grass-roots level.

The AAA program had a tremendous impact upon the economy of Idaho. By the close of the harvest season of 1936, 73,258 AAA contracts had been negotiated in the state—43,482 in wheat, 15,790 in corn and hogs, and 13,986 in sugar. The result of the AAA endeavor was a decline in crop acreage and a rise in crop values. Whereas the total cash value of Idaho crop production in 1932 had been $41,906,000, the value of the 1935 crop was $74,921,000, a 79 per cent increase. But the AAA was certainly no unqualified success. The number of Idaho tenants, significantly, increased 15 per cent from 1930 to 1935; and the average Idaho farm, worth $10,012 in 1930, was worth only $6,814 in 1935.[18] Yet the AAA could claim much of the credit for alleviating the farm crisis of 1932–33, and the federal production-control payments to the farmers immediately raised the buying power of farmers and stimulated the entire economy of Idaho.

An important supplement to the AAA was the Farm Credit Administration (FCA), established by Congress on June 16, 1933. The purpose of the FCA was to halt the rise of farm mortgage foreclosures by refinancing farm loans through the nation's twelve federal land banks. The Land Bank of Spokane served all of Idaho, and through August of 1936 it made 9,234 Idaho loans totaling $11,581,000 on first mortgages, and 5,000 loans on second and third mortgages amounting to another $10,997,000.[19] Since ninety-two dollars of every one hundred dollars of FCA loans went directly to creditors, the FCA provided an immediate stimulus to the Idaho economy. While Ross was claiming credit for keeping farmers on their land through his mortgage moratoriums, the FCA quietly supplied the necessary money.

The Home Owners' Loan Corporation (HOLC) did for debt-burdened home owners what the FCA accomplished for farmers. From June of 1933, when the HOLC began operations in Idaho, until June of 1935, when it closed its doors, this agency refinanced almost 15 per cent of the nonfarm homes in the state and negotiated loans totaling over $8,000,000. Allowing repayment over a fifteen-year period, the HOLC rarely had to foreclose. And by absorbing the overdue taxes of borrowers, which were incorporated in the loans, the HOLC disbursed about $845,000 in badly needed cash to local taxing authorities.[20]

The Federal Emergency Relief Act of May 12, 1933, was the first of many New Deal attempts to help the states carry the burden of providing relief for the unemployed. It made available five hundred million dollars in federal funds. Half of this amount was to be issued to the states on a matching basis of three dollars of state money for every one dollar from the FERA, and the other half was to be granted to areas of greatest need at the discretion of the FERA administrator, Harry Hopkins.[21]

Governor Ross agreed with Hopkins on one thing, that public works projects were superior to the "dole." For this reason, he was able to channel FERA funds initially into state highway projects and thus to use state highway appropriations as matching funds in order to qualify for federal aid. But he disagreed with Hopkins on other policies. Hopkins requested all governors to appoint nonpartisan relief commissions, "with full power to exercise supervision over local relief administration," and he demanded that the states immediately raise matching funds, by the sales tax or by other means. Ross did appoint a relief commission, but with only nominal authority. He kept control of relief in his own hands and appointed his personal secretary, Parker Carver, as state relief director. And he persistently eluded federal demands that he call a special legislative session to provide more matching relief funds, arguing that tax delinquencies made further levies impossible.[22] From the beginning, then, relief offered the most fertile field for federal-state dissension and disunity.

During the first stage of FERA aid to Idaho, Hopkins obliged Ross and allocated federal money to the state without requiring any special matching funds. In mid-May, Ross sent Carver and his trusted highway director, J. H. Stemmer, to Washington, D.C., to represent him in securing federal public works allocations. Their mission was successful, and on May 29 the FERA awarded Idaho its initial grant of $173,627. During 1933, the FERA pumped $2,424,344 into Idaho for highway projects, supplying almost 50 per cent of the total expenditure. In fact, the percentage of federal funds in the total amount spent for Idaho relief in 1933 was 68.2 per cent, while in the nation as a whole it was only 60.6 per cent.[23] Ross later boasted in his campaigns that, through his thrifty ingenuity, he had saved money for Idaho and outguessed the bureaucrats.

Because of seasonal upswing in employment, Governor Ross was able to hold down relief rolls through the spring and summer of 1933 with his federally financed, state run work projects. The demand for temporary, unskilled farm labor absorbed many of the unemployed from May through September, and Ross's road projects employed the rest. The real crisis in relief was thus postponed until the fall, when the end of the harvests would again leave the unskilled workers at the mercy of the government. Fortunately for Idaho, new relief programs would emerge in time to aid them. In the meantime, the shortcomings of federally financed—but state operated—relief had not yet become apparent.

One New Deal relief–public works agency, authorized by Congress in late March of 1933, was of particular interest to mountainous Idaho—the Civilian Conservation Corps (CCC). The purpose of the CCC was to establish work camps in the countryside where young men could earn a small wage and learn new skills while at the same time contributing toward forest and soil conservation, disease eradication, and fire prevention. Idaho's twenty million acres of timberlands made it a natural center for CCC activity. The valuable stands of white pine in northern Idaho were at that time being ravaged by blister rust fungus, and a mammoth conservation effort to halt the spread of the disease was badly needed. Ross no doubt expressed the enthusiasm of the entire state when he welcomed the CCC program as an effort to "restore self-support and confidence to many a boy who is discouraged and disgusted in feeling that he is a burden upon his parents or upon the community." [24]

Agriculture Secretary Henry Wallace notified Ross of the formation of the Emergency Conservation Work (ECW) program on March 31, 1933, and requested that the Governor send qualified representatives to meet with him on April 6 to assist in formulating plans for the execution of the program. To this meeting Ross sent Franklin Girard, the secretary of state and a former forest ranger, and, as his personal representative and administrator, Harry C. Shellworth, the secretary-manager of the South Idaho Timber Protection Association.[25] The Idaho representatives were exceptionally well prepared and, along with the other western delegates, managed to secure more than their share of CCC camps. Girard also succeeded in putting through his and Ross's pet schemes for the local purchase of CCC supplies and the priority of local men in state hiring.[26]

In the original allocation of CCC camps, Idaho was allowed one hundred, second only to California in the entire West. But federal administrators soon realized that the western states had been grossly favored in the distribution of the camps and ordered a general reduction in the eleven western states of about 37.5 per cent. The Idaho Democrats joined in the general western outcry against this reduction, and finally Idaho obtained seventy of the original one hundred camps allowed it.[27]

Construction of the camps began in late May, and on June 2 the first seven cadres of youth from the East arrived in Boise to begin work in the forests. Eventually, 18,200 young men came to Idaho to work in the CCC camps.[28] Administration of the CCC program involved cooperative efforts by the state government, private industry, and several branches of the federal government, such as the Army, Forest Service, and Bureau of Entomology and Plant Quarantine. Twenty-two of the seventy camps were located on state and private timberlands, the others in national forests. The achievement of the CCC in Idaho was considerable, not only in providing relief and local expenditures, but also in lasting accomplishments. In its first three years, the CCC treated 1,188,000 acres of white pine for blister rust; built and improved numerous roads, buildings, fences, and phone lines; developed many conservation and reclamation projects on both timber and range lands; fought fires, insects, and diseases; and paid approximately $6,755,000 to dependents of Idaho CCC workers.[29] The CCC was especially well administered in Idaho, and there seems to have been little friction or misunderstanding between federal administrators and Idahoans. Local political jealousies over hiring provided the only real controversies in the Idaho ECW.[30]

The enormous expansion of federal activity in Idaho which began during the "100 Days" had an immediate effect on local politics. The flood of new jobs whetted patronage appetites of state politicians and widened the factional fissures in the Democratic party which had begun to appear during the first Ross administration. Before the Democratic landslide of 1932, Ross had easily

Working with the New Deal: 1933-34

held the reins of patronage in his own hands. But the newly elected congressional and state officials looked to the White House, not to the statehouse, for leadership. Ross's strategy of ignoring party lines in favor of personal loyalty in dispensing jobs was bound to conflict with the ideas and ambitions of New Deal Democrats. With Congressmen Coffin and White, Senator Pope, and First Assistant Secretary of the Interior T. A. Walters now in Washington, D.C., the Governor found his voice in federal patronage distribution weakened from the beginning.

Democratic State Chairman Theodore A. Walters of Caldwell was the only citizen of Idaho to join the Roosevelt administration in a high position. He first went to Washington in February of 1933 to apply for a judgeship on the Ninth District Circuit Court of Appeals. When he failed in this, the Idaho congressional delegation backed him for the vital post of commissioner of reclamation, but with no more success. Walters' western supporters finally arranged his appointment as first assistant secretary of the interior, a position which he held until his death in 1937.[31]

Although he and Ross had been long-time political friends and allies, Walters, like the other Democratic party stalwarts, became increasingly perturbed at Ross's disregard of the organization and his personal ambitions. As the Governor's haughty independence became more apparent, following the inception of the New Deal program, the resentment of other Democrats became more and more vocal. Walters expressed his feelings to Senator Pope:

> I am not deceived or misled at all as to how or why he became a candidate. Ross has had and probably yet has a capacity to appeal to the average voter. He is, however, one of the most asinine persons I have ever come in contact with so far as appreciation of an organization or the efforts of those who have had much to do with his success is concerned.[32]

Party unrest over patronage came to a head in June, 1933, when an unduly large number of Republicans seemed to be turning up in choice CCC positions. Congressman Thomas C. Coffin, a former labor attorney, ex-mayor of Pocatello, and an outspoken liberal, raised a public furor after receiving numerous complaints from constituents that Democratic patronage interests were being neglected. First, he took the matter up with Regional Forester R. H. Rutledge. But Rutledge replied that, although he had deferred to the recommendations of Governor Ross for some positions, CCC appointments were normally made on the basis of qualifications and were usually left to local forest supervisors.[33]

Rutledge sent Coffin a list of CCC appointees, and when Coffin allegedly checked thirty of them and found twenty-eight to be Republicans, he concluded bitterly: "I have never seen a more fantastically untactful list of appointments than that made in the reforestation army in Idaho." Coffin then delivered a public harangue against Ross, blaming him for the appointments, but Ross heatedly denied the charge and claimed that his recommendations had been ignored by the Forest Service. When Coffin attempted to persuade state CCC Administrator Harry Shellworth to make more political appointments, he was rebuffed in no uncertain terms. The matter soon blew over, leaving no one quite satisfied. But Coffin's charges did prompt an investigation by the federal ECW office, which concluded that in some Idaho counties as many as one-third of the CCC positions had gone to Republicans. The investigation also concluded, however, that the real problem was the thwarted spoilsmanship of Congressman Coffin.[34]

Ross was no doubt partially responsible for the Republican appointments. His own special representative in forestry matters, Harry Shellworth, was a Republican and was thought to be the political agent for the Weyerhaeuser lumber interests in Idaho.[35] Yet, Shellworth was obviously well qualified for the job, and it would be inaccurate to conclude that most Republican appointments which Ross backed were for mere political gain. Moreover, the hiring practices of local camp supervisors were beyond the control of either Ross or the regional foresters.

Another wedge driving loyal Democrats away from Ross was

Working with the New Deal: 1933-34   65

his arrogant criticism of the Roosevelt administration. The Governor undoubtedly understood the omnipresent feeling of the average voter that the federal bureaucracy does not understand his peculiar problems, and he capitalized upon it. First he criticized the banking holiday, arguing that too much attention was being paid to bolstering weak financial institutions and not enough to controlled currency inflation. Then he attacked the FERA's dollar-matching policy because it penalized the "thrifty" states, and spoke against the CCC policy of setting the age limit for workers at twenty-five. Finally, as early as July, 1933, he lashed out at the "one-man rule" of President Roosevelt as a danger to democracy and expressed the hope that it would not last long.[36] Ross's onslaughts against the administration resembled similar outbursts by such other rural spokesmen as Senator Pat McCarran of Nevada or Governor Eugene Talmadge of Georgia. Once again, he was sacrificing party harmony to personal popularity.

No issue better revealed the difference in outlook between Ross and the New Dealers than that of prohibition repeal. In February, 1933, the lame-duck Congress submitted the Twenty-first Amendment, which would repeal the Eighteenth Amendment, to the states for ratification. One of Roosevelt's first actions as President was then to secure modification of the Volstead Act to allow the manufacture and sale of 3.2 per cent beer. In most states there was little organized resistance to repeal by 1933, but in Idaho the dries were still numerous and well organized. Even congressional legalization of 3.2 per cent beer was hamstrung in Idaho by the state Prohibition Law of 1915 which was still in effect. The Idaho wets, therefore, clamored both for a special session of the legislature to legalize 3.2 per cent beer and for a special election to ratify the Twenty-first Amendment. Until June of 1933, Ross steadfastly refused to call either, even though popular opinion turned increasingly against him.[37]

Repeal pressure soon became almost irresistible. Postmaster General James Farley, who was also Democratic national chairman, called Ross several times pleading for action. On May 29, 1933, members of the Governor's own official family hatched a so-called "Beer Putsch" against him. The conspirators publicized their complaints the next day when Secretary of State Franklin Girard, Attorney General Bert Miller, State Auditor Harry Parsons, and State Treasurer Mrs. Myrtle Enking issued a statement urging that Ross call a special session of the legislature to deal with the beer question.[38]

The crowning blow came when Mayor Barzilla Clark announced that he would ask the city council of Idaho Falls to legalize 3.2 per cent beer by city ordinance. When the council complied and the cities of Malad, Pocatello, and Mackay indicated that they would follow suit, Ross finally disappointed his dry supporters and announced that he would call the legislature into special session on June 19. Raising the specter of insurrection and martial law, Ross explained that he had no alternative.

> I came to the conclusion, after thorough investigation, that nothing short of martial law would suffice to correct the evil, and since that is a dangerous procedure I decided to call a Special Session and let the legislators act. . . . Here in Idaho the people are not enthusiastic about the beer question, they are hysterical. There are only two ways to meet the situation, one is absolute enforcement of the laws and the other is to modify them.[39]

The special session of June 19, 1933, did its work promptly and with little dissension. The legislature declared 3.2 per cent beer to be nonintoxicating and legalized its manufacture and sale. A license and excise tax was levied upon brewers, wholesalers, and retailers, and the revenue was divided evenly between the public school fund and the general fund. The special session also ratified the recently negotiated Idaho-Wyoming Water Pact concerning irrigation on the upper Snake River.[40]

Seeing that the dry battle was lost, Governor Ross then called a special election for September 19, 1933, to elect delegates to a constitutional convention to consider ratification of the Twenty-first Amendment. The delegates chosen at that election met at the state capitol building on October 17, 1933, and voted unanimously to repeal the Eighteenth Amendment.[41] But the drinking population of Idaho had to be satisfied with beer until the general election of 1934, when the voters would decide upon the proposed amendment repealing the Prohibition Law of 1915, and until the 1935 legislature had enacted laws providing for the manufacture and sale of liquor.

The summer of 1933 was thus a traumatic period for the Idaho dries. Aside from ministerial organizations and the Women's Christian Temperance Union, most of the dry leadership had come from the old Nonpartisan League and the Progressive elements. They had abandoned the Republican party in 1930 to follow Ross but now felt that neither party suited them. Their leaders considered either founding a third party or attempting to capture the Republican party through the direct primary, the same way the Nonpartisan League had seized the Democratic party in 1918.[42] They did neither. During and after 1934, their moralistic, reform energies came more and more to be absorbed by such crusades as the Townsend Movement for federal old-age pensions.

While the summer political storms raged in Idaho, the New Deal program continued to evolve. President Roosevelt signed the key measure of the early New Deal, the National Industrial Recovery Act, on June 16, 1933, calling it "the most important and far-reaching legislation ever enacted by the American Congress." The act consisted of two parts. Title I, "Industrial Recovery," established a National Recovery Administration (NRA) to supervise a program of business-government cooperation through a moratorium on the antitrust laws, the licensing of member business firms, and the negotiation of codes of fair competition. Section 7(a) of the act guaranteed collective bargaining, maximum hours, and minimum wages for labor. Title II, "Public Works and Construction

Projects," appropriated $3,300,000,000 for a mammoth, federally operated system of public works to be administered by a Public Works Administration (PWA).[43]

The organization of the NRA in Idaho began in July and August of 1933. Following the recommendation of the President's NRA director, General Hugh Johnson, Governor Ross recommended the names of eight Idaho citizens to comprise the Idaho State Recovery Board. They were to serve as a board of review in cases of code violations and to disseminate information to various businesses, consumer groups, and civic organizations. Upon Ross's recommendation, Will Simons of Boise became the state NRA director and chairman of the State Recovery Board. An excellent choice, Simons was a prominent Ross Democrat and the son-in-law of former Governor Moses Alexander. The duty of supervising compliance with the NRA codes of fair competition fell to Senator Pope's man, Walter T. Lockwood.[44]

Idaho joined in the enthusiastic national drive to sign up all industry and commerce under the codes of fair competition and to register as many consumers as possible under the "consumers' pledges" to buy only from those firms exhibiting the NRA's insignia, the "Blue Eagle." When Henry Ford refused to cooperate with the NRA, Ross urged a boycott of Ford cars and announced that henceforth the state would not purchase automobiles from any firm which did not join the NRA. Organizational drives were spearheaded by local committees, usually working through municipal chambers of commerce. In Boise, for instance, almost every business in town exhibited the Blue Eagle, and nine thousand consumers' pledges had been negotiated by the end of 1933. It was estimated that the state was 90 per cent "signed up" with the NRA by early fall.[45]

The initial enthusiasm that the NRA generated in Idaho far surpassed the results which it eventually achieved. The absence of many large industries and the fact that most employers were retailers and wholesalers meant that the NRA would not have a revolutionary impact upon Idaho. The northern mines were covered by the lead code; but lumber, a notorious NRA offender, was inspected only by a field force of the Western Pine Association, which was hostile to the NRA. No code at all covered the large railroad yards at Pocatello and Nampa. And the weakness of labor organizations in Idaho softened the impact of Section 7(a). Of 395 labor complaints handled, 258 were rejected. The 1935 legislature passed an Idaho Industrial Recovery Act which authorized a State Code Commission to draft codes of fair competition. But Ross had no chance to put it into effect, since the United States Supreme Court struck down the entire NIRA in May of 1935. The state NRA apparatus was dismantled during the summer of 1935, and few people in Idaho mourned its passing. In spite of all the excitement the NRA had caused there, it left little in the way of positive achievement.[46]

The Public Works Administration (PWA), authorized by Title II of the NIRA, was placed under the administration of Interior Secretary Harold Ickes. Its purpose was to provide work for the unemployed and to build all kinds of useful public projects. Originally, the federal government supplied 30 per cent of the costs of labor and materials on all PWA projects; the states and localities provided the remaining share of the costs either by bond issues or by other means. The Idaho PWA office opened in September, 1933, under the direction of J. V. Otter. But a month later only three projects were under way.[47]

Until it was overhauled in 1935, the Idaho PWA had approved and allocated funds for only twenty-six projects. But under the President's new work-relief program, which began in June of 1935, the government assumed 45 per cent of labor and materials costs; from then on, the tempo of PWA activity quickened. From June of 1935 through December of 1936, fifty-two more projects were approved, amounting to a total PWA commitment to Idaho by that date of almost three and a half million dollars. All PWA projects were well planned and of genuine public value, and at the insistence of Ickes political considerations were excluded from the program. The most common PWA projects in Idaho were improvement of irrigation facilities, construction and renovation of city water and sewage systems, and school construction.[48]

The slow pace at which both the PWA and the Agriculture Department made work-relief funds available prompted another outburst from Ross in September, 1933. The Governor was anxious to begin secondary-road construction projects with Agriculture Department funds before winter set in, and when the promised federal contributions were not immediately forthcoming, he launched a harsh, public protest, first at Agriculture Secretary Wallace and then at Interior Secretary Ickes. He heaped scorn on Wallace and the federal bureaucracy and invited the other western governors to join him:

> I expect that you are having the same difficulty in getting your road-public works program underway. I have made an investigation and found that the reason for delay is on account of book-rule men and red tape. . . . I hope you can see your way to join with me and the other 11 western governors in advising the President, through his secretary, ... that engineers, owing to their technical training, are obstructing the public works program to the extent that it is more or less seriously affecting the working people of this country.[49]

Only four of the governors backed Ross in this effort, since most of them were beginning to get results at the time.[50] The Agriculture Department replied to Ross's charges by pointing out that the delay had been caused by Ross's failure to authorize the Bureau of Highways to place competent engineers in charge of the desired projects.[51] If the Governor was embarrassed, he did not reveal it.

Undaunted, Ross next aimed his barbs at Interior Secretary Ickes and the PWA. In a telegram of September 17, 1933, he charged that administrative red tape threatened to delay commencement of the work program until the spring and asked that, contrary to the rules, the money be turned over directly to state authorities, who would put it to immediate work.

If you think the state of Idaho is to blame turn the money over to us and we will start work before the end of next week employing hundreds of men and guarantee to accomplish ten per cent more actual construction than under your plan of surveys maps details and whatnot. . . . Abraham Lincoln said quote If I am wrong ten thousand angels swearing I was right will not make me right unquote.[52]

This time, Ross had baited the wrong man. Ickes was well known for his volatile temperament and was never one to avoid a fight. He replied to Ross that the real problem was "your own lack of efficient organization." In a Chicago radio address, Ickes then commented with scorn about "a certain western governor," whose misapprehensions showed "his colossal ignorance." "I had a letter from a governor, raising hell about red tape and delay. . . . There is a lot of political whizbanging and sharpshooting. There are a lot of persons trying to make a record for assiduity. They want to be in a position, in case the program fails, to say 'I told you so.' "[53]

An investigation of the Governor's charges by federal officials eventually disclosed that the source of trouble lay in the fact that Ross had earlier dismissed or furloughed all highway engineers not occupied on projects in progress and had not rehired them in time to have project specifications prepared when the PWA was ready to begin considering them. Ickes pointed out to Ross that an allotment of $4,486,249 in PWA funds designated for Idaho awaited merely the reappointment of the proper number of engineers and the submission of specifications.[54]

By early October, things had quieted down again. As of October 5, 1933, projects totaling $2,628,000 had been approved. Ross promised Ickes that he would "cooperate with your new program to the fullest extent," and the two were soon on good terms once more. These controversies offer an excellent example of the problems arising from the new federal-state relationship. The application of large-scale federal programs was often hindered by local misunderstanding, incompetence, and opportunism. Like Ross's other anti-New Deal tirades, this maneuver gained him the admiration of the suspicious segment of the populace but lost him more of the support of loyal Democrats.[55]

Many students of the New Deal have pointed to President Roosevelt's pragmatic outlook and willingness to experiment as the key to his success in coping with the depression. Such experimentation on the federal level, however, frequently led to vast confusion and frustration when applied at the local level. This problem is nowhere better illustrated than in the changing federal policies toward relief during late 1933 and early 1934.

On November 8, 1933, five months after the inception of the FERA, that program was temporarily eclipsed by a new agency, the Civil Works Administration (CWA). The President's purpose in founding the CWA was to step up federal work relief rapidly, by means of simple "made work" projects, in order to meet the heavier unemployment of the winter months—to employ, that is, more men quicker. Unlike the FERA, the CWA was federally operated, and it sought to avoid the encumbrance of state administration.[56] The CWA, it was hoped, would absorb most of those able and willing to work, while the states and counties could again take full responsibility for the indigent.

By an order from Harry Hopkins, now CWA director, Governor Ross immediately designated the state and county relief boards as local offices of the CWA, responsible for screening relief applicants. Thomas J. Lloyd of Twin Falls became chairman of the state CWA organization.[57] In mid-November of 1933, Ross and Lloyd went to Washington to submit Ross's program to Hopkins. The Governor succeeded in getting approved his request for the immediate employment of twenty thousand to thirty thousand

Working with the New Deal: 1933–34

men, and by the end of November over ten thousand were already at work on CWA projects in the state.[58]

The CWA program began just in time to pull Idaho through its most trying time of the year. With the close of the farm employment season, unemployment rose from seven thousand families in late October to over twenty thousand in late November. Since most CWA projects were not of a permanent nature and generally consisted of "made work," it was able to take immediate and forthright action. By mid-January of 1934, when the CWA was functioning at its maximum capacity, it carried twenty thousand men on its payroll. In its brief career, the CWA undertook 819 projects, completed 416, and spent $5,425,000 in Idaho.[59]

In terms of its goal of employing as many as possible as rapidly as possible, the CWA was a real success in Idaho. Administrative difficulties were held to a minimum. The only serious problems involved "chiselers" who held both private and part-time relief employment, and recurrent complaints by organized labor that the county workers were often being paid less than the federal minimum wage on local projects.[60] But the agency was contemplated only as a temporary measure, and Roosevelt hastened its demise out of fear that its cost would prove unbearable and that the program would foster the growth of a permanent class of reliefers. The closing down of the CWA and the renewal of the FERA, however, set off the most difficult and complicated series of problems which the Ross administration ever had to face.

The termination of the Idaho CWA program began in mid-February of 1934, at the rate of about fifteen hundred men dropped per week, and continued until March 31, when the last eight thousand reliefers were released and the agency closed its doors. Parker Carver, the state relief director, resigned and was replaced by Edward Horsfal of Pocatello. The first two weeks in April of 1934 were allowed to lapse before the renewal of the FERA program, so that private enterprise might be allowed to absorb as many of the unemployed as possible. The new state relief organization, named the Idaho Emergency Relief Administration (IERA), then resumed the original system of state-administered work relief with the aid of federal grants. By the end of April, seventy thousand Idahoans, counting dependents, drew all or part of their income from the IERA.[61]

Local resentment at the termination of the CWA and the prolonged delay in re-establishing the FERA ran high, and it found frequent expression in mass protests by the unemployed. An orderly crowd of over three hundred Boise unemployed marched on the statehouse voicing their anger at the "dole" and at the lavish furnishings of the new IERA offices. Ross himself took up the charges and bitterly criticized Regional FERA Director Pierce Williams for moving the IERA offices out of the statehouse and beyond his personal supervision. He loosed a barrage of charges: that the new IERA would be poorly managed and wasteful, that families were being allowed to starve because of federal ineptitude, that Williams was more concerned with red tape than caring for the needy, and that the change in relief amounted to a dole. "The policy here," he proclaimed, "seems to be to dish out a dole to our people who are opposed to a dole. They want an opportunity to work and support their families and educate their children."[62] When Relief Director Horsfal questioned Ross's assertions, the Governor denounced him too.

Unlike some governors, Ross refrained from attacking Hopkins directly at this time and aimed his barbs instead at Regional Director Williams. It became obvious to the FERA leaders that they must either federalize the IERA (as had been done in Ohio and Oklahoma), thereby declaring war upon the Ross administration, or place the IERA directly under Ross's control and dispense with Pierce Williams. Following an Idaho visit by Aubrey Williams, Hopkins' lieutenant, the FERA elected to placate the Governor by making him solely responsible for the administration of relief.[63]

In thus gaining decisive control over state relief, Ross had again successfully employed his favorite tactic of marshaling public sentiment in his own favor. The IERA, in effect, became the Governor's personal bailiwick, managed by county boards partially of his choosing, yet financed for the most part by monthly stipends from the FERA. Those on relief came to realize that decisions concerning their welfare flowed directly from the Governor's office and such recognition was undoubtedly a political asset for the occupant of that office. Throughout 1934 Ross had the best of both possible worlds. The federal government paid most of the cost of relief, while he held control; yet he did not have to ask for additional tax revenue to pay for it. But, in the meantime, Hopkins and his colleagues became increasingly dissatisfied with this arrangement, and they were soon to demand that Idaho carry its share of the relief burden.[64]

By early 1934, the apparatus of the "First New Deal" had been firmly established. Until early 1935 the various new federal agencies kept up their vigorous activity in Idaho with little innovation; the AAA, FCA, HOLC, FERA, PWA, CCC and all the other relief, reform, and recovery instruments of the New Deal continued to subsidize the economic improvement of the state along the lines already established. At the personal behest of Governor Ross and Senator Pope, the Roosevelt administration agreed to allow the seventy CCC camps established in Idaho during 1933 to continue to operate through the year 1934, and to extend the blister-rust-control program as well.[65] In effect, what had happened since March of 1933 was a near revolution in nation-state relations. The federal government had assumed direct responsibility for restoring and maintaining the entire economic and social order of the nation, and in so doing had established a new prerogative in fields of endeavor which until that time had been the exclusive preserves of state and local government.

A good example of the new, expanded role of the federal government in Idaho was the response to the severe drought which hit the state during 1934. This drought was a local counterpart of the great "dust bowl" calamity that swept over the Great Plains during 1934–35. It fell upon southern Idaho during the spring of 1934 and was quickly recognized as the worst such affliction in the state's history. As the watersheds dried up and irrigation became impossible, a crop loss of twenty-five million dollars seemed imminent. Compounding the problem, dust bowl refugees from the Midwest poured into Idaho and other western states seeking jobs or relief.[66] The FERA immediately stepped in to aid the stricken areas, offering sizable grants through a special emergency drought relief program. Ross in turn appointed an Emergency Drought Relief Committee to assist localities in supplying badly needed feed and supplies and in tapping new wells with the federal funds.

During the summer of 1934 alone, the FERA poured almost one million dollars into Idaho drought relief, and the Drought Relief Committee used the money to save almost four million dollars in crops and to drill thousands of new wells for emergency water.[67] Only the prompt action of the federal government prevented the drought from reaching disastrous proportions in Idaho. Two years earlier, such prompt and decisive action would have been impossible.

By late 1934, recovery seemed well under way. Farm income had increased, the tempo of business activity was on the rise, and a new optimism was definitely in the air. The Boise Chamber of Commerce reported a general increase in business transactions of 46 per cent over February of 1933.[68] Democrats in Idaho, as elsewhere throughout the nation, faced the elections of 1934 with a solid record of reform and recovery achievement behind them. Yet the crisis of depression had not completely passed, and the work of the New Deal was far from finished.

V

THE HIGH TIDE OF REFORM: 1934-36

The hottest issue in Idaho politics during 1934 was Governor C. Ben Ross's bid for a third term. Since no man had ever served three terms as governor of Idaho, tradition ran strongly against Ross's ambitions. Even more important than tradition, however, was the desire of organization Democrats to get rid of Ross. By early 1934, the Governor's skirmishes with the Roosevelt administration, his casual disregard of influential members of his own party, and his cultivation of a highly efficient and free-wheeling personal organization had led to open mutiny in the Democratic ranks.

Ross's foes within the party were too divided by personal ambitions and an inability to heal old wounds to achieve even a semblance of unity. The wet-conservative wing of the party nursed grievances of the longest standing, but many of the leaders of this faction were also ideologically opposed to the New Deal. Some of them, in fact, joined the rightist, anti-Roosevelt Liberty League in 1934. On the other hand, the progressive Democratic faction, which was loyal to President Roosevelt, resented Ross's criticism of the New Deal and his undermining of party organization, but they also distrusted the Governor's conservative Democratic foes.[1] Furthermore, the leading elective state officials were opposed to Ross because of his practice of ignoring them, and Congressman Thomas C. Coffin still bore the wounds of his previous patronage quarrels with the Governor.

Two Democrats eventually announced against Ross in the primary race—his old foe Asher B. Wilson of Twin Falls, and former Attorney General Frank Martin of Boise. Wilson posed no serious threat, but Martin did. One of the revered old gentlemen of the party, Martin was a forceful campaigner and an organization man through and through. If anyone could unite the anti-Ross forces, he seemed to be the man. In his announcement of candidacy "General" Martin stated the issue clearly:

> Patronage is in no sense the private property of the governor and should not be used for building a personal machine to maintain him in office. I firmly believe that no man is bigger than his party and that we have reached the time when the Democratic party must decide whether it will dictate and control the policies of those whom it elects to office, or be dictated to, or ignored by, these beneficiaries of its labors.[2]

At first it seemed that Martin might succeed in weaning the county organizations away from Ross. The state Roosevelt Club issued a circular castigating Ross for his "domineering, Hitler-like attitude towards members of his own party." A meeting of party satraps held at the Boise Hotel on June 19 heard Ross flayed without mercy and compared to Kaiser Wilhelm as an autocrat to whom government was "sort of a 'me and Gott' business."[3] But Martin's supporters were more vocal than numerous; and by dividing his opposition and appealing to the masses, Ross withstood Martin's attack with relative ease.

The untimely death of Congressman Coffin further added to the problems of the anti-Ross opposition. Following his public quarrel with Coffin in June of 1933, Ross brought D. Worth Clark of Pocatello, the youngest and most promising member of the powerful Clark family, to Boise as assistant attorney general and began grooming him to run against Coffin in the 1934 primary. Meanwhile, Coffin added to his own problems by his fiery independence and his outspoken advocacy of prohibition repeal. By June of

1934, both the progressive and conservative Democratic factions openly opposed his renomination. Walters and Senator Pope served notice upon Coffin that they intended to deprive him of his patronage powers and to fight him in the primaries, but the belligerent little congressman retaliated by publicizing their threats and announcing that he intended to fight to keep his seat. The feud was cut short, however, when Coffin was struck by a car in Washington, D.C., and died on June 9, 1934.[4] His death touched off a mad scramble for the nomination, with Clark and six other Democrats contending for the office.

In the primary election of August 14, 1934, Ross proved that he was still the strongest man in his party, easily defeating his two opponents by a 14,026-vote plurality. His candidate D. Worth Clark won the Second District congressional nomination against six contenders; and his friend and ally G. P. Mix gained the nomination for lieutenant governor unopposed. Congressman Compton I. White and the elective Democratic state officials all held their positions. In the Republican column, Frank Stephan, a moderately conservative Twin Falls lawyer, defeated progressive J. Wesley Holden of Idaho Falls for the gubernatorial position.[5]

But at the Democratic platform convention, held at Hailey on August 29, Ross learned that his control of the Democratic party was no longer truly secure. The overwhelming majority of delegates to the convention supported Robert Coulter, who had demonstrated his organizational loyalty and ability many times in the past, for the position of state chairman. But Ross wanted to install his own man, John Foreman of Pocatello, in the key post. Only after an angry confrontation with Coulter did Ross decide that it would "be bad politics for me to make a hard fight against the judgement of the rest of the candidates" and acquiesce in Coulter's selection. The Democratic platform endorsed the New Deal without reservation and applauded the Ross record, and once again it demanded more federal assistance to old folks, veterans, and irrigation districts. As in the previous two campaigns, the platform evaded the repeal issue and failed to mention the amendment to abolish the state Prohibition Law of 1915.[6]

The Republican platform convention, held at Boise on September 1, was a festival honoring Senator Borah, the only Republican in the state who held a major elective office. Although he did not attempt to dictate to candidates, Borah sought and received the platform to do with as he pleased. The Senator's two-score planks assailed most New Deal administrative policies but cleverly endorsed the principle of federal relief, supported the direct-primary system and the strict regulation of liquor sales in case of passage of the repeal amendment, and demanded a universal draft of persons and property in the event of war. Surprisingly, although the Republican ticket in 1934 was more conservative than it had been in 1932, Borah supported and campaigned for all major candidates; he even endorsed Stephan by name.[7] Borah was most likely attempting to unite the Republicans behind him, in case Ross should attempt to unseat him in 1936.

As usual, Ross managed to seize the initiative and to steal the limelight during the 1934 campaign. He based his argument upon economy in government, boasting that he had demanded "one hundred cents of every dollar spent," and that he had "saved a million dollars" for each of his four years in office. The Governor commended the work of the New Deal but reserved the major credit for recovery for his own administration. "By those relief measures and by the farm mortgage moratorium," he declared, "I showed my determination that the people should not lose their homes and property and I want to say those democratic boys in the legislature gave me the finest kind of support." [8]

On the other hand, the Republicans, and especially gubernatorial candidate Stephan, failed to come up with any constructive or inspiring issues. For the most part, they had not yet digested many of the popular innovations of the New Deal. The staunchly conservative editor of the *Pocatello Tribune,* for instance, remarked that "the Democratic party in the nation has been seized by a group of socialistic theorists and has ceased to be democratic." Stephan himself committed the classic error of allowing the incumbent to choose his own issues. Stephan's only damaging charge was that a third term was too dangerous an innovation to allow any politician, especially so grasping an individual as the incumbent. Otherwise, the campaign bogged down and became tedious. He insisted that the Ross administration had really been extravagant instead of economical, that Ross's hidden taxes were unsound, and that political manipulations must be removed from state administration.[9]

Ross's real worry was less the Republican opposition than the rebellious members of his own party. "Democratic Stephan for Governor Clubs" began to emerge around the state as the campaign gathered momentum, and the number of actual Democratic votes they represented was impossible to determine. The Governor's long-time enemies also took advantage of the opportunity to snipe at him again. W. Orr Chapman made loud and boisterous charges of irregularities in the purchasing of highway equipment. When Ross declared the charges invalid, Chapman publicly retorted: "What else but a whitewash could you expect?"[10] Most of the Democratic defectors seem to have been members of the conservative faction. The progressive Democrats, whatever their misgivings about Ross, could not vote against the New Deal party.

The Idaho election of November 6, 1934, closely followed the national pattern. Even though it was an off-year election, the Democrats maintained their tremendous gains of 1932; and Borah's endorsement of the Republican slate apparently had little effect on the voting public. Every Republican contender for national or state office suffered defeat. Ross's candidate for the Second District congressional seat, D. Worth Clark, won handily, even though he was a Catholic running against a Mormon leader in a heavily Mormon district, and thus emerged as a powerful new political personality in the state. The amendments for the nonpartisan election of judges and for repeal of the state Prohibition Law both passed easily. Even in the legislature, the Democrats held their own; the Republicans lost one seat in the senate and gained four in the house.[11]

The Democratic victory of 1934, however, was far less a personal triumph for Governor Ross than it was for the New Dealers. While the other Democratic candidates won by margins ranging from 20,000 to 55,000, Ross's plurality fell from 48,000 in 1932 to 17,654 in 1934.[12] As a result of the third-term issue and Democratic defections, Ross now seemed to be weaker than his party. Nevertheless, the fact did not dampen his enthusiasm or ambition, as is shown by the assessment he expressed to National Chairman James Farley:

> During these two campaigns, I whipped two United States Senators. Senator Pope did his best, through his appointments in Idaho, to make General Frank Martin the nominee of the Democratic ticket and, therefore, I gave him a licking. Then, Sen. Borah came to Idaho, something he has not done before in a number of years, and actually endorsed and supported the nominee on the Republican ticket.... So, I say to you again, Jim, I licked two United States Senators in the year 1934, and I will lick another one in 1936.[13]

Whether he realized it or not, Ross's powerful position of two years before had been considerably weakened. The New Deal Democrats had outpolled him for the first time. Had the Roosevelt administration refused to support Ross, as it refused to support Upton Sinclair in California, he probably would not have won at all. The Governor was re-elected in 1932 on the basis of his personal reputation and record; in 1934 he probably owed his re-election to the immense popularity of the New Deal, a popularity reflected in the fact that after 1934 only seven Republican governors remained in office.

It seemed at the time that the New Deal had revolutionized Idaho politics. As the perceptive analyst Horatio Miller noted at the time, it was no longer possible to recognize certain areas as

High Tide of Reform: 1934–36

Republican and others as Democratic. The New Deal majority was strikingly uniform in all counties.[14] But only the future would tell whether the New Deal had begun a permanent revolution in state politics or whether the old patterns would reappear as the crisis passed and the reform movement lost its momentum.

The foremost concern of the third Ross administration was to keep Idaho apace with the drastic and revolutionary reforms being wrought from above by the federal government. Long overdue reforms at the state level now had to be carried through almost overnight; old laws had to be revised and new laws enacted so that the state could qualify for the benefits accruing from the welfare policies of the New Deal. For this reason, the 1935 Idaho Legislature was the busiest and most hectic such body which the state had ever seen. Three overriding problems confronted the legislature from the outset: establishing a system of liquor sales and control, harmonizing state statutes to meet the requirements of newly enacted federal reform measures, and finding new sources of state revenue with which to match the relief funds made available by the federal government.

The most controversial problem was that of liquor control. The dries, especially the Mormons, wanted outright abolition of the open bar and saloon. Their views were expressed by the Liquor Advisory Commission, appointed by the Governor over a year earlier, which recommended the sale of liquor only in privately owned liquor stores and in eating places.[15] On the other hand, those more inclined to the wet point of view favored state-owned liquor stores and the legalization of bars and saloons.

With the social security program of the New Deal pending in Congress, Ross was advised by the American Public Welfare Association that the legislature should pass an unemployment insurance law and measures to aid crippled children and the elderly. The FERA also pressured the Governor to find new sources of revenue with which to match federal relief funds. Aubrey Williams, deputy FERA administrator, believed that the county committee system was unreliable in that it allowed people to receive relief who were not entitled to it. But Ross managed to keep his system in effect by ordering more careful scrutiny of relief applicants and by cutting the relief rolls.[16] The problem of raising more tax revenue was most difficult and politically dangerous. Lacking any plausible alternative, Ross seemed inexorably drawn toward the sales tax, which could produce large amounts of revenue quickly but which was sure to offend many voters.

Whereas Governor Ross had been able to control a united Democratic majority during the 1933 legislative session, the 1935 regular session gradually broke up into warring factions and ended in a deadlock over the tax problem. Before that stalemate developed, however, Ross succeeded in putting through most of his program. Two new debtor-relief bills passed with little debate. Since the crisis over mortgage foreclosures had passed and the 1933 General Moratorium Law had now legally terminated, the legislature enacted a new, modified measure, which merely allowed mortgagors to plead in court for more time to meet payments. A delinquent tax moratorium canceled penalties and interest on unpaid taxes due from 1928 to 1933 and levied a minimal 2 per cent penalty on such delinquent taxes, allowing the unpaid balance to be paid off at six-month intervals.[17]

The 1935 legislature enacted three measures to synchronize state policy with national policy. Complying with an NRA directive, the Governor recommended and the legislature passed a law establishing a State Code Approval Board to authorize codes of fair competition and to enforce penalties for code violation; the law also guaranteed collective bargaining and labor's right to organize. An Idaho Agricultural Adjustment Act ratified the federal AAA production-limitation codes and set up the Idaho Agricultural Adjustment Board to aid in execution of AAA policies in the

High Tide of Reform: 1934–36

state. Looking toward the pending federal welfare legislation, a Workmen's Compensation Law was passed, modeled after such plans in other states.[18]

Following extensive debate between the advocates of state sale and those of private sale, the Sharp Liquor Bill passed both houses on February 19. The law was a victory for the advocates of state control and a more liberal policy, authorizing a system of state liquor stores under the control of a Liquor Control Commission and legalizing saloons and bars. Passage of the administration's Driver's License Bill on February 23, which required more stringent examinations for license applicants, ended the constructive work of the regular session.[19]

Sensing the approaching storm, Ross allowed the troublesome budget and revenue problems to drift until the rest of his program had been settled. His initial budget proposals had been violently attacked by an "economy bloc" of dissident Democrats in the house, led by Representatives Charles C. Gossett of Nampa and A. Y. Satterfield of Pocatello. Rather unrealistically, this group demanded the strictest conceivable economy in government and denounced any new tax proposals.[20] Realizing the popular appeal of this stand, as well he should from his own experience, the Governor now found himself in an extremely difficult position. Unless he could force through a tax of some kind to provide one hundred thousand dollars per month in state matching funds, the FERA threatened to terminate relief allotments to the state. He knew that the sales tax was the quickest and surest way for a state to raise revenue, and he remained firmly opposed to increasing the property or income taxes. In fact, the sales tax offered the only hope of realizing his old dream of driving down the property tax and keeping it down permanently. But he also knew that a sales tax would arouse widespread antagonism among both merchants and consumers and would be stigmatized by liberals as regressive and unfair to the poor. With good reason, Ross confided to Regional FERA Director T. J. Edmonds that he was "beginning to feel that his assumption of responsibility and his active participation in relief has ruined his political career." [21]

At first the Governor followed the vacillating course of presenting a 2 per cent sales tax measure to the legislature but refusing to endorse it as an administration bill. He also introduced bills proposing a slot machine and a tobacco tax, but violent public protests against further taxation of any kind immediately strengthened the position of the economy bloc. Tempers flared on both sides, and all legislative activity bogged down in a morass of competing tax proposals and recriminations. The regular session adjourned on March 8, 1935, in "the worst legislative log jam . . . that the state has ever known." [22]

Obviously, Ross's only recourse in this situation was to call the legislature back into special session at once, and this he did. He addressed the joint session on March 8 and advised the legislators that, if the state did not provide matching funds for relief by March 15, all FERA allocations to Idaho would cease, leaving twenty-one thousand families without support. The Governor advised against raising the property or income taxes, since this would place the burden of relief upon a relatively small and already overtaxed segment of the population, and suggested the sales tax as furnishing "the broadest base for raising revenue." Apparently, Ross even hinted to individual legislators and newsmen that Harry Hopkins demanded an Idaho sales tax, which was untrue.[23]

Determined lobbying by merchant groups and public protests against the sales tax, however, only intensified the opposition of the economy bloc. As March 15 approached, no end to the stalemate seemed in sight; and FERA Administrator Hopkins had pigeonholed the Idaho relief allotment with the notation "held pending state action." The situation became intensely dramatic when Ross went on the air to plead for passage of the sales tax and announced that, unless the legislature provided tax relief at once, he would be forced to close all the relief agencies in the state for lack of funds. The Governor had thus thrown the hot potato to the legislature. But the opposition leaders still held out, arguing that an emergency appropriation could carry relief through the month and that a slight increase in the property tax along with more stringent economizing would suffice without necessitating any further taxation.[24] Ross continued to maintain, with equal determination, that the sales tax was the only solution.

Finally, Ross was forced to make good his threat, and on March 19 he ordered the closure of all relief offices in the state. By dumping eighty thousand needy persons upon the communities, he brought immediate and irresistible pressure to bear upon the legislators, and prompted a quick reversal in the vote. By March 21, both houses had passed Ross's 2 per cent sales tax, and that evening the turbulent special session adjourned. After drawing one hundred thousand dollars from the general fund to cover costs until federal funds arrived, Ross reopened the relief agencies on the morning of March 22. The Cooperative Emergency Revenue Act of 1935 was visualized as a temporary measure, effective only until March 15, 1937. It authorized a tax of 2 per cent of gross receipts upon all retail sales and required that all businesses report their sales on the fifteenth day of each month, thereupon remitting the taxes due.[25]

The manner in which Ross had turned the tables on the opponents of his sales tax was clever and somewhat ruthless. The Republican press gave his action sensationalized coverage, pointing to it as the work of a demagogue and a tyrant, and portraying those who fought the tax as martyrs. District FERA Administrator T. J. Edmonds in effect supplied the Governor's critics with ammunition when he told reporters that neither he nor his superiors had authorized the closing down of Idaho relief offices, which was apparently true. The *Idaho Daily Statesman* commented: "Idaho has never seen a more shameful exhibition of the way a ruthless political machine can override the wishes of the majority of citizens than that presented by the forces determined to cram the sales tax down the public's throat." The FERA had put Ross in a precarious position by withholding the funds; and although the Governor realized that the sales tax was a tremendous liability, he was forced either to push it through or to bear the responsibility for the termination of relief.[26]

The legislative session of 1935 dealt a critical blow to the prestige of C. Ben Ross. A large faction of the Democratic party had revolted against his leadership and now felt that they had been coerced into ratifying his program. Furthermore, two of the key laws passed at that session—the liquor and sales tax measures—offended large segments of the Idaho populace. The dries were deeply angered at their failure to get tighter liquor controls. And when Ross appointed Democratic State Chairman Robert Coulter as chairman of the State Liquor Commission, they cried that Democratic patronage would fatten upon the traffic in booze. The old crusader Harry Kessler summed up their reaction: "Idaho has gone the limit. The last two legislative sessions have marked a backward step of almost half a century. . . . We are as yet one moral notch above Nevada." [27]

Much more damaging to Ross's popularity was the sales tax. As a source of revenue, it was quite successful, bringing in a total of $3,467,684 through 1936.[28] But the sales tax immediately stimulated a harsh reaction across the state. Charges circulated that Ross had sold out to the railroads and other corporations in passing such "regressive," pro-business taxation. Disgruntled merchants and consumers formed the Anti-Sales Tax League for the purpose of halting tax collection by means of a referendum. The league was violently hostile to Ross. Its president, lawyer Frank Kinyon of Boise, assailed him as an "irresponsible boss, drunk with power." [29] League workers and the State Grange managed to obtain the necessary seventeen thousand signatures and petitioned the Idaho supreme court to nullify the law as unconstitutional because of its discriminatory provisions. They were only partially successful: the court upheld the constitutionality of the law but allowed it to be submitted to a popular vote on a referendum at the 1936 general election, the first such use of the referendum in Idaho history.[30] Agitation against the sales tax thus continued, and the issue remained to plague Ross in his 1936 campaign.

"The year 1935," according to Arthur M. Schlesinger, Jr., "marked a watershed." Whereas the earlier New Deal had sought merely to re-establish a social equilibrium, the "Second New Deal" set out to "restore a competitive society within a framework of strict social ground rules" through a process of massive federal reform and spending. Beginning early in 1935 the Roosevelt administration began a concerted effort to achieve social justice for all citizens by means of a mammoth work-relief program, welfare legislation, and a New Deal for labor.[31] The third Ross administration struggled mightily to adjust to and help implement the new program of federally sponsored reform.

The revolution in federal work relief began with the Emergency Relief Appropriation Act of May 1, 1935. By authorizing the expenditure of almost five billion dollars, this act became the largest single appropriation in the history of any nation up until that time. The keystone of the new program was the Works Progress Administration (WPA), under the direction once again of Harry Hopkins. In establishing the WPA, the intention of the federal relief strategists was to place all "employables" on the federal payroll and to entrust the care of dependent children, the aged, and the disabled to the states, who would in turn be aided in their care by other new government programs. New Deal planners sought to do away with the dole and "made work" projects by making all WPA projects socially useful, and by allowing WPA workers to practice their special skills.[32] The state FERA organizations would be gradually terminated as the WPA employed those able to work, and eventually they would be replaced by new state welfare agencies.

During the summer of 1935, the Idaho WPA program began, taking over work on the unfinished IERA projects. The original WPA allocation to Idaho, authorized in late May, amounted to $5,035,969 and was designated for a wide variety of socially useful projects: road construction and improvement, the building and repair of school and community facilities, water-supply systems, sanitation and health benefits, water conservation, and reclamation. Especially important was the $1,600,000 earmarked for work on the Black Canyon Irrigation Project and on Arrowrock Dam. Under the supervision of Idaho Public Works Director J. Leo Hood of Pocatello, the WPA began work in July, 1935. Of the total workers and dependents on IERA relief in June, WPA officials estimated that 70,000 were employable and could be absorbed by WPA work projects and private enterprise. By the end of October, the last of the IERA projects closed down, and in mid-November 9,000 men were employed on 285 projects throughout the state.[33] The new program went into full effect on December 2, when the IERA closed its doors.

Although the WPA never fulfilled the fondest expectations of its creators, it accomplished more than any of its predecessors, both in providing useful employment and in stimulating the economy. It was, like the CWA, federally planned and administered. In late February of 1936, when the WPA operation reached full capacity, it was at work on 510 Idaho projects, employing almost 22,000 men. The WPA program of building and improving county and feeder roads was especially important to and popular in farm states like Idaho. And since the WPA allowed the unemployed to work at jobs at which they were skilled, it was popular from the outset in Idaho, both with state officials and with the populace. Men who had been ashamed to accept relief or to perform the menial tasks of "made work" greeted it with enthusiasm, as is revealed in this poignant letter:

High Tide of Reform: 1934–36

> I'm ashamed to go to the relief. I have been a rich man once. All I ask is if you would give me a job on Priest River so I can make enough money to start in business again. I'm very truthful; I would do more good in the forest. . . . I would starve before I go to relief. I been a gentleman once. Will you please send me at once out, because I got just 41¢ now, the last of the money.[34]

Unlike the previous New Deal work-relief endeavors, the WPA program was multilateral and intended to aid even select groups of the economically oppressed. The Federal Writers' Project of the WPA, for example, paid unemployed writers up to $22.77 weekly to compile useful historical, genealogical, and geographical tracts, as well as miscellaneous other works. Under the direction of the well-known local author Vardis Fisher, the Idaho Writers' Project produced some of the best government-sponsored literary works in the country.[35]

The most significant of the subdivisions of the WPA was the National Youth Administration (NYA), established by an executive order of June 26, 1935. Under the direction of Aubrey Williams, the NYA sought to do for youth in particular what the WPA did for the other unemployed; it was also designed to aid young people to stay in school through part-time employment. The youth unemployment problem in Idaho was compounded by the large demand for seasonal farm employees, which lured students out of school during the growing and harvest season and left them stranded on relief during the rest of the year.[36]

The Idaho NYA began operation during August of 1935 with the appointment of W. W. Godfrey as state NYA director. During the school year of 1935–36, over 4,000 high school and college students earned a total of $152,230 through part-time employment with the NYA. The nature of their work projects varied from the construction of recreational centers to the compilation of oral history collections. But the federal NYA directors were unhappy with the program in Idaho, complaining of the lack of originality in selecting student work and the fact that Godfrey drew his salary from the NYA but spent most of his time on other state duties. The student-aid program did not actually function at full capacity until the 1936–37 biennium.[37]

The Resettlement Administration (RA) in the Agriculture Department also performed useful activities in Idaho. Its purpose was to relocate families living on submarginal lands, to aid them in getting a new start, and to restore the land to productivity. Idaho was placed in RA Region XI along with Washington and Oregon, and the lack of any administrative apparatus within the state apparently caused considerable confusion and inefficiency. The major RA achievement during the Ross regime was its Oneida County project, under which it bought up 140,000 acres of arid rangelands and relocated the seventy-five families living there. The RA also aided over six thousand other needy rural families by distributing surplus commodities, making subsistence advances to the destitute, and helping to refinance loans.[38]

Despite the general popularity of the WPA program, difficulties in administration arose, just as they had in the earlier work-relief efforts. Like such other rural politicians as Governor Eugene Talmadge of Georgia, Ross instinctively distrusted Harry Hopkins and his coterie of trained social workers. And, it might be added, Hopkins had little patience for the carping complaints of local politicians. His opinion of Ross probably resembled what he said of Talmadge: "He doesn't contribute a dime but he's always yapping." [39]

But Ross had a legitimate complaint when Hopkins issued a WPA ruling in November of 1935 to the effect that only those who had been on relief rolls between May and October would be eligible for WPA employment. The idea behind this ruling was to cut down the number of direct relief cases as quickly as possible, but in farming areas it had the effect of discriminating against those who had been able to find private employment during the farm season and now needed government help again. "It is," wrote the Governor, "another one of their brainstorm ideas, that hasn't a particle of good reasoning in it." Ross then pointed out the problem to Hopkins in very blunt terms, arguing that the ruling served no one "except those relief clients who are satisfied to sit around pool halls and let the Government support them." [40]

When he received no satisfaction from Hopkins, Ross wrote angry letters to the President and to the state's congressional delegation, and sent copies of his protest to the other western governors. With a characteristic lack of subtlety, he expressed his ire to President Roosevelt:

> Mr. President, you do not see the common people as I do. I do not care whether it is in Chicago or San Francisco, ninety per cent of the good-thinking people of this country will tell you that ruling is unreasonable, discriminatory, and in favor of the man who is willing to be supported by the Government. . . . It has a tendency to lower the people's opinion and confidence in the ability of the man who made such a decision, and is a reflection upon you, as the President of these great United States.

Obviously, despite the Governor's lack of tact, his criticism was valid, and Senator Pope and Congressmen Clark and White joined him in keeping pressure upon Hopkins to rescind his order. Public opinion in Idaho was overwhelmingly on Ross's side. Finally, after a conference with Pope and Clark in early January of 1936 and in the face of mounting criticism from other rural areas, Hopkins dropped the ruling and agreed to allow seasonally employed workers to join the WPA.[41]

The dark side of the new federal work-relief program was the fact that it returned direct responsibility for the unemployable and for those who could not be absorbed by private enterprise and the WPA to the states and counties. This heavy responsibility put a severe strain on local government, and many of the smaller states like Idaho were physically unable to give the proper aid to those incapable of providing for themselves.[42] The termination of the FERA program thus turned the welfare problem back to local initiative, with only limited help from the federal government.

On December 2, 1935, the Idaho Emergency Relief Administration closed its doors forever, and most of its four hundred administrative employees joined the ranks of the unemployed. It was supplanted by a new state relief bureau, the Idaho Cooperative Relief Agency (ICRA). The ICRA was entirely a creature of the state government, with no direct federal connection. Ross kept the ICRA under his own control; but Peter H. Cohn, a veteran of Idaho relief work, became its active director. To meet his extremely limited budget, Governor Ross reduced the administrative staff of ICRA to a bare minimum, keeping only seventy-five employees on the agency's payroll. He told a radio audience that the laying off of four hundred IERA employees in one day caused him more anguish than any other act of his public career.[43]

The duties of the ICRA were fourfold: to distribute relief funds to the twenty thousand unemployables in the state; to certify those eligible for WPA employment; to select CCC workers from Idaho; and to recommend needy families to the Resettlement Administration. The ICRA administration resembled that of the IERA, with a central office in Boise and district offices in regional cities, but the staffs were considerably reduced in size. In each county a three-member county relief committee—composed of one county commissioner, the probate judge, and an ICRA representative—declared upon the eligibility of applicants and supervised the administration of relief. Like the IERA, the ICRA worked under the traditional disadvantages of state-sponsored relief. Local ingenuity could not compensate for the lack of trained social workers, and the system of county relief boards was always likely to foster partiality in administering relief. Characteristically, Ross weakened the organization by retaining control of relief in his own hands and refusing to delegate the proper authority to his subordinates. The resources of the ICRA were pathetically small. Its sole source of funds was the one hundred thousand dollars per month which it drew from the sales tax, plus the three hundred thousand dollars in federal funds which Ross had managed to save from FERA allot-

High Tide of Reform: 1934–36

ments.[44] Yet, with what little it had, the ICRA worked reasonably well.

The responsibilities of the ICRA were broadened in February of 1936, when the new federal social security program went into effect in Idaho. The Social Security Act, signed by the President in August of 1935, established a national system of old-age insurance and retirement benefits, financed by a compulsory tax upon both employers' payrolls and employees' earnings. This aspect of the social security program, of course, was entirely a federal operation. But the Social Security Act also authorized federal grants to the states on a matching basis to help in providing for dependent children, the blind, and destitute persons over sixty-five who would not be able to participate in the old-age insurance program.[45] It also set up a federal-state system of unemployment insurance.

In December of 1935, the federal Social Security Board approved Idaho's plan for participation in the national Social Security Assistance and Health Program. But the plan did not take effect until Congress appropriated the necessary funds in February of 1936. The Idaho program was placed under the direction of Peter Cohn and the ICRA, and the state's share of the financial burden was drawn from the sales-tax fund of the ICRA and from county donations. The state provided one-third of the funds for old-age and blind assistance and for aid to dependent children. The counties contributed one-sixth of the old-age and blind assistance funds and one-third of the aid to dependent children. Beginning with the first bimonthly stipend of $173,000, the federal government paid the remainder of the cost.[46] The social security program was administered on the county level by the ICRA committees, to which two additional citizens were added for that purpose.

The dimensions of the new welfare program expanded much more rapidly than state officials had foreseen. The number of applicants for old-age assistance, for example, rose from 3,845 in February of 1936, to 7,088 in June; and over a thousand borderline but deserving cases had to be rejected for lack of funds. Relief and welfare expenditures of the ICRA from February to July of 1936 ran almost 40 per cent above its monthly income of one hundred thousand dollars, necessitating the apportionment of direct relief on the basis of funds available rather than need. To cope with this problem, Ross called the legislature into special session again on July 28, 1936, and asked that an additional four hundred thousand dollars in sales-tax revenue be allocated to the ICRA to meet increased welfare needs through the year 1936. The legislature promptly carried out his requests and also enacted an Unemployment Compensation Law, authorizing a withholding tax to be levied on both employers and employees. Under this law, those eligible could receive up to 50 per cent of their regular wage, not over fifteen dollars per week nor under five dollars per week.[47]

The Ross administration thus made every effort to cooperate with the federal government in carrying out its social security program. By October, 1936, nearly 8,000 persons in Idaho were receiving old-age assistance; and 262 blind people and 1,548 dependent children also shared in the benefits of the expanded federal-state welfare program. Always a believer in welfare principles, Governor Ross was very proud of the improvements made in the state welfare system and heralded them as one of his key accomplishments. Idaho pension payments averaged $21.12 per person per month, compared to a national average of $19.48 per month.[48] Considering its limited resources and the heavy demands which the new welfare-relief arrangement placed upon the state, Idaho met its broadened commitments in this area admirably.

Along with the new work-relief and social security programs, federal labor legislation in 1935 rounded out the basic reforms of the Second New Deal. The National Labor Relations Act, signed by the President on July 5, 1935, reaffirmed to labor the guarantees of collective bargaining and freedom of unionizing which had been embodied in Section 7(a) of the NIRA in 1933. The act also established the National Labor Relations Board with the semijudicial responsibility to see that these provisions were fulfilled. Idaho

High Tide of Reform: 1934–36

was placed in NLRB District XIX, which also included Washington, Oregon, western Montana, and Alaska, with headquarters at Seattle.[49]

The great upsurge of labor organization and activity which followed the reform of 1935, however, barely touched Idaho, where industrial labor was numerically weak and for the most part in a primitive stage of organization. The Idaho State Federation of Labor had been organized and chartered by the American Federation of Labor in 1916 and had perennially backed such progressive reform measures as old-age pensions, workmen's compensation, and the direct primary. Yet, even as late as the 1930s, AFL activity was limited to a few cities—mainly Pocatello, Nampa, Boise, and Lewiston—where there was enough industry to sustain it. Although union organization revived following 1934, it did not compare with the mammoth strides which labor took in the more populous, industrialized states to the east.[50] Like other agricultural states, Idaho's labor force for the most part remained unorganized; and like most agrarian politicians, Governor Ross was no enthusiastic supporter of organized labor. Under Ross, the Idaho Democratic party made few overtures to labor, and there was no attempt to pass a "little Wagner Act" on the state level to strengthen labor's economic position.

The few episodes of labor unrest in Idaho during this period reflected the absence of concerted workers' organization in the state. An instance of this sort occurred in Teton County in August of 1935, when fifteen hundred imported migrant pea pickers threatened violence in protesting against low wages and deplorable working conditions. At the request of local officials and with no apparent concern for the workers' situation, the Governor placed the county under martial law and sent in more than one hundred National Guard troops to maintain law and order.[51] The strike was quickly broken and tranquillity restored.

A more dangerous situation erupted in Clearwater County near Pierce during late July and August of 1936, when striking lumber workers affiliated with the Industrial Workers of the World engaged in a gun battle with strikebreakers at a mining camp run by Potlatch Forests. When conditions threatened to degenerate into full-scale labor war, Ross again declared martial law and sent in troops to patrol the picket lines. The troops quickly restored order, but only after deporting several of the IWW ringleaders from the state. After a month of tense negotiations and threats, the "Wobblies" gained limited concessions from the lumber industry and discontinued the strike. This was one of the last attempts by the IWW to revive its moribund organization, but its extinction in Idaho soon followed. Ross's firm action won him general acclaim as a guardian of law and order, but he was criticized by some intellectuals and labor spokesmen as a strikebreaker. Actually, the Governor seemed to have no real interest in breaking the strike, but was concerned only with keeping order. Local opinion was fiercely against the "foreign agitators" who encouraged the strike, and widespread violence might have ensued had matters been allowed to drift. But once again, as in Teton County, Ross had seemingly disregarded the legitimate complaints of the unions.[52]

As they made ready to face the electorate in the fateful election of 1936, Democrats in Idaho could plausibly argue that four years of the New Deal had succeeded in moving the state far on the road to recovery. By every conceivable standard, the state's economy was much healthier in mid-1936 than it had been in 1933. Farm income had increased almost 20 per cent in 1935 over what it had been in 1933. State bank deposits had increased 42.81 per cent, and national bank deposits almost 50 per cent. State taxpayers were once again able to meet their obligations: collection of the state income tax rose from $100,000 in 1933 to $350,000 in 1934 to $610,000 in 1935.[53]

On almost every economic front, it seemed that New Deal spending had infused new life into the Idaho economy. Rising gold

High Tide of Reform: 1934–36

prices during the first Roosevelt administration stimulated an 82 per cent increase in Idaho gold production. And largely as a result of the administration's Silver Purchase Act of 1934, Idaho silver production had climbed 95 per cent. The construction and renovation of reclamation projects with massive federal aid held the promise of a new stability and affluence for farmers of the state. Perhaps most promising of all to Ross and other Northwest progressives was the potential of federally sponsored public power, an integrated system of hydroelectric and reclamation dams on the Snake and Columbia rivers similar to the Tennessee Valley Authority. Such a plan of regional development held great hope for the water-rich Northwest, and Ross along with the other governors of the region heartily sponsored it. Their efforts would yield limited results, as the future and Grand Coulee Dam would soon reveal.[54]

As his third term neared its close, Governor Ross actually boasted less about the financial recovery of his state than about his reduction of state indebtedness. During his three terms, the total indebtedness of Idaho had been reduced from $3,628,934 on December 31, 1930, to $2,403,500 on March 1, 1936.[55] Actually, however, the federal government had re-established the economic stability of Idaho, with only a minimal outlay by the state government. Ross claimed, quite correctly, that he had economized in every way and had left the matter of providing funds to Uncle Sam. "Idaho had not contributed and do you know why Idaho had not contributed and matched the Government money as Utah and all the states around us? I don't know any other reason but that we had a Scotch Governor that talked them out of it. We got by for two years and Uncle Sam paid the bill." Columnist David Lawrence cited the above statement as an instance of "state extravagance vs. federal gullibility." [56] While this view bears some truth, the essential fact was that the federal government had intervened to an unprecedented extent in order to do for the state of Idaho what it was unable to do for itself. It is impossible to compute exactly everything the New Deal accomplished in Idaho from 1933 through 1936. But, in addition to feeding the hungry and bolstering the economy, its accomplishments included a multitude of useful public works, giant strides in all aspects of conservation, protection of mortgaged homes and farms, and the beginning of a new way of life for farm people through the Rural Electrification Administration, which was just beginning its activities in 1936.

The New Deal record was, of course, a supreme political asset for Governor Ross. In effect, the New Deal had subsidized the state's economic recovery while allowing the Governor, like his Kansas counterpart Alf Landon, to practice his much-heralded ability to economize in state government. Ross's relationship to the Roosevelt administration had been one of opportunism. He welcomed Roosevelt's dynamic program of reform and enthusiastically supported those measures which were beneficial to and popular in his own state. But he opposed and loudly criticized those administration efforts which did not directly benefit Idaho and C. Ben Ross. By striking an independent pose, he shared in the glory of both the New Dealers and their critics. The Governor now felt ready and able to do battle with one of the nation's most prominent Republicans, Senator William E. Borah.

VI

1936: "THE BATTLE OF THE IDAHO TITANS"

The 1936 political campaign in Idaho promised to be one of the most exciting the state had ever seen, featuring the proverbial meeting of the irresistible force and the immovable object. At stake was the Senate seat held for thirty years by Senator William E. Borah, one of the best-known men in the United States Senate and in the Republican party. For the first time in his long senatorial career, Borah faced a really powerful opponent in the person of Governor C. Ben Ross, one of the most effective campaigners the state had ever seen. In Idaho, personalities almost overshadowed the issues in 1936. The central issue confronting the electorate, however, was both obvious and significant: whether to accept or reject the aims and accomplishments of the New Deal. The political passions stimulated by the depression and the New Deal in Idaho reached the boiling point in the 1936 campaign.

Few states have ever so honored or esteemed a politician as Idaho did William E. Borah. The "Lion of Idaho" was seventy years of age in 1935, as he approached the end of his third decade in the Senate. But he was still erect and alert, and his prestige at home had never been higher. Idaho voters revered him as their special gift to the nation and the world—the rugged independent who always placed principle above party, the friend of the common man, foe of monopoly, and stalwart spokesman of isolationism. His power in Idaho was practically beyond challenge. Even though he was still alive and active, Idaho had named her highest mountain for him. The Pacific Northwest's foremost political analyst, Richard L. Neuberger, described him as "more widely known than any other American who has not occupied the White House," and continued: "No person in American public life so typifies the magnificent promise and scant fulfillment of the Pacific Northwest as the seventy-three-year-old Idaho lawyer whom Walter Lippmann once called the region's greatest citizen. . . . People in faraway places who have no conception of where Idaho is know about Senator Borah." [1]

Borah's disregard of his party, both state and national, and his reputation as an independent had long ago become his trademark. He was, in essence, an old-fashioned, western progressive, whose liberalism consisted mainly of a nostalgic faith in individualism and the atomized society. His favorite theme was the danger of monopoly. Despite the Senator's rugged honesty and support of many commendable reforms, his critics could and did point out that no major legislative enactment carried his name and that his record had largely been one of dissent and of pointing out the follies of others.[2]

Unlike Herbert Hoover and his devotees, Borah did not voice abhorrence of all or even most of the innovations of the New Deal. In his superb study of the "old progressives" and their reaction to the New Deal, Otis L. Graham, Jr., lists Borah as an opponent of the general New Deal reform program. But, while the Senator often spoke out against various New Deal measures, he never drifted near the reactionary posture which some of the old progressives embraced during the 1930s. He remained, verbally at least, a liberal. Following the catastrophic Republican defeats of 1932 and 1934, in fact, he repeatedly demanded that the party liberalize and press reform measures of its own. On this platform, he launched his ill-starred campaign for the Republican presidential nomination in 1936. With Democratic fortunes apparently running high in 1935–36, Borah actually occupied a strategic position. Roosevelt and many other liberals held a sentimental attachment to him, as they did to other Republican progressives like Senator George Norris of Nebraska. Borah's first biographer, C. O. Johnson, noted at the time: "One may hazard a guess that the Senator could have made his peace with the Roosevelt Administration at any time he desired." [3] Borah had never actually gone over to the Democratic side before, but many Democrats were eager to welcome him in 1936 should the GOP ignore his wishes by choosing a conservative as its presidential nominee.

It is doubtful that Senator Borah would ever have endorsed the New Deal under any circumstances. But even had he been so inclined, one obstacle stood in the way—the ambitions of C. Ben Ross. Actually, the two men were far from being archenemies. They were very close in political philosophy, and Borah had not even actively opposed Ross in 1930. Yet Ross's long-standing ambition to unseat the Senator was well known. Against the advice of almost all his friends and advisors, Ross seemed sure that 1936 was the year in which he would end Borah's public career.[4] The reason for this secret and highly personal ambition remains a point of conjecture. At the time rumor had it that the soothsayer whom Ross saw occasionally had predicted that he would defeat Borah in 1936 and that the Governor had accepted it as predestined.[5] Be that as it may, there can be no doubt that Ross's burning sense of mission and belief in the invincibility of his own determination were at the root of his ambition. As he told a *Collier's* investigating team in 1936, "Mr. Borah has a number of things on his mind. I have but one. I am Idaho's next senator." [6]

Ross's desire to see Borah defeated was shared by another man in powerful position, National Democratic Chairman James A. Farley. Unlike President Roosevelt, who apparently admired Borah as a progressive, Farley held to the strictly professional view that the Senator, as a Republican and an influential critic of the

New Deal, should be defeated. During late 1934 and 1935, rumors circulated in the press that an all-out effort was afoot to "get" Borah. One story actually had Farley saying that he would see to the Senator's defeat, even if it meant moving the United States Treasury to Idaho.[7]

The dimensions of Borah's prestige were revealed by the reaction to these stories in the summer of 1935. Senator Burton K. Wheeler of Montana announced that he would go into Idaho "at the drop of a hat" to aid his fellow progressive, and similar offers came from Senators George Norris of Nebraska and Carter Glass of Virginia. Influential Democrat Bernard Baruch wrote a warm letter of support. Even former NRA Director General Hugh Johnson offered his assistance: "About all I know of politics is that I am a Democrat by inheritance but it doesn't go so far as wanting to see a national asset taken out of the Senate. I am small potatoes and few in a hill but if ever I can do anything on that score, I am yours to command." [8]

Chairman Farley denied at the time, and still denies, that he made any special effort to secure the removal of Borah from the Senate.[9] The press reports to that effect were apparently the figments of journalistic imagination. But there is no doubt that at first Farley was willing to work with Ross to plot the Senator's defeat. Using his ally, Representative D. Worth Clark, as his contact in Washington, Ross secured a promise from Farley in January of 1935 that he was "going to get Borah in 1936 if it was the last thing he did." It should not be construed, however, as it was at the time, that Chairman Farley directed the campaign against Borah. It was Ross's project from the beginning. In fact, Ross seemed to be about the only one who was really enthusiastic about it. The Governor's own attitude was that his chances would be improved if Farley and the national organization merely left the matter to the Democrats in Idaho.[10] Farley must have agreed, for in the end he left Ross largely to his own devices.

Ross's apparent confidence in the strength of his organization

1936: "Battle of the Idaho Titans"

seems to have been overly optimistic. His grip upon the Idaho Democratic party had been slipping since the 1934 election. Many of the county organizations were nearing open mutiny against the Ross administration because they resented the Governor's distribution of patronage to Republicans who had supported him in the past. Indicative of this sentiment was a meeting of Democratic delegates from seventeen southeastern Idaho counties held at Idaho Falls in June of 1935, the purpose of which was "the organization of an association to exemplify the spirit and teachings of Andrew Jackson, viz.: 'To the victors belong the spoils.' " The delegates aired their grievances over not being consulted on appointments and concluded their meeting with the resolution "that in the future no person should receive a federal and state appointment of any kind without having the endorsement of the county central committee from the county in which he resides and the endorsement of the Democratic state chairman of the state of Idaho." [11]

The rumored prospect of a Ross-Borah contest stirred mixed reactions among the Idaho Democrats. Some of the Governor's friends sought to dissuade him from running. Will Simons, for example, wanted to find a judgeship for Senator Pope, so that he might vacate his seat in Ross's favor. Pope, of course, was not interested. The anti-Ross Democrats, on the other hand, knew that Ross had no chance of outpolling Borah unless he received the undivided support of the party. As veteran Democrat T. A. Walters wrote from Washington, D.C.: "Scarcely anybody here who takes any interest in politics thinks that Borah can be defeated. They feel that the State is not going to retire not only its most outstanding character but the most outstanding figure in the United States Senate." [12]

No doubt many Democrats in Idaho shared Walters' admiration of Senator Borah and were prepared to support him against Ross. If the Governor's opponents within the Democratic party could effectively play Borah against him and at the same time nominate and elect one of their own men to succeed him in the statehouse, then they might remove Ross and his "machine" from power permanently. The problem was to find a suitable gubernatorial candidate around whom the anti-Ross forces could muster. Ross would undoubtedly back his loyal lieutenant governor, G. P. Mix of Moscow. The most likely opponent to Mix seemed to be former state chairman and present first assistant secretary of the interior, Theodore Walters. But Walters was satisfied with the security of his position and refused to run. Instead, gubernatorial candidates began to emerge from all factions—Mayor Barzilla Clark of Idaho Falls, Secretary of State Franklin Girard, and Ross's two Democratic opponents of 1934, Frank Martin and Asher B. Wilson.[13]

In assessing the relative strengths and weaknesses of Borah and Ross, one vital factor was intangible. That was the large voting bloc of agrarian reformers who had at various times epoused the creeds of Populism, the Nonpartisan League, Progressivism, and the Anti-Saloon League. Throughout his career, Borah had always appealed successfully to this group; in fact, he owed as much to their support as to that of his own party. But Ross too had won their allegiance in 1930 and 1932. While he had lost some popularity with them by calling the special session of the legislature which legalized 3.2 per cent beer in 1933, he could still count on considerable support from their ranks. Many of these old reformers were now inflamed by a new messianic creed, the Townsend movement, which swept through Idaho during and after 1934.

The Townsend movement had grown to awesome proportions since that day in the fall of 1933 when Dr. Francis E. Townsend of Long Beach, California, had watched three old women groveling in a trash can for food and had vowed to improve the plight of the nation's elderly. Townsend's organization, Old Age Revolving Pensions, Limited, had by early 1936 become one of the strongest pressure groups in the United States, boasting an active membership of five million. Like other appeals to the distressed during the hard times of the 1930s, the doctor's plan was a panacea. He proposed a federal law which would give to every person over sixty a monthly pension of two hundred dollars, with the stipulation that it must be spent within one month. The money to finance these payments would be raised through a federal sales tax, and the purchasing power thus primed would immediately rejuvenate the entire economy.[14] Townsend and his disciples thus believed that by favoring the elderly they could solve the problems of the entire country.

Townsendism appealed especially to the religiously inspired, the lower middle class, and of course the elderly. Spreading outward from California, its greatest strength was always in the far West. It seemed to strike an exceptionally responsive chord among the agrarian progressives of Idaho; and it was no doubt for that reason that the Townsend movement exerted an especially powerful force in Idaho politics. Richard Neuberger guessed in the spring of 1936 that the Townsendites were correct in their predictions that they would hold the balance of power in the coming state elections. Ross and Borah thought so too. Borah wrote to his friend William Allen White: "The situation in Idaho is exceedingly mixed. The Townsend people are very strong. . . . They are strong enough to defeat me in case they hold together." [15]

When Doctor Townsend visited Boise in September, 1935, he met a tremendous reception. A half-mile parade escorted him to the fairgrounds where he addressed the city's largest crowd in years. Ross and Representative Clark both spoke warmly of Townsend and his plan, and Borah introduced him as "the most humane, sympathetic and sincere man I have ever met. If his plan is unconstitutional, it can be made constitutional." [16] Townsend responded with the assertion that he was ready to change his registration to Republican in order to support Borah for President.

But Senator Borah evidently saw through Townsend's peculiar plan all along, for in a Brooklyn speech of January 28, 1936, he said that he favored increased pensions for the aged but that Townsend's pension plan was unworkable.[17] Both Ross and Borah remained sympathetic to the Townsend organization, but they stopped short of outright endorsement. They evidently sought to obtain Townsend support without joining the fold and thereby possibly losing more votes than they stood to gain. As the campaign opened, it remained uncertain whom the Townsend people would support.

The struggle began in June of 1936. Since February, Borah had been campaigning for the Republican presidential nomination on the platform of rescuing the GOP from reaction and disaster.[18] At the Republican national convention in Cleveland on June 9, however, he had been overwhelmingly defeated by the more conservative Governor Alf Landon of Kansas. Dissatisfied with both the nominee and the platform, Borah left Cleveland in a huff and refused to say whether he would bolt the party. There was no doubt that the Senator would seek re-election. His friend Ray McKaig of Boise, who had already announced his own candidacy for Borah's Senate seat, withdrew. While Borah had been stumping the nation, his secretary, Miss Cora Rubin, and his numerous friends in Idaho had been laying the groundwork for his campaign.[19]

Governor Ross announced his candidacy for the Senate on June 26, 1936, while the Democratic national convention was in progress. He listed for reporters the winning issues that he would demand: more liberal old-age pensions; a redistribution of wealth through a more steeply graduated income tax; allowing the states more authority in federal public works programs; and a better deal for the farmer. His announcement prompted a violent reaction in some Democratic quarters. In Philadelphia, the site of the Democratic national convention, the Idaho delegation was bitterly divided between Ross Democrats, led by Acting State Chairman Mrs. Frank Johnesse, and anti-Ross Democrats, led by the Governor's old foes Robert Elder of Coeur d'Alene and W. Orr Chapman of Twin Falls. At a caucus of the delegation, only five of the seven-

1936: "Battle of the Idaho Titans"

teen delegates approved of Ross's move, and Elder and Chapman spoke emphatically against it.[20]

Orr Chapman, who was probably the most bitter of all Ross's Democratic enemies, hatched an interesting plot to insure the Governor's defeat. Following the convention, he stopped by the Washington office of Democratic National Chairman James Farley and set forth a plan whereby the Roosevelt administration would withdraw its support of Ross and in return Borah would endorse the President for re-election. After allegedly having discussed the matter with Borah, Chapman was sure he would agree. At the same time, other mutual friends of Roosevelt and Borah, especially editor J. David Stern of the *Philadelphia Record* and philosopher-historian Will Durant, were urging Farley to get Ross out of the race. They were sure that, once this was done, Borah would come out for the New Deal and bring a host of his admirers into the Democratic column.[21]

It was a plausible scheme, and under other conditions it might have worked. But neither Borah nor Ross would agree to it. James MacGregor Burns, in his biography of Roosevelt, claims that Borah was willing to play along with the idea; but the evidence points to the contrary. The Senator wrote to his friend Stern that he would not barter his independence for a return to the Senate. Farley discussed the matter with Governor Ross on the telephone but could not talk him out of making the race. At it turned out, Borah went his own way and refused to endorse either Roosevelt or Landon, and the President lost a dollar bet to Farley:

> I appreciate now that I should have asked a hundred to one odds from you when last May I bet you one dollar that Borah would come out for me before November. I made the dollar bet on even terms on the doctrine of chances—that Borah, for the last twenty-five years or more, had threatened regularly during each three and a half years following election, to bolt his party nominee—only to backslide to said nominee during the few months before the national election. I was wrong. He ran true to form.[22]

Although the plot to win Borah's support for the New Deal never materialized, it indicated the plight of Governor Ross. Many administration supporters in Idaho and around the nation did not want to see Borah defeated.

Ross's senatorial ambitions touched off a bitterly fought contest for party control in the Democratic primary campaign. Senator Pope and his supporters, along with the leading state elected officials and other discontented elements of the party, attempted to defeat him for the nomination. In the person of John A. Carver, a blind United States district attorney and former Democratic county chairman of Bannock County, they found an anti-Ross candidate with wide appeal. Carver was Ross's opposite—thoughtful, quiet, an organization man, and a sincere New Dealer. He was reportedly reluctant to run and did so only because he was angered by Ross's criticism of the New Deal and his nonchalant attitude toward his own party.[23]

As the August primary approached, the split within the Democratic party crystallized into a determined struggle between the Ross and the anti-Ross factions. The opposition to the Governor was led by Pope, Carver, Secretary of State Franklin Girard, Auditor Harry Parsons, Treasurer Mrs. Myrtle Enking, and his perennial enemies Orr Chapman, Ramsay Walker, and Robert Elder, as well as the leading Democratic gubernatorial candidates, Barzilla Clark, Frank Martin, and Asher Wilson. On the other hand, Ross still commanded the support of Representative D. Worth Clark and the numerous appointed state officials. He met the strategy of his enemies by entering an entire slate of his own candidates to oppose the elective state officials who were against him, and he was undoubtedly behind the decision of Lieutenant Governor G. P. Mix to enter the gubernatorial race as a pro-Ross candidate. The fact that most party leaders were conspiring against him did not seem to trouble Ross. Political bigwigs, he said, did not matter. "It's the folks in denim and calico that hold the keys to political doom or fortune."[24]

1936: "Battle of the Idaho Titans"

The Republicans too had their internal disagreements, but they were settled by the time of the primary. During the spring of 1936, a so-called "Young Turk" faction attempted to oust State Chairman R. B. Parry and the dominant, conservative group which had triumphed in nominating Frank Stephan for governor in 1934. The "Young Turks" were mostly personal devotees of moderate C. A. Bottolfsen, an Arco and Blackfoot newspaperman, and they were attempting to wrest the gubernatorial nomination away from conservative Stephan. Apparently in return for the party chairmanship, however, Bottolfsen voluntarily withdrew from contention in May and left the field open for the renomination of Stephan. The only real disturbance on the GOP front stemmed from the Townsend people's anger at Borah's aloofness. The old progressive Byron Defenbach of Lewiston ran against Borah for the Senate nomination on a completely pro-Townsend plan platform.[25]

The Idaho primary election of August 11, 1936, revealed that the state was still safely Democratic but that the Ross machine had lost its grip. The Democratic Senate race was surprisingly close, with Ross defeating Carver by 29,471 to 22,788 votes. The Democratic gubernatorial contest was closer still, but in the end the Ross candidate, G. P. Mix, lost to Mayor Barzilla Clark of Idaho Falls by 200 votes. Running with only nominal opposition, Frank Stephan again gained the Republican nomination for governor; and Borah handily defeated Defenbach for the Senate nomination, 32,499 to 9,442. But the Borah enthusiasts had no more cause for jubilation than did the Ross forces. While the Senator outpolled Ross by three thousand votes, the fact remained that seven thousand more votes had been cast in the Democratic than in the Republican primary column. If Borah were to be re-elected, it would apparently have to be accomplished through New Deal Democratic votes. As *Time* aptly remarked, the acid test had come for Borah's "absentee political landlordship."[26]

As in the previous two elections, the direct-primary system focused intraparty power struggles upon the platform conventions.

Both parties held their conventions on August 27, 1936. Meeting at Pocatello, the Republicans maintained their united front. C. A. Bottolfsen easily won the state chairmanship which had been held by Stephan's man R. B. Parry, indicating a *modus vivendi* between the rival factions. The Republican platform condemned the New Deal, endorsed Landon and the national platform, demanded more economy in state government, and repudiated the sales tax as discriminatory. As a sop to Borah, it sanctioned collective bargaining and asked for a universal draft of men and property in the event of war.[27]

The Democratic platform convention met simultaneously at Boise. Mrs. Frank Johnesse, the acting state chairman and close friend of Ross, was replaced in that position by Ira Taylor of Rigby.[28] Senator Pope wrote the platform and made of it a blanket endorsement of the New Deal and a scathing denunciation of Republican presidential nominee Alf Landon. Taking a backhanded slap at Ross, Pope made no mention in the platform of the Governor's sales tax. Most other Democratic candidates correctly regarded the tax as a dangerous liability and sought to evade it as an issue.[29]

When Senator Borah returned to Idaho in July of 1936, he feared that his public career was fast approaching its close. Despite his unprecedented successes in the past, he had always harbored a seemingly real fear of defeat. And now he realized that he was facing the most powerful opponent who had ever challenged him. Ross thrived on those campaign swings through the rural hinterland which Borah had never savored, and Ross could identify with the agrarian population much easier than could the Senator.[30] Borah's chances seemed further narrowed when Byron Defenbach, whom the Senator had defeated in the primary contest, announced that he would still run for the Senate as an independent pro-Townsend candidate.

1936: "Battle of the Idaho Titans"

Governor Ross's prospects suffered a grievous setback, however, when he fell seriously ill in late August. By the end of his third term, six years of constant overwork began to take their toll in the form of high blood pressure, fatigue, nervous irritation, and a sudden appearance of aging. Ross's friends noticed that he was increasingly moody and nervous after his car accidentally struck and killed a man in Boise in April of 1936. The accident was unavoidable, and the Governor was cleared of any guilt; but Ross evidently suffered a great deal of anxiety as a result of it. Finally, on the eve of the platform convention, Ross fell ill with a severe attack of neuritis in the arms and shoulders. His doctors ordered a lengthy convalescence, and Ross's active campaign did not begin until early October.[31]

While the candidates for all other offices campaigned for and against the New Deal, each of the senatorial aspirants went his own way. Borah wisely ignored Ross altogether and spoke to the voters of his thirty-year battle against monopoly and international entanglement. He avoided all Republican attempts to force him into an endorsement of Landon and finally warned GOP leaders that if they pushed him into taking a public stand he would come out for Roosevelt. When Republican National Chairman John D. M. Hamilton visited Boise, the "Lion of Idaho" was conspicuously absent; when the national committee sent him a campaign check for twenty-five hundred dollars, he returned it. Like his opponent, Senator Borah applauded the principle embodied in the Townsend plan and promised to use his influence to bring the bill up for discussion in Congress; but neither of them would openly endorse the plan itself.[32]

Governor Ross's campaign strategy was to avoid a direct attack upon Borah and his philosophy and, rather, to caricature him as a great international statesman who had unfortunately neglected the interests of his home state. A typical Ross newspaper advertisement claimed: "C. Ben Ross is not a fence straddler. He is not an expert on the Polish Corridor or champion of oppressed peoples of

Russia or Asia. Ross has one interest—the interest of Idaho. Ross's record is one accomplishment after another for Idaho—his native state." In a characteristic statement to the press, he cleverly pointed to Borah's neglect of his own state's particular interests: "While Gifford Pinchot was in Boise recently he made a statement for publication that the people of Pennsylvania are just as much interested in the return to the senate of Borah as are the people of Idaho. I replied that the people of Pennsylvania should be interested because Borah had done as much for them as for Idaho." Orde S. Pinckney has argued that Ross actually erred in attacking Borah's national and international preoccupations. This, he argues, is precisely what Idahoans loved him for. Yet, in view of Borah's immense prestige, it is hard to see what other feasible strategy Ross could have pursued.[33]

As he had before, Ross campaigned on the New Deal reforms which had been enacted during his tenure in office and on his record of thrift and reform. But his past record was also used effectively against him. The GOP organization capitalized upon the prevailing sentiment against the sales tax, as is indicated by this bit of doggerel, which was then popular around the state.

> Benny got our penny,
> Benny got our goat;
> We will get our Benny
> When we go to vote.[34]

By the end of the campaign, Ross knew that he was defeated. The lack of enthusiasm for his cause, even among staunch Democrats, was apparent to anyone. Borah carried the solid support of the Grange and even the endorsement of William Green, president of the American Federation of Labor. The Townsend candidate Byron Defenbach, out of apparent fear that Ross might win, abandoned the race in Borah's favor late in September, thus removing the main obstacle Borah had seen in his path to re-election. On election eve, in a last-ditch effort to get the Townsend vote, Ross

1936: "Battle of the Idaho Titans"   115

even promised to vote for the bill embodying the plan, but it was too late. The Governor had begun his campaign with the boast that he would "take Borah for a cleaning"; he closed it only with "I am an optimist."[35]

The Roosevelt landslide of 1936 carried Idaho, as well as almost every other state in the union, to another overwhelming Democratic victory. With one exception, every Idaho Democratic candidate for important office won, most of them by margins of well over thirty thousand votes. The President gained a second astounding vote of approval from the Idaho electorate by outpolling Landon, 126,000 to 66,499 votes. But the state's voters confirmed once again their well-known habit of ballot-crossing. While voting a straight Democratic ticket for all the other offices, they reelected Senator Borah by a vote of 128,723 to 74,444—an even greater majority than they gave to F.D.R. Ross's sales tax was defeated on a fairly close referendum vote, 68,728 for and 75,468 against.[36]

The defeat of Governor Ross in 1936 was heralded by some rather myopic critics of the Roosevelt administration as a repudiation of the New Deal. The reactionary *Spokesman-Review* of Spokane, for instance, crowed that Borah had outwitted Farley. The *New York Times,* however, was perhaps more realistic in its comparison of Borah to the "Cowardly Lion" in *The Wizard of Oz;* the Senator had actually succeeded by shrewdly avoiding a direct confrontation with the New Deal.[37] It was Ross, not Roosevelt or Farley, who planned and executed the campaign against Borah; and the failure of that campaign was a personal setback for Ross himself, not for the Roosevelt administration. The victories of all other Democratic candidates showed clearly that Idaho remained a heavily pro-New Deal state in 1936. The removal of Ross and his machine from power, in fact, offered the New Deal Democrats their best opportunity to build within their party an enduring reform coalition. Their prospects of success in this endeavor depended both upon the qualities of leadership exercised by Senator

Pope and Governor Barzilla Clark and upon the future ambitions of C. Ben Ross.

The shock of defeat fell heavily upon Governor Ross. His supreme self-confidence and sincere belief in his own invincible political mission, reinforced by his past successes, made such an abrupt defeat almost unbearable. C. Ben Ross left office a disillusioned and despondent man.

> I set out to be governor of Idaho for three terms. There were times when I was tired of the job, but it was a task I had set myself. Now I've done it. I wanted to be senator in place of Borah, and I miscalculated. I didn't get there. But now politics strike me as something to avoid. I never thought I'd feel that way about it but I do.
>
> If I can finish my term and get back to the ranch, I'll never darken the doors of the statehouse again. I'm so sick of hearing all the complaints of people against the state government that I feel as if I could quit most any time.[38]

Few who knew the Governor could have taken this statement seriously. The same consuming ambition which had always motivated his public career would soon rise to the fore again. In a more optimistic moment, Ross expressed his continuing involvement in the struggle between organized wealth and the people: "The battle between those two elements still is being waged. I am interested in it because I am one of the common people." [39]

Ross left office at the end of 1936 a sick man, still suffering from his recent attack of neuritis and also from pleurisy. His physicians ordered complete rest, and following a brief convalescence in Boise he returned to his Parma ranch.[40] But the thousands of Ross's devoted followers still looked to him as their political Messiah and awaited the day when he would return to active leadership. As a force in Idaho politics, C. Ben Ross was far from finished.

VII

DEMOCRATS IN DECLINE: 1937-38

The years 1937-38 saw the ebbing of the New Deal reform movement which had swept over the nation from 1933 through 1936. The victorious Democratic coalition which had twice elected Franklin D. Roosevelt to the presidency and had enacted the revolutionary reform program of his first administration began to disintegrate as the sense of crisis passed and the more conservative Democrats turned away from the New Deal. Controversial actions like Roosevelt's "court-packing" plan, his cutback in federal spending, his attempt to "purge" conservative members of his own party, and his increasing involvement with foreign affairs contributed toward the disruption of that great consensus which had proven its dimensions in the Democratic landslide of 1936. During these two years, then, the New Deal passed from its initial stage of dynamic reform to a more defensive posture of guarding its innovations and consolidating its earlier gains.

The erosion of Democratic hegemony in Idaho followed the general trend against the New Deal which prevailed throughout the nation after 1936. But the primary factor behind these Democratic reversals in Idaho was indigenous and stemmed from local party feuds. Former Governor C. Ben Ross and his followers refused to accept the leadership of either Governor Barzilla W. Clark or Senator James P. Pope. Their determination to regain political control of the state, combined with a growing bipartisan dissatisfaction with the New Deal, led to the disintegration of the Democratic party into warring personal factions and brought the end of the six-year interlude during which the Democrats had gained almost complete sway over all elected offices in Idaho.

The new governor, Barzilla W. Clark, was as different from his predecessor in office as any man could be. Quiet and somewhat shy, Clark was not the dynamic leader that Ross had been, even though his dedication to the common man was just as sincere. Like Ross and Borah, Clark's political philosophy was rooted in the prairie radicalism of the 1890s and was most often expressed in attacks upon monopoly and economic exploitation. He was a civil engineer by occupation and had made his reputation as mayor of Idaho Falls and as an advocate of public power. As mayor, he gained statewide renown for his successful sponsorship of municipally owned and operated hydroelectric power plants on the upper Snake River, and for the fact that during his administration Idaho Falls had the lowest tax rate of any city of its size in the nation.[1] But like another engineer in politics, Herbert Hoover, Barzilla Clark found the complexities of public administration and politics much more difficult to master than those of applied technology.

Governor Clark's first and foremost problem was the unwieldy Democratic majority in the 1937 session of the state legislature. He proposed an ambitious and admirable program calling for the establishment of a public health department, liberalization of state liquor laws, measures which would assist municipalities in developing public power facilities, and a modest budget. But the legislature ignored Governor Clark's requests and discarded most of his program. The same "economy bloc" which had plagued Ross in 1935 arose again in 1937 to thwart Clark's well-founded request for new tax revenue, badly needed since the sales tax had expired. In the end, he had to veto almost two million dollars in appropriations because of an anticipated shortage of revenue for the biennium. This legislative deadlock seemed to many observers to keynote the period of drift which typified the next two years.²

One such critical observer was Clark's predecessor, C. Ben Ross. Although Ross continued to suffer from ill health and disillusionment, his ambition was still alive. So was his resentment at the manner in which many Democrats—including Governor Clark and Senator Pope—had opposed him in the past. His contempt for what he considered weak leadership on the part of Clark was nurtured by his many devoted followers who urged him to run again and revitalize the party in 1938. To one of them he expressed his views:

> The antics of the state administration have ceased to be funny and have reached the point where all good citizens must look upon the administration with a serious thought of what it means to the party and the great common-wealth of Idaho. I can come to no other conclusion except that the Democrats should clean their own house. If we fail to serve the best interests of the people in this particular respect, in my opinion, the Republicans will clean house for us. . . . At the present time, I am not interested in the kind of Democrats who hold political office.³

Despite his dissatisfation with the Clark administration, Ross might never have re-entered politics had it not been that his Democratic enemies in office leveled charges of mismanagement against his past administrations. Upon the recommendation of Attorney General J. W. Taylor, a staunch anti-Ross Democrat, the 1937 legislature appropriated twenty-five thousand dollars for a thorough audit of the Bureau of Highways in the Public Works Department. A team of accountants under the direction of veteran Boise accountant James Munro worked for almost two years investigating the records of the Bureau of Highways.⁴

While the highway audit was in progress, Taylor, Director of Public Accounts Karl B. Evans, and others demanded a grand jury investigation of certain officials of the Ross regime by the Ada County district court. The grand jury was ordered by Judge

Charles Koelsch of Boise, and carried on its hearings from January 31 to August 24, 1938. Most of the grand jury's attention focused upon the State Purchasing Department and the Department of Public Works, and it did uncover considerable evidence of sloppy administration and some indications of wrongdoing. In a blare of publicity furnished by the Republican press, it eventually returned forty-four indictments, most of which were subsequently dismissed. But the partisanship of at least some of the jurors was obvious. On one occasion, Judge Koelsch refused to accept an interim report from the grand jury, remarking that it was politically motivated and "unworthy of the grand jury." The principal charges, against former Public Works Commissioner G. E. McKelvey and former Director of the Bureau of Highways J. H. Stemmer, were later dropped.[5]

Much more damaging to Ross's reputation were the disclosures of the special highway audit, which Governor Clark received on September 14, 1938. The Department of Public Works, and especially its Bureau of Highways, had long been in need of reform. Ross had recognized the chaotic state of its records system and the opportunities for laxity and wrongdoing in 1931 when he fired Public Works Commissioner Alvin Harbour, but he had taken no action to reform it. Now he found himself the object of the same charges of corruption and inefficiency which he had leveled against Harbour seven years earlier. The audit disclosed "considerable informality" in the letting of contracts, the use of state machinery by private contractors, exorbitant rates charged against the state by private firms, irregularities in purchasing procedures, and discrepancies in payrolls. Not surprisingly, the investigators found strong evidence of political favoritism: "We wish to avoid reference to political aspects where such reference can be avoided but there is no question as to political influence at work with regard to purchasing, both in the regime covered by the audit and those preceding it."[6]

Governor Ross had certainly used the expenditure of road-con-

Democrats in Decline: 1937–38

struction and -improvement allocations to political advantage; to some extent most state executives do. The evidence assembled by the auditing team left little doubt that many secondary roads were constructed or improved to pay off the Governor's political debts. Ross also seems to have been partially responsible for the administrative irregularities in the Public Works Department. Always a critic of red tape and delay, he cut corners and bypassed the proper administrators to achieve quicker results, and this practice naturally fostered confusion in the bureaucracy. Neither the highway audit nor the grand jury probe revealed any evidence of unlawful activity on Ross's part.[7] But they damaged his prestige and raised the wrath of the "Ben Ross faithful" against those Democrats who had sponsored them. Ross himself felt with good reason that he had been dealt a low blow by some of his opponents within his own party and resolved to re-enter politics in order to win "vindication" of the charges against his administration.[8]

The most logical man for Ross to oppose in 1938 would have been Senator James P. Pope, with whom he had been quarreling since 1932. A native of Louisiana and a graduate of the Univesity of Chicago Law School, Pope had risen to statewide prominence as a capable Boise attorney and an active, loyal, and progressive Democrat. As mayor of Boise from 1929 to 1933, he set a record by being re-elected without opposition. Pope was an intelligent and sincere but somewhat austere and ponderous man, and it was his singular good fortune to have ridden into the Senate on the long coattails of F.D.R. in 1932.

Probably no senator was more loyal to the New Deal than was James P. Pope. He was a liberal and an internationalist, a solid supporter of every major administration bill, and a cosponsor of the second Agricultural Adjustment Act. But Pope's New Deal loyalty had become a political liability by 1938. As in most rural areas, the Idaho electorate was inherently conservative and isolationist in sentiment, and by 1938 the people were becoming increasingly suspicious of the New Deal and its urban orientation.

Anti-Roosevelt orators delighted in panning Pope as a spineless Roosevelt "yes-man," who lacked the courage of his own convictions.[9]

Had Ross's health been better, he would probably have announced his candidacy against Senator Pope early in 1938. In April, however, he committed his support for the nomination to his youthful friend and protégé, Representative D. Worth Clark, who was the nephew of Governor Barzilla Clark and the youngest member of that politically powerful clan from southeastern Idaho. Ross had recognized the potential of the handsome young lawyer from Pocatello and had supported him for the nomination to the Second District congressional seat in 1934. During his two terms in Congress, Clark remained loyal to Ross but not to Roosevelt. He described himself as an independent, conservative Democrat and openly espoused the isolationism of Senator Borah. Since 1936 he had become increasingly critical of the New Deal and had voted against the President's cabinet and court reorganization bills.[10] He announced his candidacy against Pope for the primary nomination in April of 1938, and thus gave the Idaho Democrats a clear choice between loyalty to or independence from the New Deal.

After conferring with Ross, Congressman Clark began his Senate campaign in the spring of 1938. Ross told reporters at the time: "I'd like to have made that race myself, but it looks like I'm going to be forced to run for governor again." He spent several weeks putting his organization in shape. His old friend and ally "Gub" Mix agreed to run again for the lieutenant governorship. Several other pro-Ross Democrats entered the primary race, including Calvin Wright for state auditor and former Attorney General Bert Miller for the Second District congressional post. Ross announced his gubernatorial candidacy in late June. His platform was about the same as it had always been: economy in government, aid to the farmers, and increased state welfare. His only reference to the incumbent governor was saying that he sought "vindication" and allegedly remarking that any government is "better than no government at all." [11]

The Democratic primary campaign of 1938 took on the aspect of a fratricidal war between the followers of Ross and those of Pope. The key issues were Ross's defense of his administrative methods and Representative Clark's charges that Pope had violated the trust of his constituents by supporting the New Deal without qualification. All the other candidates found themselves forced into declaring their positions on Ross and Pope. Meanwhile, under the leadership of State Chairman C. A. Bottolfsen, the Republicans kept silent on the assumption "that our opponents are becoming so hopelessly divided . . . that it would be impossible for them to heal the wound if we can keep our organization intact." [12] Bottolfsen was a party stalwart, but a moderate in his political views. Sensing that the time was finally right, he resigned as party chairman and entered the race for the GOP gubernatorial nomination.

National attention focused upon the Idaho primary in August of 1938 as a test case of New Deal popularity. President Roosevelt's current efforts to "purge" conservative Democrats in various state primaries clarified the national issue, and observers around the country watched the early primary in Idaho, especially the Pope-Clark contest, as an indication of how the voters would react to "the issue of New Deal loyalty versus independence." The Ross-Clark conspiracy against Pope in Idaho, remarked the *New York Times,* represented "perhaps the most outspoken party challenge to Roosevelt leadership yet to be reached in the primaries." [13]

The Roosevelt administration was indeed heavily committed to Pope. The President gave him a letter of commendation for his "yeoman service" in drafting the second Agricultural Adjustment Act, and Secretary of State Cordell Hull broke his customary political silence to approve of Pope's foreign policy stand. National Democratic Chairman Farley, conveniently vacationing at Sun Valley, described him as one of the most loyal New Deal senators.[14]

The problem involved in interpreting local elections as national test cases was typified in Idaho by internal complications. The 1937 legislature had revised the 1931 Primary Law so that voters could obtain the ballot of either party regardless of their own affiliation. This opened the possibility that Pope's many bitter conservative enemies and Clark's many pro-Townsend admirers in the GOP could cross over in the primary to swing the election away from Pope. Many Republicans welcomed this opportunity to embarrass the Roosevelt administration, or as one of them phrased it, "to cavort in the green fields of Democracy." That old political manipulator of Nonpartisan League days, Ray McKaig, wired Senator Borah that thousands of Republicans planned to infiltrate the Democratic primary. W. D. Gillis, a GOP stalwart, wrote to Bottolfsen: ". . . it looks like you are going to thwart me in my earnest desire to go into the Democratic primaries and vote against that dirty skunk of a Pope . . . if you are agoing to run I've got to stay out and go into the Republican primaries to vote for you. . . . Gosh how I wanted to vote agin that damn cheap skunk of a Poop [sic]."[15]

In the primary election of August 9, 1938, Ross, Representative Clark, and their allies squeezed by their incumbent opponents to regain control of the Democratic party. The margin of victory was close. Ross beat Barzilla Clark by a bare 2,200-vote plurality, 28,826 to 26,628. He might not have won at all if two other gubernatorial candidates, Charles C. Gossett and W. P. Whitaker, had not polled 20,178 and 11,223 votes, respectively. D. Worth Clark defeated Pope, 43,736 to 40,726. The other prominent pro-Ross candidates, G. P. Mix and Bert Miller, also won against several opponents. Representative Compton White easily gained renomination. On the Republican side, C. A. Bottolfsen won the gubernatorial nomination by a 6,180-vote plurality, and Donald A. Callahan of Wallace captured the Senate berth.[16]

Since Pope was the first United States senator to be defeated on the issue of New Deal loyalty or disloyalty in 1938, his failure raised a furor of claims and counterclaims across the country. The Republican press was jubilant and exclaimed that Idaho had pointed the way toward a national repudiation of the New Deal. The Portland *Oregonian,* for instance, concluded: "The great, big baked potato went to one who dared, and promises to continue daring, the vengeful presidential thunderbolts." Republican National Chairman John D. M. Hamilton called it a "stunning blow" to Roosevelt and advised the President to forget his purge and concentrate on helping his own followers. Even former President Herbert Hoover shared in the glee. "These primary returns," he said, "indicate to me that more than fifty per cent of the Democrats are against the notion of rubber stamps in Congress." [17]

Such partisan analyses ignored the change in the Idaho primary system. Pope and his followers were undoubtedly correct in their assertion that Republican crossovers swung the primary election. After conferring with Pope, the President voiced his anger and indignation at a press conference of August 23. His assessment of what happened seems largely correct:

. . . the chief question of discussion [between Roosevelt and Pope] was a matter that involves public morality. . . . The figures in the State of Idaho, for example, show that whereas in 1936 the Republican primary vote was about 42,000 and the Democratic primary vote was about 55,000, this year the Republican primary vote was only 30,000 and the Democratic primary vote was 85,000 which, of course, no matter how much you might try to hem and haw it off, was complete proof positive that the direct primary system was completely violated so far as morality went by the entrance of fifteen or twenty thousand Republicans into the Democratic primary.[18]

The defeat of Senator Pope, therefore, seems to have been due at least as much to Republican plotting as to anti-New Deal sentiment among Democrats. Pope's advocacy of internationalism probably cost him more votes in Borah country than did his enthusiasm for New Deal domestic policies. Congressman Clark had the additional advantages of more lavish financial support and the endorsement of the national Townsend organization. But, whatever the cause of Pope's defeat, it was a setback for Roosevelt and the New Deal and a portent of what was to come in other Democratic primaries around the country. As James T. Patterson notes, "The 1938 Idaho primaries offered the only example, in twenty-one chances, of successful conservative bipartisanship against an incumbent New Deal senator." The victories of such anti-administration Democrats as Senators "Cotton Ed" Smith of South Carolina and Pat McCarran of Nevada, as well as the failures of such New Dealers as Representative Maury Maverick of Texas, showed that the New Deal was losing its grip.[19]

Senator Pope and his devotees were far from willing to accept defeat at the hands of the Ross-Clark combine. Many liberal Democrats were eager to support Pope in an independent, write-in campaign for re-election. The vital question was whether the Roosevelt administration would back Pope in such a race or whether it would endorse the duly nominated candidate. Roosevelt and Farley were besieged with arguments from both sides of the controversy in Idaho, but the majority of the Idaho Democrats favored administration support of Clark. Pope went to Hyde Park on August 22 and spent the evening discussing the matter with the President and his assistants Harry Hopkins and Aubrey Williams. Rumor had it that several cabinet members, including Secretaries Ickes and Wallace, wanted administration support of Pope.[20]

Roosevelt and Farley actually had little choice but to support D. Worth Clark. He had the backing not only of the dominant Ross machine, but also that of his still powerful uncles, Barzilla and Chase Clark, whose favor he had somehow managed to keep even while allied with Ross. For the national organization to have tackled this local combination would have meant disaster. Farley sent a congratulatory note to nominee Clark and promised him the full support of the Democratic National Committee. And on September 4, Pope fell into line and pledged his loyalty to "the entire Democratic ticket." As compensation for his voluntary withdrawal, Senator Pope received an appointment to the board of directors of the Tennessee Valley Authority in early 1939.[21] The eclipse of his career seemed to symbolize the passing of the New Deal in Idaho.

If the hotly contested primary seemed to indicate a comeback for C. Ben Ross, the Democratic platform convention, held at the Boise Hotel on August 27, 1938, confirmed the fact. The Ross–D. Worth Clark forces dominated the gathering from the start, and a surface harmony prevailed from beginning to end. The smoothness of the proceedings, however, was illusory. Pope and the anti-Ross Democrats were bitter over the recent primary but were powerless in the face of the well-organized opposition. To the chagrin of Robert Coulter, who wanted the position again, the Ross forces succeeded in electing Ben Davis, a Pocatello attorney and an old confidant of Ross, as state chairman. Another Ross man, R. S. Erb of Lewiston, directed the writing of the platform. The keynoter, A. F. James of Gooding, took a backhanded slap at Pope in asserting that the Democrats had run their own primary. And, again as a concession to Clark, the platform made no mention of the many demands to reform the primary law. The platform endorsed the state and national Democratic administrations, urged more federal aid to the elderly and to reclamation, and endorsed proposals for state minimum wage and eight-hour workday laws.[22]

The Republicans held their platform convention on August 26 at the Owyhee Hotel in Boise. Ben Ross furnished the only excitement there when he boisterously turned up sporting a Bottolfsen button but campaigning for himself. Holding firm control, the Bottolfsen people easily installed Thomas Heath, a sugar producer from Preston, as state chairman. The Republican platform reflected Bottolfsen's idea that the GOP should accept the basic tenets of the New Deal and should promise the voters not to scuttle relief and reform programs without finding suitable alternatives. It carefully denounced New Deal and state waste, inefficiency, and overcentralization, but refrained from an outright repudiation of the New Deal.[23]

Since the Republicans were not campaigning directly against the New Deal as they had in 1936, local issues and personalities took the limelight. D. Worth Clark succeeded in stealing most of Republican Callahan's issues by styling himself as an independent, although he spoke more favorable of the Roosevelt administration as the campaign progressed, in an effort to mollify angry liberals.[24] In his independent stance toward the administration and in his outspoken isolationism, Clark seemed to be emulating Borah.

The prime issue in 1938 was Ross himself, and more particularly his record as an administrator. The investigations into his past administrations seemed to be timed for maximum political effect. The grand jury probe ended on August 24, and Governor Clark received the findings of the highway audit on September 14. The Governor added fuel to the flames by remarking that the practices revealed in the audit were "terrible." Instead of evading the charges, Ross met the issue head on. In countless speeches, he would first invite a member of the audience to read from the highway investigation report. Then he would leave the speaking platform and walk among his listeners, answering the allegations against him and admitting that he had evaded some cumbersome rules, but only to save money for the taxpayers. Shrewdly, Bottolfsen countered that no individual could be allowed to place himself above the law, even if his intentions were admirable.[25] The publicity given to the highway investigations had effectively turned the public against C. Ben Ross, and not even his ingenious campaign techniques could turn the scales. And, by softening their anti-Democratic attacks, Heath and Bottolfsen offered disgruntled Democrats a calculated invitation to vote Republican.

Democrats in Decline: 1937–38

In the election of November 8, 1938, the Republican strategy paid off. Bottolfsen defeated Ross by a solid 28,571 plurality, 106,268 to 77,697. The two prime pro-Ross candidates, Mix for lieutenant governor and Bert Miller for Congress, lost by slender margins (Miller was defeated by the fast-rising GOP personality, Henry Dworshak). Otherwise the Democrats fared better. D. Worth Clark beat his opponent by a convincing vote of 99,801 to 81,939, and Representative Compton White posted an easy victory. All the other state offices also went to Democrats. But the Republicans recaptured control of both houses of the legislature, reversing the trend of the last three elections.[26]

The Republican comeback in 1938 was obviously less a repudiation of the New Deal than a protest vote against the Ross machine. Nevertheless, the Democratic loss of state control in Idaho followed the national trend against the New Deal in 1938. The Republicans had increased their number of governors from seven to eighteen and had defeated such liberal incumbents as Governors Frank Murphy of Michigan, Phillip LaFollette of Wisconsin, and Elmer Benson of Minnesota. The election of Democrat Culbert Olson in California was one bright spot in an otherwise drab year for New Dealers.[27]

The key to the Republican victory, just as Bottolfsen had foreseen, was a divided opposition. Evidently over seventeen thousand Democrats deserted Ross while supporting those Democrats who were not closely allied with him. It was a personal triumph for Bottolfsen and a personal rebuke for Ross. Savoring the fruits of victory for the first time in a decade, the Republican press rejoiced in the downfall of the man who had personified their distaste for liberal innovation. As the *Idaho Daily Statesman,* citadel of conservatism, remarked, the fall of Ross proved "that the American people are tired of irresponsible radicalism and are definitely turning their backs on its exponents." Their glee was shared by Ross's enemies in his own party, whose greatest fear had apparently been that he might be re-elected. Outgoing State Auditor Harry Parsons summed up their reaction: "At last the citizens of Idaho, after long being deceived and having patiently and charitably endured the political chicanery of C. Ben Ross, yesterday arose in their righteous might and wrath and removed him and his unholy influence forever from Idaho government and politics." [28]

The 1938 campaign witnessed the end of the two most prominent New Deal careers in Idaho, those of Governor Ross and Senator Pope.[29] More significantly, the campaign saw the final breakdown of the shaky Democratic coalition which had gathered behind C. Ben Ross in 1930. That party coalition had begun as the united effort of a minority party to regain power; in 1932 it had swollen to a huge majority; in 1934 and 1936 it had started to disintegrate into personal factions. Finally in 1938, the Democratic party split apart over the basic fault which had shown itself from the time it had returned to power—the antagonism between the Ross organization and the party organization itself. In failing to submerge personal rivalries and ambitions under a united party leadership, the Idaho Democrats rejected their opportunity to forge an enduring reform party in the image of the Roosevelt coalition in the national Democratic party. Their golden age ended as it had begun, in a scuffle of personal factions.

The Idaho election of 1938 marked the end of that six-year interlude during which the Democratic party exercised complete control over state government. It also began an eight-year period in which both parties competed on an evenly matched basis for victory; until 1946 control of government alternated between them every two years. Since 1946, the year in which the gubernatorial term of office was extended to four years, the Republican party has achieved a hegemony comparable to that which existed prior to 1930.[30] The political cleverness of the Republicans in scheduling state gubernatorial elections so as never to coincide with Presidential elections only partially accounts for this long series of successes. The Democratic party in Idaho has never been able to duplicate its success under C. Ben Ross. In one sense, this is a tribute to his political acumen and appeal. In another sense, it is partially a result of his failure to unite the party behind him the way that President Roosevelt did. Like many other Idaho political leaders, Ross's independence brought him personal success but contributed to the long-term failure of his party.

For C. Ben Ross, the defeat of 1938 was the final blow. Discouraged and disillusioned, he resigned himself to private life. He expressed his attitude to his brother John:

> The election has passed into history and the people have decided that they did not like the kind of government I gave them. We can only sit by and watch the results. Your words came back to me clearly when you said that the dear people will turn against you some day. I loved it and got a lot of pleasure out of it, but I have had an awakening and that awakening is that from henceforth I must serve the Ross family.[31]

Ross remained on his family farm near Parma until his death. His last years were unhappy. Following a heart attack in 1939, his health deteriorated rapidly, and the once strong and erect man now appeared gaunt and aged. His mental powers also seem to have abated during these last years. The proud egoism of earlier days apparently lapsed into a persecution complex, through which he saw his defeats and setbacks as the work of conspirators. He complained to friends of someone trying to steal his water on the ranch and of other plots against him. His mystic religious ideas evidently became more obsessive than ever. But Ross harbored his lifelong political ambitions up to the day he died. He was interested in the gubernatorial nomination in 1940 and had to be restrained from embarking on an independent campaign on behalf of the man who actually received the nomination, Chase Clark. Less than a year before his death, he told reporter John Corlett that he would run against his old adversary Charles Gossett for Gossett's Senate seat in 1946 if his health permitted.[32]

On April 12, 1945, the day of President Roosevelt's death, C. Ben Ross suffered a cerebral hemorrhage. He lingered on as a semi-invalid for almost a year. Then, in mid-March of 1946, he was stricken by another heart attack, and he died on March 31, 1946, at the age of sixty-nine. Mrs. Ross refused to allow the former Governor's body to lay in state at the capitol building. Following a simple and quiet service at a Caldwell funeral chapel, Ross's body was buried near his Parma birthplace.[33]

The eulogies bestowed upon Ross were even more laudatory than is usual and reflect the impact he had upon those who knew him. Robert Coulter, who had often disagreed with Ross, called him "the greatest governor Idaho ever had from any standpoint," and Coulter still held to that opinion in 1965. On the floor of Congress, Representative Compton White eulogized him as a man of "sterling qualities, a gentleman, a good friend and a real statesman." Senator Glen Taylor, for whom Ross seldom had a kind word, noted that he was "probably the greatest citizen Idaho ever produced." Even the *Pocatello Tribune,* which had opposed Ross since his days as mayor, remembered him as "one of the best and most efficient governors that Idaho has ever had." Most surprisingly of all, Horatio Miller, who had so often infuriated Ross with his penetrating analyses written under his pen name of Cato the Censor, later described him as "the best governor Idaho had ever had." [34]

Ben Ross truly was a man to remember. During the hectic decade of the 1930s he dominated Idaho politics to a greater extent even than did Senator Borah. This fact has been obscured by the enormity of Borah's popularity and prestige. When Ross has been remembered at all, it has been as a colorful and somewhat eccentric rural demagogue, the Northwest's version of Huey Long or Theodore Bilbo. Ross's evangelical style of oratory, his appeal to the mind and heart of the farmer, and his dynamic demeanor were made to order for rural campaigning. Yet Ross does not appear quite so eccentric, so radical, or so demagogic when judged by his record rather than solely by his stump speaking. As an administrator, he was neither so ruthless nor so radical as the real demagogues of the depression era. Contrary to the alarmist outcries of his conservative enemies, Ross never employed or sought to employ the dictatorial methods of a Huey Long.

Judged in the proper context, C. Ben Ross was a typical Idaho politician. He was, first and last, an independent and an agrarian Democrat. In his disdain for political conventionality and party organization and in his prairie radicalism, he truly exemplified the traditional qualities of Idaho's most successful politicians—qualities which have spelled success for such other luminaries on the Idaho scene as Fred T. Dubois, William E. Borah, Glen Taylor, and even Frank Church. An instinctive politician, Ross seemed to sense the ambivalent attitude of his rural constituents toward the liberal innovations of the New Deal. And, in striking an independent pose toward the Roosevelt administration, he mirrored the political personality of the state. His meteoric rise and fall, coinciding with the rise and fall of the New Deal itself, embodied and symbolized the political dreams and passions of a turbulent decade.

An era of Idaho politics died with "Cowboy" Ben Ross. He was one of the last of that colorful breed of western politicians who left so vivid an impression of their personalities upon their times. There are many in Idaho who still hold the opinion of the eulogists that he was the state's greatest executive. Of course, the correctness of their viewpoint remains a matter of subjectivity and can never be either confirmed or denied with certainty. One editorial writer, however, was most certainly correct when he remembered Ross as "one of the most forceful and rugged creatures of Idaho politics." [35] The state has never seen anyone quite like him. In a state known for its colorful and effective campaigners, C. Ben Ross was one of the most colorful and effective of them all.

More than thirty eventful years have passed since the fall of Ross and the fading of the New Deal in Idaho, and the final question emerges: what difference did it all really make? In the parlance of current historiographical debate, was the Idaho New Deal characterized more by revolutionary change or by continuity with the past and future? Writing from a national perspective, such astute historians as Richard Hofstadter, William E. Leuchtenburg, and Carl N. Degler have emphasized the revolutionary impact which the New Deal had upon the broad course of America's historical development.[36]

Beyond dispute, the New Deal worked great changes in Idaho. Recent research by Leonard Arrington indicates that New Deal spending actually favored Idaho and other western states. The Roosevelt administration spent $177,679,871 in the state from 1933 to 1939 and loaned another $111,804,931. This amounted to a total per capita expenditure of $399, ranking Idaho eighth among the forty-eight states on this basis, and a total per capita loan expenditure of $251, ranking Idaho fourth in this category. Why such favoritism toward western states like Idaho? Perhaps because the western commonwealths held so much of the public domain, because their tremendous land holdings entitled them to greater allotments for highways, agriculture, and conservation, or because their relatively low per capita income brought them a proportionately higher share of federal tax largesse.[37]

This mammoth expenditure and the many lasting achievements which it wrought truly stabilized the economy of the state. The more sweeping New Deal reforms, such as those in agriculture and social security, worked fundamental changes on all levels of society and government, this one included. And the various efforts to expand welfare and public works did jar the local governments into a new activity. State government in Idaho, and federal involvement in Idaho, would never again be the same after the 1930s.

Yet, when all factors are weighed, one must conclude that the New Deal worked no more than a halfway revolution in this locality. Promising starts in such areas as modernized welfare and public health, reorganization of state government, and tax reform have germinated slowly. And the depression-born sales tax, which, however regressive in principle, might have paid the fare, survived only two years and did not reappear until the mid-1960s. State government and state priorities, here as elsewhere, adjusted to meet the crisis of depression but in the main showed little real transformation during the 1930s. The Idaho experience, therefore, tends to support the more cautious conclusion recently expressed by James T. Patterson:

> The New Deal produced neither federal dictation, a completely cooperative federalism, nor a new state progressivism. Instead, it helped create a rather flat mixture of achievement, mediocrity, and confusion. For all the supposed power of the New Deal, it was unable to impose all its guidelines on the autonomous 48 states.[38]

Similarly, political attitudes and organization in Idaho show a convincing twentieth-century continuity. Roosevelt and Farley usually avoided confrontations with local party "machines." As the failure of the 1938 "purge" revealed, national party leaders had little hope of realigning local organizations to suit their wishes. So they accepted the situation in Idaho, cooperating both with Ross and with anti-Ross Democrats as best they could. And in the end, the Democratic factions which polarized around this local "machine" finally disrupted the entire party coalition in the state. In Idaho, therefore, the New Deal seems to have worked few drastic changes, to have been an interlude of liberal Democratic hegemony rather than a time of truly revolutionary change.

NOTES

INTRODUCTION

1. William E. Leuchtenburg, *Franklin D. Roosevelt and the New Deal: 1932–1940* (New York: Harper and Row, 1963), p. 331.

2. James T. Patterson, *The New Deal and the States: Federalism in Transition* (Princeton: Princeton University Press, 1969); and "The New Deal and the States," *American Historical Review,* LXXIII (October, 1967), 70–84. See also Robert E. Burke, *Olson's New Deal for California* (Berkeley and Los Angeles: University of California Press, 1953); George H. Mayer, *The Political Career of Floyd B. Olson* (Minneapolis: University of Minnesota Press, 1951); and the following Ph.D. dissertations, all produced in the history departments of the universities cited: Richard M. Judd, "A History of the New Deal in Vermont" (Harvard University, 1960); Richard C. Keller, "Pennsylvania's Little New Deal" (Columbia University, 1960); John D. Minton, "The New Deal in Tennessee, 1932–1938" (Vanderbilt University, 1959); Lionel V. Patenaude, "The New Deal in Texas" (University of Texas, 1953); and James F. Wickens, "Colorado in the Great Depression: A Study of New Deal Politics at the State Level" (University of Denver, 1964). The bibliography in Patterson's work, cited above, offers the most complete guide to local studies of the New Deal.

3. Byron Defenbach *et al., Idaho: The Place and Its People* (Chicago: American Historical Society, 1933), I, 565; Vardis Fisher *et al., Idaho: A Guide in Word and Picture* (Caldwell, Ida.: Caxton Printers, 1937), pp. 73–75.

4. Benjamin E. Thomas, "Political Geography of Idaho" (Ph.D. dissertation, Harvard University, 1947), p. 1.

5. Lawrence H. Chamberlain, "Idaho: State of Sectional Schisms," in *Rocky Mountain Politics,* ed. Thomas C. Donnelly (Albuquerque: University of New Mexico Press, 1940), pp. 153–55.
6. *Ibid.,* p. 155.
7. *Ibid.,* pp. 155–56; State of Idaho, Department of Reclamation, *Seventh Biennial Report . . . 1931–1932,* p. 88.
8. Chamberlain, "Idaho," pp. 153–54, 172; Thomas, "Political Geography of Idaho," p. 257.
9. Thomas, "Political Geography of Idaho," pp. 139–42, 206, 272–73; U.S., Bureau of the Census, *Fifteenth Census of the United States, 1930. Population Bulletin, First Series, Idaho: Number and Distribution of Inhabitants,* pp. 3, 18.
10. For a contemporary discussion of political sectionalism in Idaho, see Boyd A. Martin, "Idaho: The Sectional State," in *Western Politics,* ed. Frank H. Jonas (Salt Lake City: University of Utah Press, 1961), pp. 161–79.
11. U.S., Bureau of the Census, *Fifteenth Census . . . Population Bulletin,* pp. 3, 18; U.S., Bureau of the Census, *Fifteenth Census of the United States, 1930. Unemployment Bulletin, Idaho: Unemployment Returns by Classes,* p. 6.
12. U.S., Bureau of the Census, *Fifteenth Census of the United States, 1930. Agriculture, Idaho: Statistics by Counties,* pp. 5, 13.
13. Marguerite I. Oliver, "Wealth of Idaho: An Estimate of the Amount of Wealth and the Distribution of Its Ownership Within and Without the State" (Master's thesis, University of Idaho, 1933), Table XXVIII, opposite p. 50.

CHAPTER I

1. C. Ben Ross Administration Papers, Biographical folder (MSS in the Idaho Historical Society, Boise), C. Ben Ross to L. Sage Jones, November 17, 1932. The large Ross Administration Papers collection constitutes the major source of information for this study and will be frequently referred to in the following pages. Hereafter, this collection will be cited as RAP. The appropriate folder will be designated by its heading, followed by the abbreviation "fol."
2. *Ibid.,* Ross to Mrs. C. R. Hoult, June 23, 1936; Ross to Mrs. E. F. Freeman, July 25, 1931.
3. *Ibid.,* "Idaho's Ross," unsigned, undated typescript; Lamont

Johnson, "Ex-Oregon Cowboy Idaho Governor," *The Sunday Oregonian* (Portland), May 28, 1933, magazine sec., p. 6.

4. *Ibid.;* C. J. Brosnan, *History of the State of Idaho* (4th ed., rev.; New York: Scribner's, 1948), pp. 71–72; Annie L. Bird, *Boise: The Peace Valley* (Caldwell, Ida.: Caxton Printers, 1934), pp. 360–65.

5. "C. Ben Ross—The Man Who Did It: A Personal Glimpse of Idaho's Next Governor," *Lewiston Morning Tribune,* December 14, 1930, sec. 2, p. 1. This article is signed "Norman B. Adkison," but Mr. Adkison assured me that he did not write it. It was probably written by Lamont Johnson.

6. RAP, Biographical fol., Lamont Johnson, "Governor C. Ben Ross—A Crusader," undated typescript; "Cowboy Ben Ross Wins Primary, Aims at Borah's Post," *News-Week,* VIII (August 22, 1936), 8; "Persons and Personalities," *Literary Digest,* CXX (August 17, 1935), 29.

7. Interview with Mrs. Ethel Steel, July 3, 1965; W. D. Gillis, "A Governor Guided by Divinations," *American Mercury,* XXXIII (September, 1934), 114; Johnson, "Ex-Oregon Cowboy Idaho Governor," p. 6; interview with James H. Hawley, Jr., July 23, 1965.

8. Merrill D. Beal and Merle W. Wells, *History of Idaho* (New York: Lewis Historical Publishing Company, 1959), III, 37; Hawley interview; RAP, Biographical fol., Ross to Lamont Johnson, December 23, 1932; interview with C. Ben Reavis, July 1, 1965. C. Ben Reavis is Mrs. Ross's nephew and was named after Ben Ross. He was a close friend and confidant of the Governor. The Rosses had no children of their own, but they did raise four foster children. Helen Usadel, who lived at the Ross home until her recent death, joined the family after she had reached maturity and never changed her name. Her younger nephew, Earl Usadel, was taken in later and given the Ross name. The oldest son, Dewey Ross, they found at the state children's home. Myra Casey had been a ward of Mrs. Ross's mother and came to live with the Rosses after the latter's death. Helen and Dewey are now deceased, and Earl and Myra now live near Parma.

9. Beal and Wells, *History of Idaho,* III, 37.

10. Walter Davenport, "Storm Warnings in Idaho," *Collier's,* XCVII (April 4, 1936), 11.

11. Gillis, "Governor Guided by Divinations," p. 115; interview with John Corlett, June 29, 1965; "C. Ben Ross—The Man Who Did It."

12. Interview with Robert Coulter, June 30, 1965.
13. Quoted in Johnson, "Governor C. Ben Ross—A Crusader."
14. "C. Ben Ross—The Man Who Did It"; Beal and Wells, *History of Idaho,* III, 36; "Idaho's Ross."
15. State of Idaho, State Historical Society, *Twentieth Biennial Report: 1945–1946,* p. 141; State of Idaho, State Historical Society, *Twenty-first Biennial Report: 1947–1948,* pp. 31–32; "C. Ben Ross—The Man Who Did It."
16. Reavis interview.
17. Interview with B. A. McDeavitt, July 30, 1965; RAP, Biographical fol., "C. Ben Ross: A Personal Glimpse," newspaper clipping from unknown source; "C. Ben Ross—The Man Who Did It."
18. *Ibid.;* Steel interview; "Cowboy Ben Ross," p. 8; McDeavitt interview.
19. *Pocatello Tribune,* May 3, 1930, p. 4; Robert Coulter, one of the leaders of the state Democratic party in the 1920s and 1930s, did not even know Ross in 1928. Coulter interview.
20. John Corlett, "Ex-Governor C. Ben Ross Dies in Boise," *Idaho Daily Statesman* (Boise), April 1, 1946, pp. 1–2; Steel interview.
21. Quoted by Mrs. R. S. Stringfellow; Merle Wells to the author, April 10, 1968. Many of these observations are derived from H. H. Miller in *Idaho Daily Statesman,* February 4, 1933, p. 4. The late Horatio Miller, who often wrote as "Cato the Censor," was the foremost political commentator in Idaho during the 1930s. He was a man of considerable intelligence and knowledge who probably equaled many national analysts in insight.
22. Quoted in Davenport, "Storm Warnings in Idaho," p. 11.
23. Steel interview. Mrs. Steel, who now lives near Parma, was a close personal friend of the Rosses from their earliest to their last days.
24. These rumors found their most extreme statement in Gillis, "Governor Guided by Divinations," pp. 115–17; but it must be kept in mind that Gillis was a Republican enemy of Ross. His views seem to have been accepted uncritically by Richard L. Neuberger; see his "Behind the Borah Boom," *Current History,* XLIII (February, 1936), 465.
25. Corlett interview. Ross openly discussed his acquaintance with Minnie Green with Corlett in 1944. For the first time, he admitted that he relied on her for advice and that he actually trusted in her predictions.

26. Arthur M. Schlesinger, Jr., *The Coming of the New Deal* (Boston: Houghton Mifflin, 1959), p. 18; evidence of Ross's Populist inclinations may be found in RAP, Borah Correspondence fol., Ross to Jim Hapgood, August 23, 1932; Ross to Senator William E. Borah, May 19, 1932; Richard L. Neuberger, "Battle of the Idaho Titans," *New York Times Magazine,* August 9, 1936, sec. VII, p. 20.

27. Vardis Fisher to the author, August 19, 1967; Will Rogers, "Hobnobbing with the Governors," *Kansas City Star* (Kansas City, Mo.), August 6, 1933, clipping in Ross Scrapbook No. 2 (MSS in the Idaho Historical Society, Boise); Frank Ross Peterson, "Liberal from Idaho: The Public Career of Senator Glen H. Taylor" (Ph.D. dissertation, Washington State University, 1968), pp. 1–2.

28. Quoted in Gillis, "Governor Guided by Divinations," p. 116.

29. Frank Burroughs in *The Idaho Pioneer* (Boise), August 17, 1934, p. 1; Richard L. Neuberger, "Political Notes from the Northwest," *Nation,* CXLII (May 13, 1936), 611; Dorothy O. Johansen and Charles M. Gates, *Empire of the Columbia: A History of the Pacific Northwest* (New York: Harper and Brothers, 1957), p. 642. In the second, revised edition of this standard work, Professor Johansen revised this wording by the late Professor Gates; see the 1967 edition of the same title and publisher, p. 505.

CHAPTER II

1. "Political Party Organization in Idaho, 1861–1960: A Brief Outline," *Idaho Historical Series,* IV (March, 1961), 2–3.

2. Merle W. Wells, "Fred T. Dubois and the Idaho Progressives, 1900–1914," *Idaho Yesterdays,* IV (Summer, 1960), 26–30; "Cato the Censor" in *Idaho Daily Statesman* (Boise), September 19, 1931, p. 1. "Cato the Censor" was the pen name of Horatio H. Miller, who wrote for several Idaho papers during the 1930s.

3. Merle W. Wells, "Fred T. Dubois and the Nonpartisan League in the Idaho Election of 1918," *Pacific Northwest Quarterly,* LVI (January, 1965), 17–20. The Nonpartisan League gained such political power in Idaho that its official organ called Idaho the "second League State," second that is only to North Dakota; Robert L. Morlan, *Political Prairie Fire: The Non-Partisan League, 1915–1922* (Minneapolis: University of Minnesota Press, 1955), pp. 204–5.

4. Wells, "Dubois and the Nonpartisan League," pp. 17–20; Cato the Censor in *Idaho Daily Statesman,* September 19, 1931, p. 1. Gov-

ernor Moses Alexander had appointed Nugent to the Senate to succeed the deceased Senator James H. Brady in 1918.

5. Boyd A. Martin, *The Direct Primary in Idaho* (Stanford, Calif.: Stanford University Press, 1947), pp. 69–71.

6. Garrett O. Forbes, "Dynamics of Idaho Politics: 1920–1932" (Master's thesis, University of Idaho, 1955), p. 124.

7. U.S., Bureau of the Census, *Fifteenth Census of the United States, 1930. Population Bulletin, First Series, Idaho: Number and Distribution of Inhabitants,* pp. 3–4; see Earl Pomeroy, *The Pacific Slope: A History of California, Oregon, Washington, Idaho, Utah, and Nevada* (New York: Knopf, 1965), pp. 240–42.

8. Forbes, "Dynamics of Idaho Politics," pp. 130–31; "Political Party Organization in Idaho," p. 3; James H. Shideler, *Farm Crisis: 1919–1923* (Berkeley and Los Angeles: University of California Press, 1957), p. 226.

9. Martin, *Direct Primary in Idaho,* pp. 75–81; Marian C. McKenna, *Borah* (Ann Arbor: University of Michigan Press, 1961), pp. 193–94.

10. McKenna, *Borah,* pp. 193–94; interview with W. Lloyd Adams, July 31, 1965. W. Lloyd Adams of Rexburg, one of the masterminds of the Gooding organization, still feels that the return to the direct primary was a political disaster.

11. Forbes, "Dynamics of Idaho Politics," p. 128; G. C. Hobson *et al., The Idaho Digest and Blue Book* (Caldwell, Ida.: Caxton Printers, 1935), chap. iii, abstract table 18. This valuable reference work contains abstracts of all Idaho primary and general election results from 1890 through 1934.

12. Cato the Censor in *Idaho Daily Statesman,* November 22, 1934, p. 4. For biographical information on these and other prominent Idaho figures of the period, see the biographical section in Hobson *et al., Idaho Digest and Blue Book.*

13. *Ibid.;* interview with Robert Coulter, June 30, 1965.

14. Merrill D. Beal and Merle W. Wells, *History of Idaho* (New York: Lewis Historical Publishing Company, 1959), II, 249; Forbes, "Dynamics of Idaho Politics," pp. 67–72.

15. Coulter interview; Herbert Asbury, *The Great Illusion: An Informal History of Prohibition* (Garden City, N.Y.: Doubleday, 1950), pp. 321–25; William E. Leuchtenburg, *The Perils of Prosperity: 1914–1932* (Chicago: University of Chicago Press, 1958), pp. 237–38; Norman H. Clark, *The Dry Years: Prohibition and Social Change in*

NOTES TO CHAPTER II

Washington (Seattle: University of Washington Press, 1965), p. 204.

16. Tom Noswal in *Boise Capital News,* November 11, 1928, p. 1; Claudius O. Johnson, *Borah of Idaho* (2nd ed. rev.; Seattle: University of Washington Press, 1967), p. 427. Governor Baldridge appointed John Thomas of Gooding to succeed Senator Gooding upon the latter's death on June 30, 1928. Thomas was a long-time ally of Gooding and assumed leadership of his organization.

17. James P. Pope Law Office Papers (MSS in the Idaho Historical Society, Boise), James P. Pope to Ben Davis, February 8, 1928; Pope to Robert Elder, February 7, 1928.

18. James H. Hawley Papers (MSS in the Idaho Historical Society, Boise), James H. Hawley to David Rose, July 7, 1928; Hawley to Franklin D. Roosevelt, September 29, 1928.

19. *Ibid.,* James H. Hawley to Ross, June 25, 1928; Pope Law Office Papers, Ross to James P. Pope, August 13, 1928.

20. *Idaho Daily Statesman,* August 28, 29, 1928, p. 1; *Pocatello Tribune,* August 28, 29, 1928, p. 1; Coulter interview; *Idaho County Press* (Grangeville), August 30, 1928, p. 1; interview with Chase A. Clark, July 27, 1965; interview with James H. Hawley, Jr., July 23, 1965.

21. *Pocatello Tribune,* August 29, 1928, p. 1.

22. *Idaho Daily Statesman,* October 5, 1928, p. 2; October 7, 1928, p. 9; November 1, 1928, p. 1; *The Idaho Pioneer* (Boise), October 12, 19, 1928, p. 1.

23. Tom Noswal in *Boise Capital News,* November 11, 1928, p. 1; on Adams' career, see William E. Davis, "W. Lloyd Adams: A Kingmaker's King," *Idaho Yesterdays,* XII (Summer, 1968), 2–19; C. Ben Ross Personal Papers, E. M. Holden to Herbert H. Lehman, August 7, 1928. (The personal papers of Governor Ross are in the possession of Mrs. Ethel Steel of Parma, Idaho, at whose home the author used them. This collection will eventually be sent to the University of Idaho Library at Moscow.) Hereafter cited as Ross Personal Papers.

24. State of Idaho, Department of State, "Abstract of Votes . . . Nov. 6, 1928," *Nineteenth Biennial Report . . . 1927–28,* appended to p. 79; *Idaho Daily Statesman,* November 7, 1928, p. 1; November 8, 1928, pp. 1, 7; E. E. Robinson, *The Presidential Vote: 1896–1932* (Stanford, Calif.: Stanford University Press, 1934), p. 27.

25. *Idaho Daily Statesman,* November 8, 1928, pp. 1, 7; *Spokesman-Review* (Spokane), November 8, 1928, p. 10; *Morning Oregonian* (Portland), November 8, 1928, p. 8; Dorothy O. Johansen and

Charles M. Gates, *Empire of the Columbia: A History of the Pacific Northwest* (New York: Harper and Brothers, 1957), p. 638.

26. Forbes, "Dynamics of Idaho Politics," pp. 95–99; Keith J. Adams, "An Economic Analysis of the Idaho Income Tax Law" (Master's thesis, University of Idaho, 1951), pp. 17–27.

27. Coulter interview; *Pocatello Tribune,* May 3, 1930, p. 4.

28. *Lewiston Morning Tribune,* February 13, 1930, p. 1; March 16, 1930, p. 6.

29. *Idaho Daily Statesman,* May 3, June 26, 1930, p. 1; *Pocatello Tribune,* May 3, 1930, p. 1; *Boise Capital News,* June 27, 1928, p. 6. According to a much-discussed *Literary Digest* poll, Idaho voted 3,419 for "enforcement," 1,965 for "modification," and 3,208 for "repeal"; this reversed the national pattern, which favored repeal by at least 30 per cent. *Literary Digest,* CV (April 26, 1930), 6.

30. Pope Law Office Papers, Robert Coulter to James P. Pope, August 12, 1930; Tom Noswal in *Boise Capital News,* July 28, 1930, p. 14; Tom Noswal in *Lewiston Morning Tribune,* July 27, 1930, sec. 2, p. 1.

31. *Pocatello Tribune,* August 27, 1930, pp. 1, 8; *Lewiston Morning Tribune,* August 28, 1930, pp. 1–2.

32. *Ibid.*

33. *Idaho Daily Statesman,* August 28, 1930, pp. 1, 7; August 29, 1930, p. 1.

34. Quoted in *ibid.,* October 26, 1930, p. 1.

35. William E. Borah Papers (MSS in the Library of Congress, Washington, D.C.), Box 317, Ray McKaig to Borah, August 6, 1930; *New York Times,* September 14, 1930, sec. 2, p. 1; Coulter interview.

36. Interview with Joe R. Williams, July 26, 1965; interview with Mrs. Ethel Steel, July 3, 1965; Adams interview. Joe Williams, now a prominent Idaho Democrat, was then a Young Democrat working in a Boise service station, where he serviced the car McMurray was using and then reported it to Democratic headquarters. Ross later told him that this episode was the decisive factor in the campaign. W. Lloyd Adams, who was McMurray's campaign manager, claims that the Democrats unearthed the state car issue by planting a spy as secretary in his office.

37. The Borah Papers are, typically, unrevealing on this matter. Despite his unparalleled power of re-election, Borah always seemed to have an unusual fear of defeat; it remains a matter of speculation

whether this fear was genuine or whether it was feigned to motivate his supporters to greater efforts on his behalf. Adams interview.

38. "Abstract of Votes Cast in . . . the State of Idaho . . . at the General Election Held November 4, 1930," Hobson et al., *Idaho Digest and Blue Book,* chap. iv, abstract table 21.

39. Cato the Censor in *Idaho Daily Statesman,* November 7, 1930, pp. 1, 9; Tom Noswal in *Boise Capital News,* November 9, 1930, p. 1.

40. *Ibid.*

41. Cato the Censor in *Idaho Daily Statesman,* November 15, 1931, p. 4.

42. *Idaho Daily Statesman,* November 6, 1930, p. 4; *Weiser American,* November 6, 1930, p. 4; *Twin Falls Daily News,* November 6, 1930, p. 1; *Pocatello Tribune,* November 5, 1930, p. 4; *Idaho Falls Post,* November 7, 1930, p. 4; *Lewiston Morning Tribune,* November 8, 1930, p. 2; *Spokesman-Review,* November 7, 1930, p. 4.

CHAPTER III

1. *Arco Advertiser,* December 12, 1930, p. 1; "LEX" in *Lewiston Morning Tribune,* December 21, 1930, sec. 2, p. 1.

2. Cato the Censor in *Idaho Daily Statesman,* September 30, 1932, p. 4; for a listing of the various appointive as well as elective positions and who filled them, see *Official Directory of Congressional, State, Judicial, and Legislative Officers of the State of Idaho: 1931–1932,* copy in Ross Scrapbook No. 2 (MSS in the Idaho Historical Society, Boise).

3. Cato the Censor in *Idaho Daily Statesman,* November 22, 1934, p. 4.

4. Ross quoted in *ibid.,* January 1, 1931, p. 1; *Boise Capital News,* January 5, 1931, pp. 1, 3.

5. Ross Administration Papers (RAP), Senate: 1931–32 fol., "Governor's Message to the Twenty-first Session of the Legislature of the State of Idaho, 1931."

6. Keith J. Adams, "An Economic Analysis of the Idaho Income Tax Law" (Master's thesis, University of Idaho, 1951), pp. 28–30; Tom Noswal in *Boise Capital News,* February 15, 1931, p. 7.

7. *Lewiston Morning Tribune,* January 30, February 8, 1931, p. 1; Adams, "Economic Analysis," pp. 31–32.

8. Tom Noswal in *Lewiston Morning Tribune,* February 15, 1934,

sec. 2, p. 1; State of Idaho, *General Laws . . . Passed at the Twenty-first Session of the State Legislature: 1931,* pp. 16–26, 29.

9. RAP, Senate: 1931–32 Correspondence fol., Ross to G. P. Mix, February 28, 1931; Ross Personal Papers, Ross to M. C. Rose, February 28, 1931; *New York Times,* April 12, 1931, sec. 3, p. 6; "Reno's New Rivals," *Literary Digest,* CIX (April 4, 1931), 11. Ross's fear that the ninety-day divorce law would arouse criticism of Idaho was borne out by the outspoken disapproval of most newspapers around the country.

10. *Lewiston Morning Tribune,* March 6, 1931, p. 1.

11. RAP, House of Representatives: 1931–32 fol., "Message from the Governor to Members of the Legislature of the State of Idaho, Convened in Extraordinary Session, March 6, 1931," copy; *Idaho Daily Statesman,* March 14, 1931, p. 1.

12. State of Idaho, *General Laws . . . Passed at the Extraordinary Session . . . 1931,* pp. 6–57, 59–61; Tom Noswal in *Boise Capital News,* March 22, 1931, pp. 1, 8; August 20, 1931, p. 1; *Pocatello Tribune,* March 12, 1932, p. 1.

13. Quoted in *Pocatello Tribune,* March 15, 1931, p. 1; *Idaho Falls Post,* March 13, 1931, p. 1.

14. *Emmett Index and Emmett Examiner,* March 19, 1931, p. 1; *Idaho Daily Statesman,* April 28, May 31, 1931, p. 4.

15. Reconstruction Finance Corporation, Statistical Division, "Idaho," December 23, 1932, unsigned typescript in U.S., National Archives and Records Service, *Records Relating to Emergency Relief to the State of Idaho. Record Group 234, Records of the Reconstruction Finance Corporation* (microfilmed; Washington, D.C.: General Services Administration, 1964); hereafter cited as *Idaho RFC Records.*

16. RAP, Planning Board fol., J. D. Wood *et al.,* "Public Works in Idaho during the Emergency Period: A Supplement to the Idaho State Planning Consultant's Six Months' Summary Progress Report, June–December, 1935" (Boise: Idaho State Planning Board, 1936), p. 5, mimeographed copy. Cited hereafter as "Public Works in Idaho."

17. Mark Sullivan in *Idaho Daily Statesman,* September 27, 1932, p. 1; *Idaho RFC Records.*

18. RAP, HOLC: 1933–36 fol., "Accomplishments of the Home Owners' Loan Corporation in Idaho," unsigned, undated, mimeographed copy; State of Idaho, State Auditor, *Twenty-third Biennial Report . . . October 1, 1934,* p. 5; Clara A. Aldrich, *The History of Banking in Idaho* (Boise: Syms-York, 1940), p. 71.

NOTES TO CHAPTER III

19. *Lewiston Morning Tribune,* August 3, 1931, p. 8; *Arco Advertiser,* June 26, October 9, 1931, pp. 1, 8; December 11, 1931, p. 1; RAP, Mackay Controversy fol., telegram, D. Worth Clark to Ross, February 28, 1935; Bruce Schmalz, "Headgates and Headaches," *Idaho Yesterdays,* IX (Winter, 1965–1966), 22–25.

20. *Idaho County Press* (Grangeville), September 3, 1931, pp. 1, 4; *Times-Register* (Idaho Falls), September 10, 1931, p. 1.

21. *Boise Capital News,* August 30, 1931, pp. 1–2; *Pocatello Tribune,* January 7, 1932, pp. 1, 6; *Idaho Daily Statesman,* March 2, 1932, pp. 1–2; RAP, Special Session of June 19, 1933, Misc. fol., H. C. Parsons, State Auditor, "Report to the Special Session of June 19, 1933," copy.

22. Barzilla W. Clark Administration Papers (MSS in the Idaho Historical Society, Boise), K. B. Evans and T. Barraclough, "Report of Investigation of State Highway Department with Summary of Gusman Case . . . ," bound typescript; RAP, Gusman Contract fol., Ross, "Implications of Defenbach's Lewiston Speech," copy of address delivered at Lewiston, October 12, 1932; *Idaho Daily Statesman,* November 6, 1931, p. 1; November 9, 1931, p. 4; *Lewiston Morning Tribune,* April 30, May 3, 1932, p. 1.

23. *Idaho Evening Times* (Twin Falls), November 4, 1931, pp. 1, 4; November 23, 1931, p. 1; *Boise Capital News,* November 23, 1931, p. 1; *Idaho Daily Statesman,* November 25, December 16, 1931, p. 1; Preston L. Grover in *Idaho Post* (Moscow), January 1, 1932, p. 2.

24. *Pocatello Tribune,* July 12, 14, 1932, p. 1; RAP, Gas Price Reduction fol., George Donart to Ross, July 13, 1932.

25. "Public Works in Idaho," p. 5; Ross quoted in Joseph M. Clark, "Relief: The Nation's Stepchild," *Today,* III (January 12, 1935), 20; compare FERA State File (Idaho) (MSS in Record Group 69, National Archives, Washington, D.C.), Box 73, Ross to Harry Hopkins, December 14, 1934.

26. Harris G. Warren, *Herbert Hoover and the Great Depression* (New York: Oxford University Press, 1959), pp. 195–96; John D. Hicks, *Republican Ascendancy: 1921–1933* (New York: Harper and Row, 1960), p. 271; Albert U. Romasco, *The Poverty of Abundance: Hoover, the Nation, the Depression* (New York: Oxford University Press, 1965), pp. 189–191.

27. Marriner S. Eccles, *Beckoning Frontiers: Public and Personal Recollections* (New York: Knopf, 1951), pp. 50–55, 69–70; *Idaho Daily Statesman,* February 13, 1932, pp. 1, 7; February 14, 1932, p.

1; Aldrich, *History of Banking,* p. 71. Marriner Eccles later became governor of the Federal Reserve Board and a trusted economic advisor to President Roosevelt.

28. Warren, *Hoover,* pp. 206–8.

29. *Idaho RFC Records,* telegram, Pierce Williams to F. C. Croxton, August 19, 1932; *ibid.,* letters, Williams to Croxton, August 20, October 1, 1932.

30. *Ibid.,* Ross to RFC, August 20, September 12, 1932; *ibid.,* "Final Report of Governor's Account of Relief Funds Made Available by the Reconstruction Finance Corporation under the Emergency Relief and Construction Act of 1932," typescript; *ibid.,* Pierce Williams to F. C. Croxton, October 1, 1932.

31. RAP, Clark Controversy fol., E. M. Holden to Ross, September 22, 1932; open letter, Ross to B. W. Clark, September 23, 1932; *Pocatello Tribune,* September 20, October 1, 1932, p. 1; *Lewiston Morning Tribune,* October 1, 1932, p. 1.

32. James H. Hawley, Jr., Papers (MSS in the Idaho Historical Society, Boise), Hawley to Franklin D. Roosevelt, September 7, 1932.

33. Interview with Calvin Wright, July 25, 1965.

34. *Pocatello Tribune,* January 14, 1932, pp. 1, 10; *Idaho Daily Statesman,* January 15, 17, February 19, 1932, p. 1; February 26, 1932, pp. 1, 3.

35. *Idaho Pioneer* (Boise), February 5, 26, April 29, 1932, p. 1; Harry S. Kessler Papers (MSS in the Idaho Historical Society, Boise), Kessler to G. E. Huntsberger, April 21, 1932.

36. *Post-Register* (Idaho Falls), March 20, 1932, p. 1; *Idaho Daily Statesman,* April 23, 1932, p. 1.

37. "Abstract of Votes at the Primary Election, May 24, 1932," G. C. Hobson *et al., The Idaho Digest and Blue Book* (Caldwell, Ida.: Caxton Printers, 1935), chap. iv, abstract table 29; *Emmett Index and Emmett Examiner,* May 26, July 21, 1932, p. 1; *Idaho Daily Statesman,* May 24, August 25, 1932, p. 1.

38. *The Idaho Pioneer,* June 17, 1932, p. 14; *Idaho Daily Statesman,* June 10, 11, 1932, p. 1; June 14, 1932, p. 4; Frank Freidel, *Franklin D. Roosevelt: The Triumph* (Boston and Toronto: Little, Brown, 1956), p. 289.

39. *Lewiston Morning Tribune,* June 11, 1932, p. 1; *Idaho Daily Statesman,* June 11, 1932, p. 1.

40. Ross Personal Papers, "Defenbach's Speech Made at Boise, on

NOTES TO CHAPTER IV   149

November 2, 1932," typewritten copy; *Idaho Daily Statesman,* October 30, 1932, p. 6.

41. *Idaho Daily Statesman,* July 1, 5, September 19, 1932, p. 1; *Lewiston Morning Tribune,* September 20, 1932, p. 1; *Pocatello Tribune,* September 19, 1932, p. 1.

42. *Wallace Miner,* November 10, 1932, p. 1; *Lewiston Morning Tribune,* December 11, 1932, sec. 2, p. 1; *Morning Oregonian* (Portland), November 10, 1932, p. 3; "Abstract of Votes . . . in the State of Idaho . . . at the General Election Held November 8, 1932," Hobson et al., *Idaho Digest and Blue Book,* chap. iv, abstract table 22; Marian C. McKenna *Borah* (Ann Arbor: University of Michigan Press, 1961), p. 337; *Biographical Directory of the American Congress: 1774–1961* (Washington, D.C.: U.S. Government Printing Office, 1961), pp. 916, 1612; William E. Borah Papers (MSS in the Library of Congress, Washington, D.C.), Box 339, Borah to J. H. Peterson, November 11, 1932.

43. *New York Times,* November 9, 1932, pp. 2–3; *Morning Oregonian,* November 9, 1932, p. 1; Dorothy O. Johansen and Charles M. Gates, *Empire of the Columbia: A History of the Pacific Northwest* (New York: Harper and Brothers, 1957), p. 638; Edgar E. Robinson, *They Voted for Roosevelt: The Presidential Vote, 1932–1944* (Stanford, Calif.: Stanford University Press, 1947), p. 52.

44. Hobson et al., *Idaho Digest and Blue Book,* chap. iv, abstract table 22.

45. Cato the Censor in *Idaho Daily Statesman,* November 2, 1932, p. 4; interview with James H. Hawley, Jr., July 23, 1965.

CHAPTER IV

1. *Lewiston Morning Tribune,* January 2, 1933, p. 1.

2. Ross Administration Papers (RAP), House of Representatives: 1933–34 fol., "Governor's Message to the Twenty-second Session of the Legislature of the State of Idaho, 1933," copy. This emphasis on thrift and budget slashing characterized most state legislatures in 1933; see James T. Patterson, *The New Deal and the States: Federalism in Transition* (Princeton: Princeton University Press, 1969), pp. 46–49.

3. "Governor's Message to Twenty-second Session."

4. *Boise Capital News,* January 31, February 23, 1933, p. 1.

5. Interview with Chase A. Clark, July 27, 1965; interview with

Robert Coulter, June 30, 1965; Cato the Censor in *Idaho Daily Statesman* (Boise), March 5, 1933, p. 1; State of Idaho, *General Laws . . . Passed at the Twenty-second Session of the State Legislature: 1933*, pp. 230, 468–73.

6. *Lewiston Morning Tribune*, February 22, 1933, p. 1.

7. *Idaho Free Press* (Nampa), February 11, 1933, p. 1; William E. Leuchtenburg, *Franklin D. Roosevelt and the New Deal: 1932–1940* (New York: Harper and Row, 1963), p. 25.

8. State of Idaho, *General Laws . . . Passed at the Twenty-second Session . . .* , pp. 60, 179.

9. *Ibid.*, p. 229; Therman Evans in *Boise Capital News*, March 1, 1933, p. 1; *Idaho Post* (Moscow), March 24, 1933, p. 6; *Pocatello Tribune*, March 24, 1933, p. 1; Leuchtenburg, *F.D.R. and the New Deal*, pp. 25–26; G. H. Mayer, *The Political Career of Floyd B. Olson* (Minneapolis: University of Minnesota Press, 1951), pp. 125–27.

10. *Lewiston Morning Tribune*, March 2, 1933, p. 1.

11. *Boise Capital News*, March 2, 1933, p. 1.

12. RAP, Misc. Correspondence "J" fol., "The Ross Plan for National Rehabilitation," enclosure in letter, Lamont Johnson to Ross, April 26, 1933; Ross Personal Papers, Earl Bunting, "An Analysis of the Ross Plan . . . ," undated typescript; *Idaho Daily Statesman*, March 7, 1933, pp. 1, 7.

13. Ross Personal Papers, Earl Bunting to Ross, April 3, 1933.

14. Clara A. Aldrich, *The History of Banking in Idaho* (Boise: Syms-York, 1940), p. 71; *Boise Capital News*, March 3, 6, 9, 1933, p. 1.

15. RAP, Banking: 1933 fol., telegrams, Ross to Parker Carver, March 6, 1933; Ben Diefendorf to Ross, March 10, 1933; Cordell Hull to Ross, March 10, 1933; Ross to James P. Pope, March 12, 1933; E. G. Bennett to Ross, March 14, 1933; *Boise Capital News*, March 14, 19, 1933, p. 1.

16. Edwin G. Nourse *et al.*, *Three Years of the Agricultural Adjustment Administration* (Washington, D.C.: The Brookings Institution, 1937), pp. 15–35; Murray R. Benedict, *Farm Policies of the United States: 1790–1950* (New York: Twentieth Century Fund, 1953), pp. 282–84.

17. RAP, USDA fol., telegram, Henry Wallace to Ross, April 26, 1933.

18. *Ibid.*, Accomplishments of Federal Agencies fol., U.S. Depart-

NOTES TO CHAPTER IV

ment of Agriculture, Agricultural Adjustment Administration, Division of Information, "Changes in the Agricultural Situation in Idaho: 1932–1935," *State Summary Series* (September, 1936), pp. 1, 6; *ibid.*, USDA Statistics fol., U.S., Bureau of the Census, *United States Census of Agriculture, 1935: Summary by States,* p. 7, copy.

19. *Ibid.,* Accomplishments of Federal Agencies fol., "Accomplishments of the Farm Credit Administration in Idaho," unsigned, undated transcript.

20. *Ibid.,* HOLC fol., "Accomplishments of the Home Owners' Loan Corporation in Idaho," unsigned, undated transcript.

21. Josephine C. Brown, *Public Relief: 1929–1939* (New York: Henry Holt, 1940), pp. 146–51; J. D. Wood *et al.,* "Public Works in Idaho during the Emergency Period . . ." (Boise: Idaho State Planning Board, 1936), p. 5; Patterson, *The New Deal and the States,* pp. 56–57, 65.

22. FERA State File (Idaho) (MSS in Record Group 69, National Archives, Washington, D.C.), Box 73, Ross to Harry Hopkins, June 23, 1933; Parker Carver to Hopkins, July 25, 1933; RAP, CWA Projects: 1933 fol., telegrams, Harry Hopkins to Ross, June 9, 22, 1933; Ross to Hopkins, June 9, 1933; Parker Carver to Ross, June 26, 1933; Harry Hopkins Papers (MSS in the Franklin D. Roosevelt Library, Hyde Park, N.Y.), Pierce Williams to Hopkins, June 1, July 11, 1933; telegrams, Williams to Hopkins, August 22, October 15, 1933; *Idaho Post,* August 25, 1933, p. 1.

23. RAP, Emergency Relief to CWA: 1933 fol., telegram, Harry Hopkins to Ross, May 29, 1933; "Public Works in Idaho," p. 28.

24. CCC Selection Division State File (Idaho) (MSS in Record Group 35, National Archives, Washington, D.C.), Ross to F.D.R., May 3, 1933; Elmo R. Richardson, "Western Politics and New Deal Policies: A Study of T. A. Walters of Idaho," *Pacific Northwest Quarterly,* LIV (January, 1963), 15; State of Idaho, Land Department, *Twenty-third Biennial Report . . . 1935–1936,* p. 37. For a national perspective on the CCC, see John A. Salmond, *The Civilian Conservation Corps, 1933–1942: A New Deal Case Study* (Durham, N.C.: Duke University Press, 1967).

25. RAP, CCC Administrative: 1933 fol., telegrams, Henry Wallace to Ross, March 31, 1933; Ross to R. H. Rutledge, n.d.; *Idaho Daily Statesman,* April 2, 8, 1933, p. 1; interview with Harry C. Shellworth, February 1, 1964.

26. *Boise Capital News,* April 21, 1933, p. 1; Harry J. Brown in *Idaho Daily Statesman,* April 8, 1933, p. 1; RAP, Reforestation Camps: 1933 fol., "Recommendations of Delegations of Western States," April 7, 1933, typed copy.

27. Richardson, "Western Politics," p. 15; *Idaho Daily Statesman,* April 21, 1933, p. 1; RAP, CCC Administrative: 1933 fol., Robert Fechner to George H. Dern, May 11, 1933; E. W. Kelley to Ross, June 10, 1933; telegrams, Fechner to Ross, May 10, 1933; Ross to F.D.R., May 15, 1933; Ross to Borah, May 29, 1933; James P. Pope to Ross, May 30, 1933; Ross to W. F. Persons, June 4, 1933; Persons to Ross, June 6, 1933; *ibid.,* Coffin Correspondence fol., T. C. Coffin to Ross, June 6, 1933.

28. Merrill D. Beal and Merle W. Wells, *History of Idaho* (New York: Lewis Historical Publishing Company, 1959), II, 257; *Boise Capital News,* May 1, 3, 11, 29, June 2, 6, 8, 1933, p. 1.

29. "Public Works in Idaho," pp. 36–42; RAP, CCC: 1935–1936 fol., ECW, Office of the Director, "Idaho," press release of July 13, 1936, enclosure in letter, Robert Fechner to Ross, July 3, 1936; State of Idaho, Land Department, *Twenty-third Biennial Report . . . 1935–1936,* pp. 37–38; E. W. Kelley, quoted in *Clearwater Tribune* (Orofino), January 18, 1935, p. 1.

30. RAP, Forestry Board: 1933–34 fol., A. W. Middleton to Ross, January 19, 1933; Shellworth interview. Shellworth was Ross's most trusted advisor on forestry and CCC matters.

31. Richardson, "Western Politics," pp. 9–10; RAP, C. I. White Correspondence fol., White and T. C. Coffin to F.D.R., March 20, 1933.

32. T. A. Walters File (MSS in Record Group 48, National Archives, Washington, D.C.), Walters to James P. Pope, October 26, 1933; July 28, 1936; Walters to Robert Elder, September 15, 1933; RAP, Walters Correspondence fol., Ross to T. A. Walters, July 8, 1933; Walters to Ross, July 11, 1933; Ross Personal Papers, Walters to Ira Masters, June 23, 1933; Richardson, "Western Politics," p. 11.

33. RAP, CCC Administrative: 1933 fol., R. H. Rutledge to T. C. Coffin, June 7, 1933.

34. *Ibid.,* telegrams, T. C. Coffin to B. G. Lane, June 15, 1933; Coffin to Ross, June 16, 1933; Ross to Coffin, June 15, 1933; Parker Carver to Ross, June 15, 1933; *Lewiston Morning Tribune,* July 11, 1933, p. 1; Shellworth interview; CCC-300 (Idaho) File (MSS in Record Group 35, National Archives, Washington, D.C.), James R.

Williams, "Memorandum Relative to Political Controversy over Appointments of Overhead on CCC Camps in Idaho," typed copy.

35. CCC-300 (Idaho) File, Hugh Rankin to Robert Fechner, August 15, 1933; RAP, Forestry Board: 1933–34 fol., R. H. Rutledge to "The Forester," Washington, D.C., August 26, 1933.

36. Cato the Censor in *Idaho Daily Statesman,* July 7, 1933, p. 4.

37. *Ibid.;* Herbert Asbury, *The Great Illusion: An Informal History of Prohibition* (Garden City, N.Y.: Doubleday, 1950), pp. 328–30.

38. *Boise Capital News,* May 30, 1933, p. 1; *Idaho Daily Statesman,* May 30, 31, 1933, p. 1.

39. RAP, Misc. Correspondence "D": 1933–34 fol., Ross to J. A. Dunbar, June 8, 1933; *Lewiston Morning Tribune,* June 3, 1933, p. 1; *Idaho Daily Statesman,* June 4, 1933, p. 1; Harry Kessler Papers (MSS in the Idaho Historical Society, Boise), Kessler to Ross, May 31, 1933.

40. State of Idaho, *General Laws . . . Passed at the Extraordinary Session . . . 1933,* pp. 4–5.

41. *Journal of the Idaho Repeal Convention . . .* (Caldwell, Ida.: Caxton Printers, 1933), pp. 7, 12.

42. Harry S. Kessler in *The Challenge,* I (July, 1933), 2.

43. Leverett S. Lyon, *The National Recovery Administration: An Analysis and an Appraisal* (Washington, D.C.: The Brookings Institution, 1935), pp. 3–26; Arthur M. Schlesinger, Jr., *The Coming of the New Deal* (Boston: Houghton Mifflin, 1958), pp. 98–99.

44. Telegrams, Ross to C. F. Horner, July 31, 1933; Horner to Ross, July 7, 1933; Horner to Will Simons, August 7, 1933; Simons to Horner, August 8, 1933, in U.S., National Archives and Records Service, *Papers Relating to the State of Idaho in Selected Records Series. Record Group 9, Records of the National Recovery Administration* (microfilmed; Washington, D.C.: General Services Administration, 1964); cited hereafter as *Idaho NRA Records;* RAP, NRA fol., telegrams, Hugh Johnson to Ross, August 9, 1933; Ross to C. F. Horner, July 21, 1933.

45. *Idaho Daily Statesman,* September 7, 1933, p. 10; September 10, 1933, p. 1; RAP, Chambers of Commerce: 1931–33 fol., Boise Chamber of Commerce, "Annual Report: 1933," undated pamphlet.

46. *Idaho NRA Records,* W. T. Lockwood, "An Analysis of Compliance Conditions in Idaho," undated typescript; *ibid.,* W. T. Lockwood to Control Section, Compliance Division, NRA, April 12, 1935; Lockwood to A. N. D. Attaya, July 13, 1935; Donald Renshaw to

A. L. Merrill, July 29, 1935; Renshaw to Lockwood, August 9, 1935.

47. "Public Works in Idaho," pp. 13–14; RAP, PWA No. 1 fol., Ivan C. Crawford to Ross, October 23, 1933.

48. PWA Reclamation File (MSS in Record Group 135, National Archives), Box 85, D. W. Ross to Fred E. Schnepfe, November 17, 1933; RAP, PWA No. 3 fol., J. V. Otter, "The First Three Years: The Story of the Public Works Administration in Idaho," transcript of radio broadcast over station KIDO, Boise, November 6, 1936.

49. RAP, Ickes Controversy fol., telegram, Ross to F. B. Balzar, September 9, 1933.

50. See the correspondence in RAP, Ickes Controversy fol.

51. *Ibid.*, telegrams, Ross to Henry Wallace, September 9, 1933; C. F. Martin to Ross, September 19, 1933; *ibid.*, Coffin Correspondence fol., T. C. Coffin to Ross, September 19, 23, 1933; Martin to Coffin, September 21, 1933; B. J. Finch to Coffin, September 22, 1933; *Boise Capital News,* September 9, 26, 1933, p. 1.

52. RAP, President of the U.S. fol., telegram, Ross to Harold Ickes, September 17, 1933.

53. *Ibid.*, Ickes Controversy fol., telegram, Harold Ickes to Ross, September 21, 1933; Ickes was quoted in *Idaho Daily Statesman,* September 27, 1933, p. 1; *Teton Peak Chronicle* (St. Anthony, Ida.), September 28, 1933, p. 1.

54. Harry J. Brown in *Idaho Daily Statesman,* September 17, 1933, p. 12; RAP, Ickes Controversy fol., Harold Ickes to Ross, October 7, 1933; Ross to Ickes, October 19, 1933.

55. RAP, Ickes Controversy fol., Harold Ickes to Ross, October 7, 1933; Ross to Ickes, October 10, 1933; Richardson, "Western Politics," p. 12; Walters File, W. T. Lockwood to T. A. Walters, October 4, 18, 1933; Walters to Robert Elder, September 15, 1933.

56. Brown, *Public Relief,* pp. 159–60; Leuchtenburg, *F.D.R. and the New Deal,* pp. 121–24; "Public Works in Idaho," p. 12; Searle F. Charles, *Minister of Relief: Harry Hopkins and the Depression* (Syracuse, N.Y.: Syracuse University Press, 1963), pp. 44–52.

57. RAP, CWA fol., telegrams, Harry Hopkins to Ross, November 8, 1933; Hopkins to T. J. Lloyd, November 13, 1933; *Kellogg Evening News,* December 6, 1933, p. 1. Lloyd was replaced by Relief Director Parker Carver in December, 1933, because of a federal order that no CWA administrator could be paid a salary from the federal allotments.

58. *Power County Booster* (American Falls, Ida.), November 16,

1933, p. 1; *Lewiston Morning Tribune,* November 20, 22, 1933, p. 1.
 59. *Kellogg Evening News,* October 31, 1933, p. 1; *Pocatello Tribune,* January 17, 1934, p. 1; "Public Works in Idaho," pp. 12–13.
 60. *Power County Booster,* January 18, 1934, p. 1; *Pocatello Tribune,* January 15, 17, 1934, p. 1; August Rosqvist Papers (MSS in the Idaho Historical Society, Boise), Rosqvist to T. C. Coffin, April 4, 1934; RAP, Labor Union Correspondence fol., Rosqvist to Ross, April 5, 1934; George Johnson to Ross, April 6, 1934; *ibid.,* Misc. Subjects: 1934 fol., Ross to W. P. Whitaker, September 16, 1934.
 61. *Idaho Daily Statesman,* February 18, April 4, 1934, p. 1; March 15, 1934, p. 5; March 30, May 11, 1934, p. 11.
 62. CWA State File (Idaho) (MSS in Record Group 69, National Archives, Washington, D.C.), Box 12, J. C. Lindsay to John M. Carmody, April 30, 1934; Hopkins Papers, telegrams, Ross to T. C. Coffin, April 10, 12, 1934; letter, Pierce Williams to Harry Hopkins, April 18, 1934; Ross was quoted in *Pocatello Tribune,* April 12, 13, 14, 18, 1934, p. 1; *Idaho Daily Statesman,* May 12, 1935, p. 4.
 63. FERA State File (Idaho) (MSS in Record Group 69, National Archives, Washington, D.C.), Box 73, telegram, Corrington Gill to Aubrey Williams, May 15, 1934; letter, J. C. Lindsay to Aubrey Williams, May 31, 1934; *Idaho Daily Statesman,* May 19, 1934, p. 7; June 1, 1934, p. 3; *Lewiston Morning Tribune,* April 22, 1935, sec. 2, p. 1; Hopkins Papers, telegrams, Harry Hopkins to Pierce Williams, April 16, 1934; T. C. Coffin to John Carmody, April 21, 1934.
 64. FERA State File (Idaho), Box 73, Harry Hopkins to Ross, November 13, 1934; *Idaho Daily Statesman,* May 12, 1935, p. 4; H. H. Miller in *Lewiston Morning Tribune,* April 22, 1935, sec. 2, p. 1.
 65. Official File 268 (MSS in the Franklin D. Roosevelt Library, Hyde Park, N.Y.), memos, F.D.R. to Robert Fechner, February 16, 1934; Fechner to F.D.R., February 19, 1934; letters, Ross to F.D.R., February 28, 1934; F.D.R. to Ross, March 12, 1934.
 66. RAP, Drought Relief: 1934–35 fol., telegram, Ross to Universal News Service, Chicago, July 26, 1934; State of Idaho, Department of Reclamation, *Eighth Biennial Report . . . 1933–1934,* pp. 6–8; Richard L. Neuberger, "Refugees from the Dust Bowl," *Current History,* L (April, 1939), 32–35.
 67. RAP, Drought Relief: 1934–35 fol., "Report of the Governor's Special Emergency Drought Relief Committee, May 22, 1934," typescript; "Public Works in Idaho," p. 12.

68. RAP, Chambers of Commerce: 1931–33 fol., "Boise Commerce," undated pamphlet.

CHAPTER V

1. T. A. Walters File (MSS in Record Group 48, National Archives, Washington, D.C.), Robert Coulter to Walters, April 27, 1934; interview with Calvin Wright, July 25, 1965; *Idaho Pioneer* (Boise), November 17, 1933, p. 1; Ross Personal Papers, Walters to Ira H. Masters, June 23, 1933.
2. Quoted in *Idaho Pioneer,* May 11, 1934, p. 1; *Wallace Miner,* March 1, 1934, p. 2; *Post-Register* (Idaho Falls), February 23, 1934, p. 1; Ross Personal Papers, Frank Martin to E. G. Osterberg, June 2, 1934.
3. Quoted in *Idaho Pioneer,* April 10, June 23, 1934, p. 1; *Aberdeen Times,* August 2, 1934, p. 1; Ross Personal Papers, E. W. Rising to Ross, September 3, 1934.
4. *Pocatello Tribune,* June 3, 5, 6, 1934, p. 1; H. J. Brown in *Idaho Daily Statesman,* June 3, 1934, p. 1; June 5, 1934, pp. 1–2; *Idaho State Journal* (Pocatello), June 12, 1934, p. 1; T. A. Walters File, T. C. Coffin to Walters and James P. Pope, June 4, 1934; Official File 300-Idaho (MSS in the Franklin D. Roosevelt Library, Hyde Park, N.Y.), T. E. Mading to James A. Farley, June 20, 1934.
5. "Abstract of Votes at the Primary Election, August 14, 1934," in G. C. Hobson *et al., The Idaho Digest and Blue Book* (Caldwell, Ida.: Caxton Printers, 1935), chap. iv, abstract table 30.
6. Interview with Robert Coulter, July 30, 1965; Ross Personal Papers, Ross to John Foreman, August 18, 1934; *Idaho Daily Statesman,* August 31, 1934, p. 1.
7. William E. Borah Papers (MSS in the Library of Congress, Washington, D.C.), Box 372, J. A. Stewart to Borah, November 16, 1934; *Pocatello Tribune,* September 2, 1934, p. 1; Claudius O. Johnson, *Borah of Idaho* (2nd ed., rev.; Seattle: University of Washington Press, 1967), pp. 485–86.
8. Ross Personal Papers, "Radio Speech Given by Governor C. Ben Ross at Idaho Falls, Idaho, November 1, 1934," typescript; *Lewiston Morning Tribune,* October 7, 1934, p. 10.
9. *Pocatello Tribune,* November 5, 1934, p. 4; Ross Personal Papers, "Frank L. Stephan Speech Made at Emmett, Idaho, October 10, 1934," typed copy; *Wallace Miner,* October 18, 1934, p. 1.

NOTES TO CHAPTER V 157

10. Ross Personal Papers, B. L. McLaughlin to Robert Coulter, October 31, 1934; *Idaho Daily Statesman,* October 19, 20, 1934, p. 1.
11. "Abstract of Votes . . . at the General Election Held November 6, 1934," in Hobson *et al., Idaho Digest and Blue Book,* chap. iv, abstract table 23; *Morning Oregonian* (Portland), November 8, 1934, p. 7; *Spokane Daily Chronicle,* November 8, 1934, p. 6; *New York Times,* November 7, 1934, p. 2; November 8, 1934, p. 1; *Post-Register* (Idaho Falls), November 7, 1934, p. 1; *Idaho Post* (Moscow), November 9, 1934, p. 1; *Idaho Daily Statesman,* November 7, 1934, p. 1; *Lewiston Morning Tribune,* November 9, 1934, p. 1.
12. "Abstract of Votes . . . 1934," in Hobson *et al., Idaho Digest and Blue Book,* chap. iv, abstract table 23.
13. Ross Personal Papers, Ross to James A. Farley, November 8, 1934.
14. Arthur M. Schlesinger, Jr., *The Coming of the New Deal* (Boston: Houghton Mifflin, 1959), p. 507; H. H. Miller in *Lewiston Morning Tribune,* November 11, 1934, p. 3; Cato the Censor in *Idaho Daily Statesman,* November 11, 1934, p. 4.
15. Ross Administration Papers (RAP), Liquor Legislation fol., Alvin Denman to Ross, December 12, 1934; Ezra T. Benson to Ross, January 12, 1935; *ibid.,* Liquor Control Commission fol., "Summary Report of the Governor's Liquor Advisory Commission," undated typescript; *Pocatello Tribune,* December 12, 1934, p. 1.
16. FERA State File (Idaho) (MSS in Record Group 69, National Archives, Washington, D.C.), Box 73, memo of telephone call from Aubrey Williams to T. J. Edmonds, January 23, 1935; telegrams, Edmonds to Williams, January 17, 1935; Edmonds to Robert T. Lansdale, January 21, 1935; RAP, American Public Welfare fol., Glen Leet to Ross, December 27, 1934, January 23, 1935; Ross Personal Papers, memo, "Telephone Conversation between Gov. C. Ben Ross and Aubrey Williams, Washington, D.C., Jan. 31, 1935—10:15 A.M."; *Pocatello Tribune,* January 25, 1935, p. 1; February 10, 1935, p. 8; *Idaho County Press* (Grangeville), April 11, 1935, p. 1.
17. State of Idaho, *General Laws . . . Passed at the Twenty-third Session of the State Legislature: 1935,* pp. 11–13, 61–66.
18. *Ibid.,* pp. 214–21, 263–75, 301–4.
19. *Ibid.,* pp. 222–52; *Lewiston Morning Tribune,* February 19, 1935, p. 1; *Boise Capital News,* February 23, 1935, p. 1.
20. George Donart, quoted in *Weiser Signal,* April 18, 1935, p. 1; A. Y. Satterfield, quoted in *Clearwater Tribune* (Orofino), April 5,

1935, p. 1; *Idaho Daily Statesman,* February 10, 1935, p. 1; *Lewiston Morning Tribune,* February 10, 1935, p. 1; *Pocatello Tribune,* February 10, 1935, p. 1; interview with Chase A. Clark, July 27, 1965.

21. Harry Hopkins Papers (MSS in the Franklin D. Roosevelt Library, Hyde Park, N.Y.), telegram, T. J. Edmonds to Aubrey Williams, February 5, 1935.

22. *Boise Capital News,* February 27, March 7, 21, 1935, p. 1; Ross Personal Papers, "Notes on Telephone Conversation between Aubrey Williams, Asst. FERA Administrator, and Gov. C. Ben Ross, March 1, 1935, at 2:05 P.M.," transcript.

23. RAP, Extra Session of March, 1935, fol., "Governor's Message, Members of the Legislature of the State of Idaho, Convened in Extraordinary Session, March 8, 1935," typescript; FERA State File (Idaho), Box 73, telegram, T. J. Edmonds to Aubrey Williams, March 19, 1935.

24. *Idaho Daily Statesman,* March 19, 1935, p. 1; *Lewiston Morning Tribune,* March 15, 1935, p. 1.

25. FERA State File (Idaho), Box 73, telegram, T. J. Edmonds to Aubrey Williams, March 21, 1935; *Boise Capital News,* March 19, 20, 1935, p. 1; *Idaho Daily Statesman,* March 20, 21, 22, 1935, p. 1; State of Idaho, *General Laws . . . Passed at the Extraordinary Session . . . 1935,* pp. 26–42.

26. *Idaho Daily Statesman,* March 20, 1935, p. 4; March 21, 1935, p. 1; *Post-Register,* April 7, 1935, p. 1; Ross Personal Papers, "Telephone Conversation between Gov. Ross and D. Worth Clark at Washington, D.C., March 19, 1935," typescript. Ross seems to have been deeply angered by the pressure which the FERA put upon him during the session. He instructed Clark to tell Aubrey Williams "not to interfere here."

27. Harry S. Kessler in *The Challenge,* II (March, 1935), 1–2; Coulter interview.

28. RAP, Sales Tax: 1935–36 fol., Sales Tax Bulletin of September 3, 1935, enclosure in letter, Ben Diefendorf to Ross, September 3, 1935; Ross to E. H. Ramsey, December 21, 1936.

29. Quoted in *Lewiston Morning Tribune,* April 7, 1935, p. 1.

30. Hopkins Papers, T. J. Edmonds to Harry Hopkins, April 3, 1935; *Post-Register,* April 4, 7, 1935, p. 1; May 1, 1935, pp. 1, 3; *Weiser Signal,* May 2, 1935, p. 1.

31. Arthur M. Schlesinger, Jr., *The Politics of Upheaval* (Boston:

Houghton Mifflin, 1960), p. 385; Basil Rauch, *The History of the New Deal* (New York: Creative Age Press, 1944), pp. 156–58.

32. Josephine C. Brown, *Public Relief: 1929–1939* (New York: Henry Holt, 1940), p. 167.

33. WPA File 610 (Idaho) (MSS in Record Group 69, National Archives, Washington, D.C.), Box 1155, telegram, Corrington Gill to J. L. Hood, June 25, 1935; *Idaho Daily Statesman,* May 17, June 25, 28, 1935, p. 1; U.S., Department of the Interior, Bureau of Reclamation, "Boise Project History: 1935," in U.S., National Archives and Records Service, *Project Histories of the Boise and Owyhee Reclamation Projects: 1934–1935–1936. Record Group 115, Records of the Bureau of Reclamation* (microfilmed; Washington, D.C.: General Services Administration, 1964); *Star-Mirror* (Moscow), July 19, 1935, p. 1; *Boise Capital News,* November 4, December 2, 1935, p. 1.

34. RAP, WPA Applications No. 2 fol., Andy Balangyan to Ross, June 18, 1935; *ibid.,* Planning Board fol., "Public Works in Idaho," pp. 25–26; *ibid.,* WPA Projects fol., "Report of WPA Projects . . . Feb. 24, 1936," typescript; WPA State File (Idaho) (MSS in Record Group 69, National Archives, Washington, D.C.), "Final Report of Idaho Work Projects Administration," pp. 3, 9, 10, mimeographed copy.

35. Ronald W. Taber, "Vardis Fisher and the Idaho Guide," *Pacific Northwest Quarterly,* LIX (April, 1968), 68–76; see also Vardis Fisher et al., *Idaho: A Guide in Word and Picture* (Caldwell, Ida.: Caxton Printers, 1937).

36. "The National Youth Administration of Idaho . . . 1935–43," in U.S., National Archives and Records Service, *Final Report: National Youth Administration for the State of Idaho. Record Group 119, Records of the National Youth Administration* (microfilmed; Washington, D.C.: General Services Administration, 1964).

37. *Ibid.;* telegram, Aubrey Williams to W. W. Godfrey, August 1, 1935; letters, Williams to "Mr. Corson," August 21, 1935; O. H. Lull to Richard Brown, March 19, 1936, in U.S., National Archives and Records Service, *Administrative, Budget, and Personnel Correspondence Relating to Idaho . . . . Record Group 119, Records of the National Youth Administration* (microfilmed; Washington, D.C.: General Services Administration, 1964).

38. RAP, Representative D. W. Clark Correspondence fol., Clark to Rexford G. Tugwell, January 9, 1936; *ibid.,* RA fol., "The Resettle-

ment Administration in Oregon, Washington, and Idaho" (January, 1936), pamphlet.

39. Quoted in Schlesinger, *Politics of Upheaval,* p. 353.

40. WPA File 610 (Idaho), Box 1155, Ross to Harry Hopkins, November 29, 1935; Ross to F.D.R., November 29, 1935; RAP, WPA Rulings fol., telegram, Hopkins to J. L. Hood, November 2, 1935; Ross to D. Worth Clark, May 17, 1936.

41. WPA File 610 (Idaho), Box 1155, Ross to F.D.R., December 23, 1935; *Idaho Daily Statesman,* January 18, 1936, p. 1. See the extensive correspondence on this matter in RAP, WPA Rulings fol.

42. James T. Patterson, *The New Deal and the States: Federalism in Transition* (Princeton: Princeton University Press, 1969), pp. 85–94.

43. *Pocatello Tribune,* December 2, 1935, p. 1; *Boise Capital News,* December 2, 1935, p. 1; *Lewiston Morning Tribune,* December 13, 1935, p. 1; RAP, NEC fol., "Welcoming Address by Gov. Ross to the NEC Federal Coordination Meeting, Hotel Boise, Dec. 4, 1935," typescript.

44. RAP, ICRA Administrative fol., Ross to Oscar Naser, January 7, 1936; P. H. Cohn to Ross, April 25, 1936; State of Idaho, Department of State, *Twenty-third Biennial Report . . . 1935–1936,* p. 51; "Welcoming Address by Gov. Ross . . . Dec. 4, 1935"; *Boise Capital News,* December 2, 1935, p. 1.

45. Lewis Meriam, *Relief and Social Security* (Washington, D.C.: The Brookings Institution, 1946), pp. 16–17; Schlesinger, *Politics of Upheaval,* pp. 309–14; Rauch, *History of New Deal,* pp. 161–63.

46. *Boise Capital News,* February 20, 1936, p. 1; State of Idaho, Department of State, *Twenty-third Biennial Report . . . 1935–1936,* p. 51; *Idaho Daily Statesman,* March 12, 1936, p. 3; *Lewiston Morning Tribune,* February 21, 1936, p. 1.

47. RAP, Special Session, July 28, 1936: House fol., "Governor's Message to the Members of the Twenty-third Legislature . . . Extraordinary Session, July 28, 1936," typescript; *Northern Idaho News* (Sandpoint), July 31, August 7, 1936, pp. 1, 5; *Lewiston Morning Tribune,* July 29, 1936, pp. 1, 3; August 1, 1936, p. 1; State of Idaho, *General Laws . . . Passed at the Third Extraordinary Session of . . . 1936,* pp. 3, 8–9, 20–48.

48. State of Idaho, Department of State, *Twenty-third Biennial Report . . . 1935–1936,* pp. 51–52.

49. William E. Leuchtenburg, *Franklin D. Roosevelt and the New*

NOTES TO CHAPTER VI

Deal: 1932–1940 (New York: Harper and Row, 1963), pp. 151–52; RAP, National Re-employment: 1935–36 fol., C. W. Hope to Ross, September 25, 1935.

50. August Rosqvist, "Idaho State Federation of Labor: When Organized and Why," *Official State Yearbook of Organized Labor: Idaho, 1930* (Pocatello: State Journal–Union Printers, 1930), p. 10; August Rosqvist, "Idaho Unions Revived in 1934," *Idaho State Federation of Labor Yearbook: 1935* (Pocatello: Graves and Potter–The Tribune Press, 1935), p. 5; August Rosqvist Papers (MSS in the Idaho Historical Society, Boise), Rosqvist to R. S. Breckinridge, February 24, 1934.

51. *Post-Register*, August 14, 18, 1935, p. 1.

52. Robert L. Tyler, *Rebels of the Woods: The I.W.W. in the Pacific Northwest* (Eugene: University of Oregon Books, 1967), pp. 225–26; Tyler, "I.W.W. in the Pacific N.W.: Rebels of the Woods," *Oregon Historical Quarterly*, LV (March, 1954), 41; "Wobblies in the Northwest," *Nation*, CXLV (November 13, 1937), 543; *Kootenai County Leader* (Coeur d'Alene), August 7, 1936, p. 1; *Clearwater Tribune* (Orofino), August 7, 14, 21, 28, 1936, p. 1; RAP, Clearwater County Strike fol., Daniel Murphy to Ross, July 26, 1936; Ross to Murphy, July 30, 1936; Lewis Williams to Ross, July 28, 1936; telegrams, Hobart Burns to Ross, August 4, 1936; Ross to F. W. Thompson, August 6, 1936.

53. RAP, NEC fol., chart enclosed in letter, W. T. Lockwood to Ross, March 2, 1936.

54. *Ibid.*, Mines and Geology: 1935–36 fol., John C. Reed, "Early and Recent Mining Activity in North-Central Idaho," University of Idaho press release (May, 1936); *ibid.*, Columbia River Development fol., Ross to T. A. Walters, May 10, 1933.

55. *Ibid.*, Special Session, July 28, 1936: House fol., "Governor's Message to the Members of the Twenty-third Legislature . . . Extraordinary Session, July 28, 1936," typescript.

56. Quoted by David Lawrence in *Washington Star* (Washington, D.C.), August 25, 1936, clipping in William E. Borah Scrapbook No. 20 (MSS in the University of Idaho Library, Moscow), p. 132.

CHAPTER VI

1. Richard L. Neuberger, *Our Promised Land* (New York: Macmillan, 1938), p. 164.

2. Arthur M. Schlesinger, Jr., *The Politics of Upheaval* (Boston: Houghton Mifflin, 1960), pp. 527–28.

3. Claudius O. Johnson, *Borah of Idaho* (2nd ed., rev.; Seattle: University of Washington Press, 1967), p. 488; Otis L. Graham, Jr., *An Encore for Reform: The Old Progressives and the New Deal* (New York: Oxford University Press, 1967), pp. 182–83, 192; James T. Patterson, *Congressional Conservatism and the New Deal* (Lexington: University of Kentucky Press, 1967), p. 104; Marian C. McKenna, *Borah* (Ann Arbor: University of Michigan Press, 1961), pp. 306–18; Marian McKenna to the author, February 10, 1966.

4. Interviews with C. Ben Reavis, July 1, 1965; W. Lloyd Adams, July 31, 1965; James H. Hawley, Jr., July 23, 1965; Chase A. Clark, July 27, 1965.

5. W. D. Gillis, "A Governor Guided by Divinations," *American Mercury,* XXXIII (September, 1934), 117. According to Gillis' account, which is undoubtedly partisan, the soothsayer had predicted three gubernatorial victories, followed by the defeat of Borah in 1936, and ultimately the presidency.

6. Quoted in Walter Davenport, "Storm Warnings in Idaho," *Collier's,* XCVII (April 4, 1936), 10–11.

7. McKenna, *Borah,* p. 337; *Daily Bulletin* (Blackfoot), clipping in Borah Scrapbook No. 8 (MSS in the University of Idaho Library, Moscow); Harry J. Brown in *Salt Lake Tribune,* November 18, 1934, p. 1; see the typed summaries of newspaper reactions to the Farley "plot" in William E. Borah Papers (MSS in the Library of Congress, Washington, D.C.), Box 401.

8. Hugh S. Johnson to Borah, July 29, 1935, Borah Scrapbook No. 14, p. 153; Bernard M. Baruch to Borah, August 7, 1935, Borah Scrapbook No. 15, p. 177; Carter Glass to Borah, September 17, 1936, Borah Scrapbook No. 20, p. 155; *Chicago Daily Tribune,* July 30, 1935, p. 5; *New York Times,* July 30, 1935, p. 12; McKenna, *Borah,* p. 338.

9. James A. Farley to the author, December 10, 1965; Marian McKenna to the author, February 10, 1966. Professor McKenna interviewed Mr. Farley in 1957. Farley assured both her and the author that, while he made an all-out effort to defeat Borah in 1936, he made no *special* attempt to do so.

10. Ross Personal Papers, D. Worth Clark to Ross, January 17, 1935; Ross to Will Simons, October 10, 1935; Official File 300-Idaho (MSS in the Franklin D. Roosevelt Library, Hyde Park, N.Y.), Ross

to James A. Farley, August 2, 1935; *Idaho Daily Statesman* (Boise), November 25, 1935, p. 1.

11. Mrs. Frank Johnesse Papers (MSS in the Idaho Historical Society, Boise), "Minutes of Meeting of Representatives of Democratic Central Committees of Seventeen Southeastern Idaho Counties, Held in Idaho Falls . . . June 7, 1935," typescript.

12. T. A. Walters File (MSS in Record Group 48, National Archives, Washington, D.C.), Walters to William Healy, December 26, 1935.

13. *New York Times,* May 11, 1936, p. 1; Walters File, Will Simons to T. A. Walters, May 29, 1935; Walters to Simons, June 18, September 26, 1935; Walters to Ira Masters, July 8, 1935; Mrs. Frank Johnesse to Walters, October 23, 1935; Ramsay Walker to Walters, April 14, 1936; Walters to Walker, March 28, 1936.

14. Schlesinger, *Politics of Upheaval,* pp. 29–41; RAP, Old Age Pensions: 1933–34 fol., "Townsend Plan of Old Age Revolving Pensions," undated pamphlet enclosed in letter, R. D. Danby to Ross, October 26, 1934; on Townsendism, see Abraham Holtzman, *The Townsend Movement* (New York: Twayne, 1962).

15. Borah Papers, Box 400, Borah to William Allen White, July 23, 1936; Richard L. Neuberger and Kelley Loe, "The Old People's Crusade: The Townsend Plan and Its Astonishing Growth," *Harper's Magazine,* CLXXII (March, 1936), 426–34; Richard L. Neuberger, "Political Notes from the Northwest," *Nation,* CXLII (May 13, 1936), 611.

16. Quoted in *Idaho Daily Statesman,* September 8, 1935, p. 1; Davenport, "Storm Warnings in Idaho," p. 28.

17. Schlesinger, *Politics of Upheaval,* p. 528; McKenna, *Borah,* p. 324.

18. For a detailed discussion of Borah's presidential and senatorial campaigns in 1936, see McKenna, *Borah,* pp. 319–44; and Orde S. Pinckney, "William E. Borah and the Republican Party, 1932–1940" (Ph.D. dissertation, University of California at Berkeley, 1958), pp. 84–140.

19. McKenna, *Borah,* pp. 335–36; Orde S. Pinckney, "Lion Triumphant," *Idaho Yesterdays,* III (Summer, 1959), 12–14. Pinckney disagrees with Richard Neuberger's assertion that Borah staged his presidential campaign merely to bolster his chances of re-election to the Senate from Idaho. See Neuberger's "Behind the Borah Boom," *Current History,* XLIII (February, 1936), 463–66.

20. *Clearwater Tribune* (Orofino), June 26, 1936, p. 1; *Washington Star* (Washington, D.C.), June 21, 25, 1936, clippings in Borah Scrapbook No. 20, pp. 45, 46; *Idaho Daily Statesman,* June 26, 1936, p. 8.

21. President's Personal File 2358 (MSS in the Franklin D. Roosevelt Library, Hyde Park, N.Y.), W. Orr Chapman to Harllee Branch, July 1, 1936; Branch to F.D.R., July 7, 1936; J. David Stern to James A. Farley, July 24, 1936; Will Durant to Marvin McIntyre, June 26, 1936; McIntyre to Farley, July 16, 1936.

22. James M. Burns, *Roosevelt: The Lion and the Fox* (Harvest Books ed.; New York: Harcourt, Brace and World, 1956), p. 279; President's Personal File 2358, Borah to J. David Stern, July 24, 1936; James A. Farley to Will Durant, July 24, 1936; Farley to Stern, July 28, 1936; Borahs' most recent biographer, Marian McKenna, also notes that Burns offers "no authority" for his claim that Borah was willing to cooperate; McKenna, *Borah,* p. 338; F.D.R. to Farley, February 19, 1937, in Elliott Roosevelt (ed.), *F.D.R., His Personal Letters: 1928–1945* (New York: Duell, Sloan, and Pearce, 1950), I, 660–61.

23. Cato the Censor in *Idaho Daily Statesman,* July 12, 1936, p. 4.

24. Interview with Calvin Wright, July 25, 1965; Hawley interview; *Idaho Pioneer* (Boise), August 14, 1936, p. 1; Ross was quoted in *Lewiston Morning Tribune,* May 17, 1936, p. 1.

25. Cato the Censor in *Idaho Daily Statesman,* May 17, 1937, p. 4; *Idaho Pioneer,* August 9, 1935, May 22, 1936, p. 1.

26. State of Idaho, Department of State, "Abstract of Votes . . . Aug. 11, 1936," *Twenty-third Biennial Report . . . 1935–1936,* appended to p. 77; *Time,* XXVIII (August 24, 1936), 22; *News-Week,* VIII (August 22, 1936), 8–9.

27. *Pocatello Tribune,* August 27, 1936, p. 1; August 28, 1936, p. 3; *Idaho Daily Statesman,* August 28, 1936, p. 1; *Lewiston Morning Tribune,* August 28, 1936, p. 1.

28. Mrs. Johnesse had replaced Robert Coulter as Democratic state chairman when he was appointed to the Liquor Commission in March, 1935. At that time she was the only woman in the country to hold such a position.

29. *Idaho Daily Statesman,* August 28, 1936, p. 1; *Lewiston Morning Tribune,* August 28, 1936, p. 1.

30. Adams interview; Pinckney, "Lion Triumphant," p. 14; Richard

NOTES TO CHAPTER VII

L. Neuberger, "Battle of the Idaho Titans," *New York Times Magazine*, August 9, 1936, sec. VII, pp. 9, 20.

31. *Idaho Daily Statesman*, April 23, 25, October 5, 1936, p. 1; August 29, 1936, p. 6; *New York Times*, September 1, 1936, p. 6; interview with Mrs. Ethel Steel, July 3, 1965.

32. McKenna, *Borah*, pp. 339–41; Pinckney, "Lion Triumphant," p. 22; *New York Times*, October 11, 1936, sec. IV, p. 6; *Kootenai County Leader* (Coeur d'Alene), October 30, 1936, pp. 1, 4; Borah Papers, Box 400, Borah to Thomas E. Whitten, December 5, 1936.

33. *Idaho Daily Statesman*, November 1, 1936, p. 2; Ross was quoted in *Lewiston Morning Tribune*, October 20, 1936, p. 12; Pinckney, "Lion Triumphant," p. 24.

34. Quoted in *News-Week*, VIII (August 22, 1936), 9.

35. Clark interview; Hawley interview; William Green to Senator William E. Borah, July 9, 1935, reprinted in *Idaho State Federation of Labor Yearbook: 1936* (Boise: Strawn and Company, 1936), p. 2; Ross quoted in McKenna, *Borah*, p. 341; Pinckney, "Lion Triumphant," p. 19; *Pocatello Tribune*, November 2, 1936, p. 6.

36. State of Idaho, Department of State, "Abstract of Votes . . . Nov. 3, 1936," *Twenty-third Biennial Report . . . 1935–1936*, appended to p. 77; *Morning Oregonian* (Portland), November 4, 1936, p. 17; *Pocatello Tribune*, November 3, 1936, p. 1; *Idaho Daily Statesman*, November 4, 1936, p. 1; November 5, 1936, p. 4; *Lewiston Morning Tribune*, November 8, 1936, sec. 2, p. 1. Ross polled over twice the number of votes of any of Borah's previous opponents.

37. *Spokesman-Review* (Spokane), November 4, 1936, p. 1; *New York Times*, November 6, 1936, p. 24.

38. Quoted in *Idaho Daily Statesman*, December 19, 1936, p. 12; Reavis interview.

39. Quoted in *Pocatello Tribune*, November 20, 1936, p. 1.

40. *Buhl Herald*, December 31, 1936, p. 1.

CHAPTER VII

1. Barzilla W. Clark Papers (MSS in the University of Idaho Library, Moscow), Barzilla Clark, "Biography of Barzilla W. Clark," undated typescript; Byron Defenbach *et al.*, *Idaho: The Place and Its People* (Chicago: American Historical Society, 1933), III, 122–24; Merrill D. Beal and Merle W. Wells, *History of Idaho* (New York:

Lewis Historical Publishing Company, 1959), III, 475–76; G. C. Hobson *et al., The Idaho Digest and Blue Book* (Caldwell, Ida.: Caxton Printers, 1935), p. 785.

2. Beal and Wells, *History of Idaho,* II, 263; interview with John Corlett, June 29, 1965.

3. Interview with C. Ben Reavis, July 1, 1965; interview with Mrs. Ethel Steel, July 3, 1965; Ross Personal Papers, Ross to A. H. Hartshorn, January 4, 1938.

4. Interview with Truman Joiner, July 29, 1965; interview with Calvin Wright, July 25, 1965.

5. *Idaho Pioneer* (Boise), September 30, 1938, p. 1; *Idaho Daily Statesman* (Boise), November 7, 1936, August 4, 1938, p. 1; *Boise Capital News,* August 16, 1938, March 21, 1939, p. 1; August 17, 1938, p. 5; August 24, 1938, March 22, 1939, p. 2; *Lewiston Morning Tribune,* August 13, 1938, p. 1.

6. James Munro *et al., Special Highway Fund Audit: January 1, 1933 to December 31, 1936* (typed copy; Boise, 1938), I, 1–35, quotation on p. 27.

7. These conclusions are in general agreement with those of Truman Joiner, a member of the investigating team, which were stated to the present author in an interview of July 29, 1965.

8. Wright interview.

9. *Literary Digest,* CXX (September 7, 1935), 27; Chesley Manly in *Chicago Daily Tribune,* August 11, 1938, p. 1; *Biographical Directory of the American Congress, 1774–1961* (Washington, D.C.: U.S. Government Printing Office, 1961), pp. 1469–70; Defenbach, *Idaho,* II, 11; Hobson *et al., Idaho Digest and Blue Book,* pp. 875–76; George E. Mowry, *The Urban Nation: 1920–1960* (New York: Hill and Wang, 1965), p. 127; for a conservative assessment of Pope, see Cobb-Ailshie Papers (MSS in the Idaho Historical Society, Boise), Margaret Cobb Ailshie to Bob Allen, August 17, 1938.

10. Ross Personal Papers, Ross to D. Worth Clark, April 4, 1938; Ross to E. W. Equals, April 4, 1938; Ross to L. G. Lacey, April 20, 1938; *Biographical Directory of the American Congress,* p. 697; Defenbach, *Idaho,* III, 292–94.

11. Ross was quoted by W. R. Bottcher in *Pocatello Tribune,* September 4, 1938, p. 1; C. E. Arney, "Ross and Pope Reach End of Political Trail," *Lewiston Morning Tribune,* November 13, 1938, sec. 2, p. 1.

12. Wright interview; C. A. Bottolfsen Papers (MSS in the University of Idaho Library, Moscow), Bottolfsen to Borah, April 8, 1938.
13. *New York Times,* August 8, 1938, p. 2.
14. *Ibid.,* July 14, August 8, 1938, p. 2; August 9, 1938, p. 3; William E. Leuchtenburg, *Franklin D. Roosevelt and the New Deal: 1932–1940* (New York: Harper and Row, 1963), p. 267; President's Personal File 5209 (MSS in the Franklin D. Roosevelt Library, Hyde Park, N.Y.), F.D.R. to James P. Pope, February 22, 1938.
15. James T. Patterson, *Congressional Conservatism and the New Deal* (Lexington: University of Kentucky Press, 1967), p. 270; William E. Borah Papers (MSS in the Library of Congress, Washington, D.C.), Box 423, telegram, Ray McKaig to Borah, August 9, 1938; Bottolfsen Papers, W. D. Gillis to C. A. Bottolfsen, May 16, 1938.
16. State of Idaho, Department of State, "Abstract of Votes . . . August 9, 1938," *Report of the Secretary of State . . . 1937–1938,* appended to p. 88.
17. *The Oregonian* (Portland), August 11, 1938, pp. 1, 22; *Seattle Daily Times,* August 11, 1938, p. 6; *Spokesman-Review* (Spokane), August 11, 1938, p. 1; *Chicago Daily Tribune,* August 11, 1938, p. 1; *Pocatello Tribune,* August 9, 10, 1938, p. 1; *Idaho Daily Statesman,* August 10, 1938, p. 1; August 11, 1938, pp. 1, 4; *Idaho Pioneer,* August 12, 1938, p. 2; *Lewiston Morning Tribune,* August 11, 1938, p. 1; Turner Catledge in *New York Times,* August 11, 1938, pp. 1–2; August 12, 1938, p. 10.
18. U.S., National Archives and Records Service, *Press Conferences of Franklin D. Roosevelt* (microfilmed; Hyde Park, N.Y.: Franklin D. Roosevelt Library, n.d.), roll 6, vol. 12, pp. 036–037.
19. *Time,* XXXII (August 22, 1938), 21; Boyd A. Martin, *The Direct Primary in Idaho* (Stanford, Calif.: Stanford University Press, 1947), pp. 130–33; Patterson, *Congressional Conservatism,* p. 270; Leuchtenburg, *F.D.R. and the New Deal,* pp. 267–69.
20. Official File 300-Idaho (MSS in the Franklin D. Roosevelt Library, Hyde Park, N.Y.), telegrams, S. E. Bradford to F.D.R., August 15, 1938; D. Worth Clark to F.D.R., August 16, 1938; I. H. Masters to F.D.R., August 25, 1938; R. H. Elder to James A. Farley, n.d.; M. E. Zener to Farley, n.d.; letters, Beecher Hitchcock to F.D.R., August 11, 1938; F.D.R. to Hitchcock, August 17, 1938; Lewis Williams to Farley, August 16, 1938; A. F. James to Farley, August 29, 1938; C. A. Clark to Farley, August 26, 1938; Farley to F.D.R., Sep-

tember 14, 1938; *New York Times,* August 21, 1938, p. 26; August 22, 1938, p. 3.

21. *New York Times,* September 4, 1938, p. 1; *Coeur d'Alene Press,* August 25, 1938, p. 1; President's Personal File 5209, F.D.R. to Ellison D. Smith, January 5, 1939; *Scholastic,* XXXIII (January 21, 1939), 8.

22. *Lewiston Morning Tribune,* August 28, 1938, p. 1; *Boise Capital News,* August 27, 1938, p. 1; August 29, 1938, p. 5; *Idaho Daily Statesman,* August 28, 1938, p. 1; W. R. Bottcher in *Pocatello Tribune,* September 4, 1938, p. 1.

23. *Boise Capital News,* August 26, 1938, p. 2; *Idaho Daily Statesman,* August 26, 1938, p. 1.

24. *New York Times,* November 6, 1938, p. 41.

25. *Boise Capital News,* August 24, 1938, p. 2; *Pocatello Tribune,* September 14, 1938, p. 1; Wright interview.

26. State of Idaho, Department of State, "Abstract of Votes . . . Nov. 8, 1938," *Report of the Secretary of State . . . 1937–1938,* appended to p. 88.

27. Robert E. Burke, *Olson's New Deal for California* (Berkeley and Los Angeles: University of California Press, 1953), p. 34.

28. *Idaho Daily Statesman,* November 10, 1938, p. 4; *Pocatello Tribune,* November 10, 1938, p. 4; *Idaho Pioneer,* November 11, 1938, p. 1; *Boise Capital News,* November 10, 1938, p. 1; November 11, 1938, p. 2; *Lewiston Morning Tribune,* November 10, 1938, p. 4; November 13, 1938, sec 2, p. 1; Parsons was quoted in *Pocatello Tribune,* November 9, 1938, p. 1.

29. C. E. Arney in *Lewiston Morning Tribune,* November 13, 1938, sec. 2, p. 1; Cato the Censor in *Boise Capital News,* November 11, 1938, p. 2.

30. "Political Party Organization in Idaho, 1861–1960: A Brief Outline," *Idaho Historical Series,* IV (March, 1961), 4.

31. Ross Personal Papers, Ross to John F. Ross, November 19, 1938.

32. Corlett interview; Steel interview; John Corlett, "Ex-Governor C. Ben Ross Dies in Boise," *Idaho Daily Statesman,* April 1, 1946, pp. 1–2.

33. Corlett, "Ross Dies in Boise"; *Coeur d'Alene Press,* April 1, 1946, p. 1; *Lewiston Morning Tribune,* April 1, 1946, p. 1; *Post-Register* (Idaho Falls), April 1, 1946, p. 1.

NOTES TO CHAPTER VII

34. Coulter quoted in *Pocatello Tribune*, April 1, 1946, p. 1; interview with Robert Coulter, June 30, 1965; *Pocatello Tribune*, April 2, 1946, pp. 1, 3–4; Miller quoted in Orde S. Pinckney, "Lion Triumphant," *Idaho Yesterdays*, III (Summer, 1959), 18. Miller expressed this opinion in an unpublished manuscript entitled "An Idaho Generation." The manuscript has apparently been lost, and to my knowledge Pinckney is the only scholar who ever saw it.

35. *Post-Register*, April 1, 1946, p. 1.

36. Richard Hofstadter, *The Age of Reform* (Vintage ed.; New York: Random House, 1955), pp. 302–28; Leuchtenburg, *F.D.R. and the New Deal*, pp. 326–48; Carl N. Degler, *Out of Our Past: The Forces That Shaped Modern America* (Colophon ed.; New York: Harper and Row, 1959), pp. 410–16; an excellent historiographical assessment of change and continuity in the New Deal is Richard S. Kirkendall, "The New Deal as Watershed: The Recent Literature," *Journal of American History*, LIV (March, 1968), 839–52.

37. These statistics are drawn from Leonard Arrington, "The New Deal in the West: A Preliminary Statistical Inquiry," an article read by the author in galleys, which was subsequently published in the August, 1969, issue of the *Pacific Historical Review*. This issue is devoted to "The New Deal in Western States" and contains articles by James T. Patterson on the New Deal in the West and by the present author on Idaho. For an interesting and informative summation of New Deal economic aid to Idaho and its results by 1939, see "Report No. 10, Volume II: Idaho—Federal Loans and Expenditures 1933–1939, State Statistics, Narrative Review of Agency Operations, Work Accomplishments" (n.p.: Office of Government Reports, Statistical Section, 1940), mimeographed copy in Utah State University Library, Logan, Utah. I am much indebted to Professor Arrington for supplying me with this material.

38. James T. Patterson, *The New Deal and the States: Federalism in Transition* (Princeton: Princeton University Press, 1969), p. 202.

BIBLIOGRAPHY

MANUSCRIPT COLLECTIONS

The most important source of information for this work is the collection of C. Ben Ross Administration Papers, deposited at the Idaho Historical Society Archives in Boise, Idaho. These papers are filed in 110 boxes and in two separate series and are arranged in folders according to specific subjects. Much of this collection consists of routine paperwork and is of little historical value. The Ross Administration Papers are, of course, most valuable as a source for administrative history. Since they contain most of the federal-state correspondence of the New Deal period, these papers are also of special interest to the student of the New Deal in general and of specific federal agencies in particular. These manuscripts contain relatively little material pertaining to state politics as such. Two large scrapbooks devoted to the Governor's political career are also grouped with this collection.

The C. Ben Ross Personal Papers are presently in the possession of Mrs. Ethel Steel of Parma, Idaho. Mrs. Steel, a long-time friend and neighbor of Ross, found and preserved these papers after the death of Ross's adopted daughter, Helen Usadel. Mrs. Steel is presently filing the manuscripts and will eventually send them to the University of Idaho Library at Moscow. This collection is only a fragment of the papers which Ross left at the time of his death; the rest were apparently destroyed by his children. Nevertheless, the Ross Personal Papers contain a considerable amount of material invaluable to the study of the Governor's political career, especially correspondence relating to his private political ambitions.

Several other manuscript collections at the Idaho Historical Society in Boise are of special interest to the student of the depression era in Idaho. The James P. Pope Law Office Papers, James H. Hawley, Jr., Papers, and the last few boxes of the James H. Hawley Papers contain valuable information concerning state politics prior to 1933. Senator Pope's post-1933 papers have apparently been either lost or destroyed. The Harry S. Kessler Papers are of special interest to the student of the repeal issue, and the August Rosqvist Papers reveal much about the labor situation. The political file in the Frank E. Johnesse Collection contains the correspondence which Mrs. Johnesse accumulated as Democratic state chairman during 1935–36, and the Cobb-Ailshie Papers are also of incidental value. For the period 1937–38, the Barzilla W. Clark Administration Papers serve the same function as do the Ross Administration Papers for 1931–36.

The William E. Borah Papers at the Library of Congress in Washington, D.C., although voluminous, are not well indexed and are not particularly revealing on state political affairs. The scholar interested in Idaho political issues should consult the general correspondence files for the 1930s, especially examining those folders designated "political" and "Idaho." At the University of Idaho Library in Moscow is the William E. Borah Collection, which consists of the many scrapbooks Senator Borah accumulated during his long career. These scrapbooks, which have been microfilmed by the Library of Congress, contain a mass of newspaper clippings and also the originals of much significant correspondence. The Barzilla W. Clark and C. A. Bottolfsen Personal Papers, also at the University of Idaho Library, are relatively thin.

The National Archives in Washington, D.C., houses the records and much of the correspondence relating to the activities of the various New Deal federal agencies in Idaho, and much of this material can be obtained on microfilm. For the purposes of this state study, the records of the Federal Emergency Relief Administration and of the Works Progress Administration in Record Group 69 were easily the most revealing. But the records of several other agencies were consulted and also proved valuable: Bureau of Reclamation, Civilian Conservation Corps, Civil Works Administration, National Recovery Administration, National Youth Administration, Public Works Administration, and Reconstruction Finance Corporation. As a source of insight into Idaho politics, the correspondence in the file of T. A. Walters, First Assistant Secretary of the Interior, in Record Group 48, is extremely valuable.

The Franklin D. Roosevelt Library at Hyde Park, New York, is naturally a key depository for New Deal source material on local as well as national topics, and many of these files can be obtained on microfilm. The following files contain material immediately pertinent to Idaho: Official Files 300-Idaho (Democratic National Committee) and 2596 (C. Ben Ross), and President's Personal Files 2358 (William E. Borah), 4936 (C. I. White), 5209 (James P. Pope), and 5550 (D. Worth Clark). The Harry Hopkins Papers are disappointingly sparse in Idaho material. Even the penetrating field reports of Lorena Hickok, so valuable for most states, say little of Idaho.

PUBLIC DOCUMENTS

Evans, Karl B., and T. Barraclough. *Report of Investigation of State Highway Department with Summary of Gusman Case*. . . . Boise, n.d. (Mimeographed.)

Munro, James, Truman Joiner, Willard S. Bowen, and Elmer Fox. *Special Highway Fund Audit: January 1, 1933 to December 31, 1936*. 4 vols. Boise, 1938. (Typed.)

"Report No. 10, Volume II: Idaho—Federal Loans and Expenditures 1933–1939, State Statistics, Narrative Review of Agency Operations, Work Accomplishments." N.p.: Office of Government Reports, Statistical Section, 1940. (Mimeographed copy in Utah State University Library, Logan.)

State of Idaho. *General Laws of the State of Idaho, Passed at the Twenty-first Session of the State Legislature: 1931*.

———. *General Laws of the State of Idaho, Passed at the Extraordinary Session of the State Legislature: 1931*.

———. *General Laws of the State of Idaho, Passed at the Twenty-second Session of the State Legislature: 1933*.

———. *General Laws of the State of Idaho, Passed at the Extraordinary Session of the Twenty-second Legislature: 1933*.

———. *General Laws of the State of Idaho, Passed at the Twenty-third Session of the State Legislature: 1935*.

———. *General Laws of the State of Idaho, Passed at the Extraordinary Session of the State Legislature: 1935*.

———. *General Laws of the State of Idaho, Passed at the Third Extraordinary Session of the Twenty-third Legislature: 1936*.

———. *Journal of the Idaho Repeal Convention*. . . . Caldwell: Caxton Printers, 1933.

―――. Department of Reclamation. *Seventh Biennial Report of the Department of Reclamation, State of Idaho: 1931–1932.*

―――. ―――. *Eighth Biennial Report of the Department of Reclamation, State of Idaho: 1933–1934.*

―――. Department of State. *Nineteenth Biennial Report of the Secretary of State of the State of Idaho and Report of the Department of Law Enforcement: 1927–1928.*

―――. ―――. *Twenty-third Biennial Report of the Secretary of State of the State of Idaho: 1935–1936.*

―――. ―――. *Report of the Secretary of State and Roster of State, County and City Elective Officials and the Judiciary: 1937–1938.*

―――. Land Department. *Twenty-third Biennial Report of the State Land Department of the State of Idaho: 1935–1936.*

―――. State Auditor. *Twenty-third Biennial Report of the State Auditor, State of Idaho: October 1, 1934.*

―――. State Historical Society. *Twentieth Biennial Report of the Idaho State Historical Society: 1945–1946.*

―――. ―――. *Twenty-first Biennial Report of the Idaho State Historical Society: 1947–1948.*

―――. State Planning Board. *A Study of Taxing Units in Idaho, Part I: County Comparisons, 1929–1936–1937.* Works Progress Administration of Idaho Official Project No. 564-92-3-49. (Mimeographed.)

U.S. Bureau of the Census. *Fifteenth Census of the United States, 1930. Agriculture, Idaho: Statistics by Counties.*

―――. *Fifteenth Census of the United States, 1930. Population Bulletin, First Series, Idaho: Number and Distribution of Inhabitants.*

―――. *Fifteenth Census of the United States, 1930. Unemployment Bulletin, Idaho: Unemployment Returns by Classes.*

―――. *United States Census of Agriculture, 1935. Summary by States.*

U.S. National Archives and Records Service. *Administrative, Budget, and Personnel Correspondence Relating to Idaho: July 1, 1935–December 31, 1938.* Record Group 119, Records of the National Youth Administration. Washington, D.C.: General Services Administration, 1964. (Microfilmed.)

―――. *Final Report: National Youth Administration for the State of Idaho.* Record Group 119, Records of the National Youth Administration. Washington, D.C.: General Services Administration, 1964. (Microfilmed.)

―――. *Papers Relating to the State of Idaho in Selected Records Series.* Record Group 9, Records of the National Recovery Admin-

istration. Washington, D.C.: General Services Administration, 1964. (Microfilmed.)

―――. *Press Conferences of Franklin D. Roosevelt.* Hyde Park, N.Y.: General Services Administration, n.d. (Microfilmed.)

―――. *Project Histories of the Boise and Owyhee Reclamation Projects: 1934–1935–1936. Record Group 115, Records of the Bureau of Reclamation.* Washington, D.C.: General Services Administration, 1964. (Microfilmed.)

―――. *Records Relating to Emergency Relief to the State of Idaho. Record Group 234, Records of the Reconstruction Finance Corporation.* Washington, D.C.: General Services Administration, 1964. (Microfilmed.)

Wood, J. D., et al. "Public Works in Idaho during the Emergency Period: A Supplement to the Idaho State Planning Consultant's Six Months' Summary Progress Report, June–December, 1935." Boise: Idaho State Planning Board, 1936. (Mimeographed copy in Ross Administration Papers, Planning Board folder.)

NEWSPAPERS
(Consulted for the years 1928–46)

Aberdeen Times (Aberdeen, Ida.).
Arco Advertiser (Arco, Ida.).
Boise Capital News.
Buhl Herald (Buhl, Ida.).
Chicago Daily Tribune.
Clearwater Tribune (Orofino, Ida.).
Daily Bulletin (Blackfoot, Ida.).
Emmett Index and Emmett Examiner (Emmett, Ida.).
Idaho County Press (Grangeville, Ida.).
Idaho Daily Statesman (Boise).
Idaho Evening Times (Twin Falls).
Idaho Falls Post.
Idaho Free Press (Nampa).
Idaho Pioneer (Boise).
Idaho Post (Moscow).
Idaho State Journal (Pocatello).
Kellogg Evening News (Kellogg, Ida.).
Kootenai County Leader (Coeur d'Alene).
Lewiston Morning Tribune.

New York Times.
Northern Idaho News (Sandpoint, Ida.).
The Oregonian (Portland).
Pocatello Tribune.
Post-Register (Idaho Falls).
Power County Booster (American Falls, Ida.).
Salt Lake Tribune.
Seattle Daily Times.
Spokane Daily Chronicle.
Spokesman-Review (Spokane).
Star-Mirror (Moscow).
Teton Peak Chronicle (St. Anthony, Ida.).
Times-Register (Idaho Falls).
Twin Falls Daily News.
Wallace Miner (Wallace, Ida.).
Washington Star (Washington, D.C.).
Weiser American (Weiser, Ida.).
Weiser Signal.

BOOKS

Aldrich, Clara A. *The History of Banking in Idaho.* Boise: Syms-York, 1940.
Asbury, Herbert. *The Great Illusion: An Informal History of Prohibition.* Garden City, N.Y.: Doubleday, 1950.
Beal, Merrill D., and Merle W. Wells. *History of Idaho.* 3 vols. New York: Lewis Historical Publishing Company, 1959.
Benedict, Murray R. *Farm Policies of the United States: 1790–1950.* New York: Twentieth Century Fund, 1953.
Biographical Directory of the American Congress: 1774–1961. Washington, D.C.: U.S. Government Printing Office, 1961.
Bird, Annie L. *Boise: The Peace Valley.* Caldwell, Ida.: Caxton Printers, 1934.
Brosnan, C. J. *History of the State of Idaho.* 4th ed., rev. New York: Scribner's, 1948.
Brown, Josephine C. *Public Relief: 1929–1939.* New York: Henry Holt, 1940.
Burke, Robert E. *Olson's New Deal for California.* Berkeley and Los Angeles: University of California Press, 1953.

Burns, James M. *Roosevelt: The Lion and the Fox.* Harvest Books ed. New York: Harcourt, Brace and World, 1956.

Charles, Searle F. *Minister of Relief: Harry Hopkins and the Depression.* Syracuse, N.Y.: Syracuse University Press, 1963.

Clark, Norman H. *The Dry Years: Prohibition and Social Change in Washington.* Seattle: University of Washington Press, 1965.

Defenbach, Byron, et al. *Idaho: The Place and Its People.* 3 vols. Chicago: American Historical Society, 1933.

Degler, Carl N. *Out of Our Past: The Forces That Shaped Modern America.* Colophon ed. New York: Harper and Row, 1962.

Eccles, Marriner. *Beckoning Frontiers: Public and Personal Recollections.* New York: Knopf, 1951.

Fisher, Vardis, et al. *Idaho: A Guide in Word and Picture.* Prepared by the Federal Writers' Project of the Works Progress Administration. Caldwell, Ida.: Caxton Printers, 1937.

Freidel, Frank. *Franklin D. Roosevelt: The Triumph.* Boston and Toronto: Little, Brown, 1956.

Graham, Otis L., Jr. *An Encore for Reform: The Old Progressives and the New Deal.* New York: Oxford University Press, 1967.

Hicks, John D. *Republican Ascendancy: 1921–1933.* New York: Harper and Row, 1960.

Hobson, G. C., et al. *The Idaho Digest and Blue Book.* Prepared by the Idaho Works Progress Administration. Caldwell, Ida.: Caxton Printers, 1935.

Hofstadter, Richard. *The Age of Reform: From Bryan to F.D.R.* Vintage ed. New York: Random House, 1955.

Holtzman, Abraham. *The Townsend Movement.* New York: Twayne, 1962.

Johansen, Dorothy O., and Charles M. Gates. *Empire of the Columbia: A History of the Pacific Northwest.* New York: Harper and Brothers, 1957. 2nd ed., rev. New York: Harper and Row, 1967.

Johnson, Claudius O. *Borah of Idaho.* 2nd ed., rev. Seattle: University of Washington Press, 1967.

Leuchtenburg, William E. *Franklin D. Roosevelt and the New Deal: 1932–1940.* New York: Harper and Row, 1963.

———. *The Perils of Prosperity: 1914–1932.* Chicago: University of Chicago Press, 1958.

Lyon, Leverett S. *The National Recovery Administration: An Analysis and an Appraisal.* Washington, D.C.: The Brookings Institution, 1935.

Martin, Boyd A. *The Direct Primary in Idaho*. Stanford, Calif.: Stanford University Press, 1947.
Mayer, George H. *The Political Career of Floyd B. Olson*. Minneapolis: University of Minnesota Press, 1951.
McKenna, Marian C. *Borah*. Ann Arbor: University of Michigan Press, 1961.
Meriam, Lewis. *Relief and Social Security*. Washington, D.C.: The Brookings Institution, 1946.
Morlan, Robert L. *Political Prairie Fire: The Non-Partisan League, 1915–1922*. Minneapolis: University of Minnesota Press, 1955.
Mowry, George E. *The Urban Nation: 1920–1960*. New York: Hill and Wang, 1965.
Neuberger, Richard L. *Our Promised Land*. New York: Macmillan, 1938.
Nourse, Edwin G., et al. *Three Years of the Agricultural Adjustment Administration*. Washington, D.C.: The Brookings Institution, 1937.
Patterson, James T. *Congressional Conservatism and the New Deal: The Growth of the Conservative Coalition in Congress, 1933–1939*. Lexington: University of Kentucky Press, 1967.
———. *The New Deal and the States: Federalism in Transition*. Princeton: Princeton University Press, 1969.
Pomeroy, Earl. *The Pacific Slope: A History of California, Oregon, Washington, Idaho, Utah, and Nevada*. New York: Knopf, 1965.
Rauch, Basil. *The History of the New Deal*. New York: Creative Age Press, 1944.
Robinson, Edgar E. *The Presidential Vote: 1896–1932*. Stanford, Calif.: Stanford University Press, 1934.
———. *They Voted for Roosevelt: The Presidential Vote, 1932–1944*. Stanford, Calif.: Stanford University Press, 1947.
Romasco, Albert U. *The Poverty of Abundance: Hoover, the Nation, the Depression*. New York: Oxford University Press, 1965.
Roosevelt, Elliott (ed.). *F.D.R., His Personal Letters: 1928–1945*. 4 vols. New York: Duell, Sloan, and Pearce, 1950.
Salmond, John A. *The Civilian Conservation Corps, 1933–1942: A New Deal Case Study*. Durham, N.C.: Duke University Press, 1967.
Schlesinger, Arthur M., Jr. *The Coming of the New Deal*. Boston: Houghton Mifflin, 1959.
———. *The Politics of Upheaval*. Boston: Houghton Mifflin, 1960.
Shideler, James H. *Farm Crisis: 1919–1923*. Berkeley and Los Angeles: University of California Press, 1957.

Tyler, Robert L. *Rebels of the Woods: The I.W.W. in the Pacific Northwest.* Eugene: University of Oregon Books, 1967.
Warren, Harris G. *Herbert Hoover and the Great Depression.* New York: Oxford University Press, 1959.

ARTICLES

Arrington, Leonard. "The New Deal in the West: A Preliminary Statistical Inquiry," *Pacific Historical Review,* in press.
Chamberlain, Lawrence H. "Idaho: State of Sectional Schisms," in *Rocky Mountain Politics,* ed. Thomas C. Donnelly. Albuquerque: University of New Mexico Press, 1940.
Clark, Joseph M. "Relief: The Nation's Stepchild," *Today,* III (January 12, 1935), 20–21.
"Cowboy Ben Ross Wins Primary, Aims at Borah's Post," *News-Week,* VIII (August 22, 1936), 8–9.
Davenport, Walter. "Storm Warnings in Idaho," *Collier's,* XCVII (April 5, 1936), 10–11, 28, 30, 32.
Davis, William E. "W. Lloyd Adams: A Kingmaker's King," *Idaho Yesterdays,* XII (Summer, 1968), 2–19.
Gillis, W. D. "A Governor Guided by Divinations," *American Mercury,* XXXIII (September, 1934), 113–17.
"Idaho: Debt of Gratitude," *Time,* XXVIII (August 24, 1936), 22.
Kirkendall, Richard S. "The New Deal as Watershed: The Recent Literature," *Journal of American History,* LIV (March, 1968), 839–852.
Malone, Michael P. "C. Ben Ross: Idaho's Cowboy Governor," *Idaho Yesterdays,* X (Winter, 1966–67), 2–9.
———. "The New Deal in Idaho," *Pacific Historical Review,* XXXVIII (August, 1969), 293–310.
Martin, Boyd A. "Idaho: The Sectional State," in *Western Politics,* ed. Frank H. Jonas. Salt Lake City: University of Utah Press, 1961.
Neuberger, Richard L. "Battle of the Idaho Titans," *The New York Times Magazine,* August 9, 1936, sec. VII, pp. 9, 20.
———. "Behind the Borah Boom," *Current History,* XLIII (February, 1936), 463–66.
———. "Political Notes from the Northwest," *Nation,* CXLII (May 13, 1936), 610–12.
———. "Refugees from the Dust Bowl," *Current History,* L (April, 1939), 32–35.

———, and Kelley Loe. "The Old People's Crusade: The Townsend Plan and Its Astonishing Growth," *Harper's Magazine*, CLXXII (March, 1936), 426–38.

Patterson, James T. "The New Deal and the States," *American Historical Review*, LXXIII (October, 1967), 70–84.

———. "The New Deal and Western States," *Pacific Historical Review*, in press.

"Persons and Personalities," *Literary Digest*, CXX (August 17, 1935), 29; (September 7, 1935), 27.

Pinckney, Orde S. "Lion Triumphant," *Idaho Yesterdays*, III (Summer, 1959), 12–15, 18–24.

"Political Party Organization in Idaho, 1861–1960: A Brief Outline," *Idaho Historical Series*, IV (March, 1961), 1–4.

"Primaries: Symbols and Shibboleths," *Time*, XXXII (August 22, 1938), 21.

"Reno's New Rivals," *Literary Digest*, CIX (April 4, 1931), 11.

Richardson, Elmo R. "Western Politics and New Deal Policies: A Study of T. A. Walters of Idaho," *Pacific Northwest Quarterly*, LIV (January, 1963), 9–18.

Rosqvist, August. "Idaho State Federation of Labor: When Organized and Why," in *Official State Yearbook of Organized Labor: Idaho, 1930*. Pocatello: State Journal–Union Printers, 1930.

———. "Idaho Unions Revived in 1934," in *Idaho State Federation of Labor Yearbook: 1935*. Pocatello: Graves and Potter–The Tribune Press, 1935.

Schmalz, Bruce. "Headgates and Headaches," *Idaho Yesterdays*, IX (Winter, 1965–66), 22–25.

Scholastic, XXXIII (January 21, 1939), 8.

Taber, Ronald W. "Vardis Fisher and the Idaho Guide," *Pacific Northwest Quarterly*, LIX (April, 1968), 68–76.

"Topics of the Day," *Literary Digest*, CV (April 26, 1930), 5–6.

Tyler, Robert L. "I.W.W. in the Pacific N.W.: Rebels of the Woods," *Oregon Historical Quarterly*, LV (March, 1954), 3–44.

Wells, Merle W. "Fred T. Dubois and the Idaho Progressives, 1900–1914," *Idaho Yesterdays*, IV (Summer, 1960), 24–30.

———. "Fred T. Dubois and the Nonpartisan League in the Idaho Election of 1918," *Pacific Northwest Quarterly*, LVI (January, 1965), 17–29.

"Wobblies in the Northwest," *Nation*, CXLV (November 13, 1937), 543.

BIBLIOGRAPHY

THESES AND DISSERTATIONS

Adams, Keith J. "An Economic Analysis of the Idaho Income Tax Law." Master's thesis, University of Idaho, 1951.

Forbes, Garrett O. "Dynamics of Idaho Politics: 1920–1932." Master's thesis, University of Idaho, 1955.

Johnson, Edward H. "The Administration of the Social Security Program in Idaho." Master's thesis, University of Idaho, 1940.

Judd, Richard M. "A History of the New Deal in Vermont." Ph.D. dissertation, Harvard University, 1959.

Keller, Richard C. "Pennsylvania's Little New Deal." Ph.D. dissertation, Columbia University, 1960.

Minton, John D. "The New Deal in Tennessee, 1932–1938." Ph.D. dissertation, Vanderbilt University, 1959.

Oliver, Marguerite I. "Wealth of Idaho: An Estimate of the Amount of Wealth and the Distribution of Its Ownership Within and Without the State." Master's thesis, University of Idaho, 1933.

Patenaude, Lionel V. "The New Deal in Texas." Ph.D. dissertation, University of Texas, 1953.

Peterson, Frank Ross. "Liberal from Idaho: The Public Career of Senator Glen H. Taylor." Ph.D. dissertation, Washington State University, 1968.

Pinckney, Orde S. "William E. Borah and the Republican Party, 1932–1940." Ph.D. dissertation, University of California, Berkeley, 1958.

Thomas, Benjamin E. "Political Geography of Idaho." Ph.D. dissertation, Harvard University, 1947.

Wickens, James F. "Colorado in the Great Depression: A Study of New Deal Politics at the State Level." Ph.D. dissertation, University of Denver, 1964.

PERSONAL INTERVIEWS BY THE AUTHOR

Adams, W. Lloyd. Rexburg, Idaho. July 31, 1965.
Clark, Chase A. Boise, Idaho. July 27, 1965.
Corlett, John. Boise, Idaho. June 29, 1965.
Coulter, Robert. Boise, Idaho. June 30, 1965.
Hawley, James H., Jr. Boise, Idaho. July 23, 1965.
Joiner, Truman. Boise, Idaho. July 29, 1965.
McDeavitt, B. A. Pocatello, Idaho. July 30, 1965.

Reavis, C. Ben. Boise, Idaho. July 1, 1965.
Shellworth, Harry C. Boise, Idaho. February 1, 1964.
Steel, Mrs. Ethel. Parma, Idaho. July 3, 1965.
Williams, Joe R. Boise, Idaho. July 26, 1965.
Wright, Calvin. Boise, Idaho. July 25, 1965.

INDEX

Ada County district court, 119
Adams, W. Lloyd, 22, 29, 142n
Agricultural Adjustment Act, 57-58, 121, 123
Agricultural Adjustment Administration: described, 58; in Idaho, 58, 75, 84
Alexander, Moses, 18, 68
Allen, O. K., 56
American Federation of Labor, 97, 114
American Public Welfare Association, 83
Anti-Sales Tax League, 88
Anti-Saloon League, 20, 106
Arrington, Leonard, 134
Arrowrock Dam, 90

Baldridge, H. C., 7, 19, 20, 22; and 1929 legislative session, 23
Banks and banking: impact of the depression upon, 42; and the RFC, 42; 1933 "banking holiday," 56-57
Bannock County, 8
Baruch, Bernard, 104
"Beer Putsch," 66
Benson, Elmer, 129
Big Lost River reclamation district, 38
Bilbo, Theodore: Ross compared to, 13, 132
Black Canyon irrigation project, 90
Boise, Ida., xi, xii, xiii; and political sectionalism, xiii-xiv; NRA program in, 68
Boise Basin, 4
Boise Chamber of Commerce, 76
Boise City National Bank, 42
Bone, Homer T., 49
Borah, William E.: compared to Ross, 3; and 1930 campaign, 26-28; and 1932 campaign, 47, 49; and 1934 campaign, 80, 81, 82; characterized, 101-2; attitude toward New Deal, 102-3, 109-10; Democratic "plots" against, 103-4; Democratic allegiance to, 104-5; and Townsend Movement, 106, 107, 108; 1936 presidential campaign, 108; 1936 primary campaign, 111; re-election in 1936, 112-18 *passim*, 122, 124, 126, 128, 132, 133, 144n; mentioned, 13, 14, 17, 20
Bottolfsen, C. A.: house speaker in 1931, 32; Republican state chairman in 1936, 111-12; quoted, 123; 1938 gubernatorial candidacy, 123, 124, 127, 128, 129
Brady, James H., 142n
Bryan, William Jennings, 7
Burns, James McGregor, 109, 164n
Burroughs, Frank: quoted, 13

Caldwell, Ida., xii
Callahan, Donald A., 35, 125, 128
Campaigns, political. *See* Elections

183

Canyon County, Ida., 4; Ross as commissioner of, 7-8
Carver, John A., 110, 111
Carver, Parker, 43, 60, 73
Casey, Myra, 139n
Chain Store Licensing Tax Law, 54
Chapman, W. Orr, 18, 20, 21, 31, 43, 110; breaks with Ross, 40; 1932 Senate candidacy, 45; quoted, 81; anti-Ross conspiracy in 1936, 108-9
Church, Frank, 13, 133
Civilian Conservation Corps: described, 61-62; in Idaho, 61-62; controversy over political appointments, 63-64, 65; mentioned, 75, 94
Civil Works Administration: program in Idaho, 72-74, 90
Clark, Barzilla: disputes Ross's relief policy in 1932, 43; 1932 gubernatorial candidacy, 46, 47; opposes Ross on prohibition repeal issue, 66; 1936 gubernatorial candidacy, 110-11; described, 118; tenure as governor, 118-19; defeated in 1938 primary, 124; mentioned, 116, 117, 122, 126, 128
Clark, Chase A., 21, 52, 126, 131
Clark, D. Worth: in 1934 campaign, 78, 79, 81; described, 122; and 1938 primary, 123-27; election to Senate, 127, 128, 129; mentioned, 93, 104, 107, 110
Clearwater County strike, 97-98
Coeur d' Alene, Ida., xii, xiv
Coffin, Thomas C.: in 1932 campaign, 46, 47; and 1933 CCC controversy, 63-64; 1934 controversy and death, 78-79; mentioned, 77
Cohn, Peter H., 94, 95
Collier's Magazine: quoted, 103
"Committee of St. Peter," 31
Comstock, W. A., 56
Coolidge, Calvin, 16
Co-operative Emergency Revenue Act of 1935, 87
Corlett, John, 131; quoted, 10, 11

Coulter, Robert, 18, 20, 21, 32, 51, 52, 127, 164n; quoted, 25, 132; as Democratic state chairman, 79; as state liquor commission chairman, 88

Davis, Ben, 31, 127
Day, J. J., 45
Day brothers, 18
Defenbach, Byron: and 1930 campaign, 24, 26; 1932 gubernatorial candidacy, 46, 47, 48, 49; in 1936 campaign, 111, 112, 114
Degler, Carl N., 134
Delinquent Tax Moratorium Law, 84
Democratic National Committee, 127
Democratic party in Idaho, 14; and 1918 election, 15, 16; in 1920s, 17-30; in 1931, 31-32; and 1932 campaign, 44-50; and 1933 legislature, 51; internal dissension in 1933, 62-66; in 1934 campaign, 77-83; and labor, 96-98; internal dissension in 1935-36, 105-6; and 1936 campaign, 108-16; decline in 1937-38, 117-18; and 1938 campaign, 123-30; and New Deal in Idaho, 130-31, 135
Democratic state central committee, 45
"Democratic Stephan for Governor Clubs," 81
Depression, ix; impact upon Idaho, 37-42; effect on Idaho politics in 1932, 44; mentioned *passim*
Dern, George H., 47
Diefendorf, Ben, 57
Direct primary, issue and law: repeal of Direct Primary Law in 1919, 15; as issue in 1920s, 17; veto of bill embodying, 18; issue in 1928 election, 21, 22; in 1930 election, 24, 26, 27, 29; in 1931 legislative session, 33, 34; Direct Primary Law of 1931, 34, 36; revision of law in 1937, 124;

INDEX

used to defeat Pope in 1938, 124, 125; mentioned, 46
Dodge, Roy, 33
"Dodge Plan," 33
Driver's License Bill, 85
Dubois, Fred T., 13, 14, 133
Durant, Will, 109
"Dust Bowl," 76

Eccles, Marriner, 42, 148n
"Economy Bloc": in 1935 legislature, 85, 86, 87; in 1937 legislature, 118
Edmonds, T. J., 86, 87
Eighteenth Amendment: Idaho's vote for repeal of, 55, 65, 67
Elder, Robert, 108, 110
Elections and political campaigns: of 1918, 15; of 1922, 18; of 1926, 18-19; of 1928, 19-23; of 1930, 24-29; of 1932, 44-50; of 1934, 77-83; of 1936, 101-16; of 1938, 123-30
Emergency Conservation Work program. *See* Civilian Conservation Corps
Emergency Drought Relief Committee, 76
Emergency Relief and Construction Act, 42
Emergency Relief Appropriation Act, 89
Enking, Mrs. Myrtle, 66, 110
Erb, R. S., 127
Evans, Karl B., 119

Faris, R. W., 39
Farley, James A., 65, 82, 109, 115, 124, 126, 135, 162n; rumored plot to defeat Borah, 103-4
"Farm Bloc": in 1931 legislature, 34; in 1933 legislature, 52
Farm Bureau, xiv; Ross as leader of, 8
Farm Credit Administration, 58-59
Federal Emergency Relief Act, 59
Federal Emergency Relief Administration: initial activity in Idaho, 1933; 59-60; Ross's criticism of,
65, 74-75; and the CWA, 72, 74; renewal of in Idaho, 1934, 73-75; and 1934 drought relief, 75-76; and 1935 legislature, 83, 85, 86, 87, 88; termination in 1935, 89, 90, 158n
Federal Writers' Project of the WPA, 91
First Security Corporation, 42
Fisher, Vardis: quoted, 12; and the Idaho Writers' Project, 91
Ford, Henry, 68
Foreman, John, 79
Fort Boise, 4
Fouch brothers, 4
Fremont County, Ida., 23
French, Burton, 26, 28, 46, 49

Gasoline Tax Law, 54
Gates, Charles M.: quoted, 13
General Moratorium Law, 84; passed by 1933 legislature, 54-55; Ross's enforcement of, 54
Gillis, W. D., 24, 26; quoted, 124
Girard, Franklin, 61, 66, 106, 110
Glass, Carter, 104
Godfrey, W. W., 91
Gooding, Frank, 16, 17, 19, 29, 143n
Gooding-Thomas "machine," 16, 17, 23, 46, 143n; and 1928 election, 22; collapse of, 24-29 *passim*
Gossett, Charles, 7, 85, 124, 131
Gould, Jay, 3
Graham, Otis L., Jr.: quoted, 102
Grand Coulee Dam, 99
Grange, xiv, 88, 114
Grebe, George W., 32
Green, Minnie, 11, 140n
Green, William, 114
Gusman, Henry, 40

Hall, W. Scott, 22
Hamilton, John D. M., 113; quoted, 125
Harbour, Alvin, 31, 45, 50, 120; Ross's dismissal of, 40
Harding, Warren G., 16
Hass, Herman, 4

Hawley, James H., 18, 21; quoted, 20
Hawley, James H., Jr., 50
Heath, Thomas, 127, 128
Hill, George, 56
Hitchcock, Beecher, 20
Hofstadter, Richard, 134
Holden, E. M., 21, 22, 25, 26
Holden, J. Wesley, 34, 35, 45, 79
Home Owners' Loan Corporation, 59, 75
Hood, J. Leo, 90
Hoover, Herbert, 16, 19, 23, 26, 28, 102, 118; and Idaho relief in 1932, 41, 42; and 1932 Idaho election, 44, 45, 47, 48, 49; quoted, 125
Hopkins, Harry, 42, 72, 126; and early FERA activity in Idaho, 59-60; and 1934 Idaho relief difficulties, 74, 75; and relief controversy in 1935 legislature, 86; as WPA director, 89; quoted, 92; Ross's charges against in 1935, 92-93
Horsfal, Edward, 73, 74
Hull, Cordell, 123

Ickes, Harold, 69, 70, 126; controversy with Ross, 70-71; quoted, 71
Idaho: and the New Deal, x-xi, 75-76, 98-100; described, xi-xiv; politics, 13, 14, 82-83, 130-31, 132-33, 135; impact of depression upon, 37-39; new role of federal government in, by 1934, 75-76; by 1936, 98-100; and the New Deal, 134-35
Idaho Agricultural Adjustment Act, 84
Idaho Agricultural Adjustment Board, 84
Idaho Bureau of Highways, 119, 120
Idaho Co-operative Relief Agency, 94-96
Idaho Daily Statesman: quoted, 29, 87, 129

Idaho Department of Public Works, 40, 119, 120, 121
Idaho Emergency Relief Administration: founding and initial activities, 73-75; phase out in 1935, 90, 93, 94
Idaho Falls, Ida., xi, xiii, xiv, 66, 118
Idaho First National Bank, 42
Idaho Industrial Recovery Act, 69
Idaho National Guard, 39, 97-98
Idaho Pioneer: quoted, 13
Idaho State Code Commission, 69
Idaho State Federation of Labor, 97
Idaho State Purchasing Department, 120
Idaho State Recovery Board, 68
Idaho State University, xiii
Idaho Supreme Court: upholds 1931 Income Tax Law, 36; ruling on sales tax, 88, 89
Idaho Writers' Project, 91
Idaho-Wyoming Water Pact, 66
Income tax, 52; instituted in 1931, 33, 35, 36
Industrial Workers of the World, 98
Interstate Commerce Commission, 8

Jackson, Andrew, 105
James, A. F., 127
Johnesse, Mrs. Frank, 108, 112, 164n
Johnson, Claudius O.: quoted, 20, 103
Johnson, Hugh, 68; quoted, 104
Johnson, Lamont, 7

Kessler, Harry: 1932 Senate candidacy, 45-46; quoted, 88
Kilowatt Tax Law, 35, 36
Kinyon, Frank: quoted, 88
"Kitchen Kabinet," 50
Koelsch, Charles, 120

Labor, 96-98
LaFollette, Phillip, 129
Land Bank of Spokane, 59

INDEX

Landon, Alf: Ross compared to, 100; 1936 presidential campaign, 108, 112, 113, 115
Langer, William, 54
Lawrence, David: quoted, 99
Legislative sessions: of 1929, 23-24; of 1931, 32-37; of 1933, 51-55; of June, 1933, 66-67; of 1935, 83-89; of March, 1935, 86-87; of July, 1936, 96; of 1937, 118-19
Leuchtenburg, William E., 19, 134; quoted, x
Lewiston, Ida., xi, xii, xiii, xiv; banking panic of 1933, 57
Liberty League, 77
Liberty party, 46-47
Lincoln, Abraham, 7, 71
Liquor Advisory Commission, 83
Liquor Control Commission, 85
Lloyd, Thomas J., 72
Lockwood, Walter T., 68
Long, Huey: Ross compared to, 13, 132, 133

McAdoo, William G., 19
McCarran, Patrick, 65, 126
McKaig, Ray, 15, 16, 20, 108, 124
Mackay, Ida., 66
Mackay Dam, 38
McKelvey, G. E., 120
Malad, Ida., 66
McMurray, John, 22; in 1930 campaign, 24, 26, 27, 28, 29, 144n
Martin, Frank, 78, 82, 106, 110
Maverick, Maury, 126
Maw, Henry, 53
Mellon, Andrew, 45
Michaud Flats irrigation district, 8, 9
Miller, Bert, 66, 122, 124, 129
Miller, Horatio H., 140n, 141n, 169n; quoted, 82, 132
Miller, Leslie, 56
Mix, G. P., 25, 28, 79, 122, 124, 129; 1932 Senate candidacy, 45, 46; 1936 gubernatorial candidacy, 106, 110, 111
Moore, C. C., 18, 19
Morgan, William, 18, 19

Mormonism and Mormons, xiii, 14; and 1930 election, 27, 29; and repeal controversy, 83
Morrison, John T., 7
Mortgage foreclosures, 38; as issue in 1933 legislature, 53, 54, 55; 1935 legislation concerning, 84. *See also* General Moratorium Law
Moscow, Ida., xii, xiv
Munro, James, 119
Murphy, Frank, 129
Murray, "Alfalfa Bill," 11
Mussolini, Benito: Ross compared to, 55

Nampa, Ida., xii, xiv
National Industrial Recovery Act, 67-68
National Labor Relations Act, 96-97
National Labor Relations Board, 96-97
National Recovery Administration, 84; functions, 67; program in Idaho, 68-69
National Youth Administration, 91-92
Neuberger, Richard L.: quoted, 11-12, 13, 102; mentioned, 107
New Deal: impact upon states, ix-xi, 55; and Idaho, x-xi, xv, 75-76, 98-100, 134-35; local effects of 1932 election, 48-50; 1933 program and Idaho, 55-64, 67-72; impact upon Idaho politics by 1934, 82-83; 1935-36 program and Idaho, 89-97; assessment of, in Idaho, as of 1936, 98-100; and 1936 election, 101, 115; decline in 1937-38, 117; and 1938 election, 121-26, 128-30; impact, 134-35; mentioned *passim*
New York Times: quoted, 115, 123
Ninety-day divorce law, 34-35, 146n
Nonpartisan League, 7; in 1918 election, 15-16; and politics in 1920s, 16, 17; mentioned, 67, 106, 124, 141n

Norris, George, 103, 104
Northern Idaho: described as region, xii; banking crisis of 1933, 56, 57
Nugent, John F., 14-19 *passim,* 142n

Old Age Pension Law, 34
Old Age Revolving Pensions, Ltd., 106
Olson, Culbert, 129
Olson, Floyd B., 13, 54
"One-Hundred Days," 55-62
Oneida County project, 92
Oregonian (Portland): quoted, 125
Otter, J. V., 69

"Panhandle" region. *See* Northern Idaho
Parma, Ida., 4, 131, 132
Parry, R. B., 111, 112
Parsons, Harry, 66, 110; quoted, 129-30
Patterson, James T.: *The New Deal and the States,* x; quoted, 126, 135
Payette, Francois, 4
Philadelphia Record, 109
Pinchot, Gifford, 114
Pinckney, Orde S., 114
Pocatello, Ida., xi, xiii, xiv, 66; Ross as mayor, 9-10; Roosevelt's 1932 visit to, 48
Pocatello Tribune: quoted, 9-10, 80-81, 132
Political campaigns. *See* Elections
Pope, James P., 18, 19, 20, 21, 63, 75, 82, 93, 105, 116, 117, 130; 1932 Senate campaign, 45-46, 47, 48; enmity with Ross, 50; efforts to defeat Ross in 1936, 110; writes 1936 Democratic platform, 112; characterized, 121-22; defeated in 1938 primary, 123-26; appointment to TVA, 127
Populism and Populist Movement, 7, 11, 14, 16, 106
Potlatch Forests, Inc., 98
Primary elections. *See* Elections
Progressive Movement, 14-15

Progressive party, 15, 16, 17, 19, 20
Progressives, 14, 15; in politics of 1920s, 16-29 *passim;* cooperate with Ross in 1931 legislature, 34, 35, 36; and failure of Idaho prohibition, 67; and Townsend Movement, 106-7
Prohibition Law of Idaho, 53, 65, 67, 80, 82
Prohibition (Repeal) issue: in 1928 campaign, 19-22, 144n; in 1930 campaign, 24-25, 29; in 1932 campaign, 45-48; in 1933 legislature, 52, 53; climax of controversy in Idaho, 65-67; in 1934 campaign, 80; in 1935 legislature, 83, 85, 88
Property Tax: Ross's philosophy, 33, 34, 35; and 1931 legislature, 33, 34, 35; and 1933 legislature, 52, 53; and 1935 legislature, 84, 85, 86, 87
Public Works Administration, 68, 75; functions, 69; program in Idaho, 69-70; Ross's criticism of, 70-71

Raskob, John J., 19
Reavis, C. Ben, 139n
Reavis, Ellen, 6
Reavis, John, 6
Reconstruction Corporation of Idaho, 42
Reconstruction Finance Corporation, 42-44
Relief. *See* Unemployment relief
Repeal issue. *See* Prohibition
Republican party, 6-7, 14-15; in 1920s, 16-29; in 1932 campaign, 44-47, 49; in 1934 campaign, 79, 80, 81; in 1936 campaign, 102, 108, 111, 112, 113; in 1938 campaign, 123-30 *passim;* in Idaho since 1938, 130
Resettlement Administration, 92, 94
Roosevelt, Franklin D.: and 1932 election, 47, 48, 49, 50; 1932 Idaho visit, 48; inauguration, 55; Ross's criticism of, 65; quoted,

INDEX

67, 109, 125; Ross's plea to concerning WPA inequities, 93; re-election in 1936, 115; mentioned *passim*
Roosevelt Club of Idaho, 78
Ross, Charles Benjamin, xv; characterized, 3, 10-12, 13, 132-33; ancestry, 3-4; boyhood, 5-6; education, 5-6; as politician, 6-7, 11-13, 31-32, 50, 101, 130-31, 132-33, 135; as Canyon County commissioner, 7-8; Farm Bureau connections, 8; as mayor of Pocatello, 9-10; personal and political philosophy, 10-13; and spiritualism, 10-11; demagoguery of, 12-13; and 1928 campaign, 21-23; and 1930 campaign, 24-30; and 1931 legislature, 32-37; attempts to cope with depression in 1931-32, 39-44; and 1932 campaign, 44-50; and 1933 legislature, 51-55; and "Ross Plan," 56, 58; and beginnings of New Deal relief, 59-61; conflicts with opposing Democrats in 1933, 62-66; criticism of Roosevelt Administration, 65; unsuccessful dry stand in 1933, 65-67; and the NRA, 68; attacks upon Secretaries Wallace and Ickes, 70-72; and relief problems of 1933-34, 72-75; and the 1934 campaign, 77-82; and 1935 legislature, 83-89; charges against WPA, 92-93; and welfare in 1935-36, 94-96; and labor, 97-98; posture toward New Deal in 1936, 99-100; ambition to unseat Borah, 103-4; and Democratic enemies in 1936, 105-6; and Townsend Movement, 107-8; announces Senate candidacy in 1936, 108-110; 1936 primary campaign, 110-11; defeat in 1936, 112-16; criticizes Barzilla Clark, 119; investigations of past administrations in 1937-38, 119-21; re-enters politics in 1938, 121-23, 123-24, 126, 127-30; last years and death, 131-32; eulogies of, 132
Ross, Dewey, 139n
Ross, Earl, 139n
Ross, Edna Reavis, 6, 132
Ross, Jeannette Hadley, 4
Ross, John, 131
Ross, John M., 3-4
Ross, W. H., 6
Ross-Davis Building, 9
"Ross Machine," 44, 122, 129, 130, 135
Ross Park, 9
"Ross Plan for National Rehabilitation," 56
Rubin, Cora, 108
Rural Electrification Administration, 100
Rutledge, R. H., 64

Sales tax: and 1931 legislature, 34; and 1933 legislature, 52; and 1935 legislature, 84-89; issue in 1936 campaign, 89, 112, 114; defeated in 1936 election, 115; mentioned, 118, 135. *See also* Co-operative Emergency Revenue Act
Salmon River, xii
Samuels, H. F., 20
Sandpoint Bridge, 43
Satterfield, A. Y., 85
Scatterday, Ralph, 26
Schlesinger, Arthur M., Jr.: quoted, 89
Sectionalism: in Idaho, xiii-xiv
Sharp Liquor Bill, 85
Shellworth, Harry C., 61, 64
Silver Purchase Act, 99
Simons, Will, 68, 105
Sinclair, Upton, 82
Smith, Addison T., 26, 28, 46, 49
Smith, Alfred E., 19, 20, 21, 23, 24, 48
Smith, "Cotton Ed," 126
Smoot, Reed, 49
Smoot-Hawley Tariff, 47
Snake River, xi, 99
Social Security Act, 95
Social Security program, 95-96, 134

Southeastern Idaho: described as region, xii-xiii
South Idaho Timber Protection Association, 61
Southwestern Idaho: described as region, xii
Spokesman-Review (Spokane), 115
"Statehouse Gang," 44
Steiwer, Frederick, 49
Stemmer, J. H., 60, 120
Stephan, Frank: gubernatorial candidacy in 1934, 79, 80, 81; in 1936, 111, 112
Stern, J. David, 109
Steunenburg, Frank, 7
Stratton, Owen T., 45, 46, 52
Sullivan, Mark: quoted, 37

Talmadge, Eugene: Ross compared to, 13, 92; mentioned, 56, 65
Tannahill, Sam O., 31, 47
Taylor, Glen, 12, 13, 133; quoted, 132
Taylor, Ira, 112
Taylor, J. W., 119
Tennessee Valley Authority, 99, 127
Teton County Strike, 97, 98
Thomas, Benjamin E.: quoted, xiii
Thomas, Elbert, 49
Thomas, Elmer, 11
Thomas, John, 20, 22, 24, 29; defeat in 1932, 45, 46, 48, 143n
Time Magazine: quoted, 111
Townsend, Francis, 106, 107
Townsend Movement, 67, 126; role in 1936 campaign, 106-8, 111, 112, 113, 114
Twenty-first Amendment, 65; ratified by Idaho, 66-67
Twin Falls, Ida., xii, xiv
Tyler, Joe, 26

Unemployment Compensation Law, 96
Unemployment relief: Ross's philosophy of, 41; RFC and Idaho, 42-44; FERA efforts in Idaho, 1933, 59-61; CWA-FERA in Idaho, 1933-34, 72-75; issue in 1935 legislature, 83-88 *passim;* and WPA, 89-91, 92-93; and ICRA-Idaho social security program, 94-95
United States Army, 62
United States Bureau of Entomology and Plant Quarantine, 62
United States Department of Agriculture, 58, 70
United States Forest Service, 62
United States Social Security Board, 95
University of Idaho, xiii-xiv
Usadel, Helen, 139n
Utah Construction Co., 38, 39
Utah Power and Light Co., 35-36

Van Hoesen, E. G., 32-33, 51
Volstead Act, 65

Walker, Ramsay, 18, 31, 45, 110
Wallace, Henry, 58, 61, 70, 126
Wallace Miner: quoted, 49
Walters, Theodore A., 18, 79, 106; as Idaho Democratic state chairman, 25, 26, 27, 29, 31, 47, 50; First Assistant Secretary of the Interior, 63; quoted, 63, 105
Weiser Institute, 6
Welfare. *See* Federal Emergency Relief Administration; Social Security; Unemployment relief
Western Pine Association, 69
Wheeler, Burton K.: quoted, 104
Whitaker, W. P., 124
White, Compton I.: in 1932 campaign, 46; quoted, 132; mentioned, 63, 79, 93, 124, 129
White, William Allen, 107
Wilhelm, Kaiser: Ross compared to, 78
Williams, Aubrey, 74, 84, 91, 126, 158n

Williams, Pierce, 43, 74
Wilson, Asher B., 18, 20, 21, 22, 106, 110; gubernatorial candidacy of 1930, 25; of 1934, 78
"Wizard of Oz," 115
"Wobblies," 98
Women's Christian Temperance Union, 67

Workmen's Compensation Law, 34, 85
Works Progress Administration: in Idaho, 89-91; Ross's attack upon, 92-93
Wright, Calvin, 122

"Young Turks," 111